CANONIZING HYPERTEXT

Also by Astrid Ensslin

Language in the Media

CANONIZING HYPERTEXT

Explorations and Constructions

ASTRID ENSSLIN

continuum

Continuum International Publishing Group
The Tower Building, 11 York Road, London SE1 7NX
80 Maiden Lane, Suite 704, New York, NY 10038

British Library Cataloguing-in-Publication Data
A catalogue record for this book is available from the British Library.

ISBN-10: HB: 0-8264-9558-3
ISBN-13: HB: 978-0-8264-9558-7

Library of Congress Cataloging-in-Publication Data
Ensslin, Astrid.
    Canonizing hypertext : explorations and constructions / Astrid Ensslin.
        p. cm.
    Includes bibliographical references and index.
    ISBN-13: 978-0-8264-9558-7
    ISBN-10: 0-8264-9558-3
    1. Criticism—Data processing. 2. Canon (Literature) 3. Hypertext systems. I. Title.

PN98.E4E57 2007
801′.9590285—dc22

                                                                    2006034641

Typeset by Aarontype Limited, Easton, Bristol
Printed and bound in Great Britain by Biddles Ltd, King's Lynn, Norfolk

Contents

Acknowledgements

I would like to extend my gratitude to Peter Paul Schnierer, Thomas Rommel, Sally Johnson, Frank Finlay, Ingo Cornils, Paul Cooke, Danielle Hipkins, Ingrid Sharp, Atik Baborie, Wolfgang Ensslin, Angela Ensslin, Fred Bridgham, Mark Pike, Deena Larsen, Rebecca O'Rourke, Syd Donald, Bronwen Thomas, Alice Bell, Anthea Fraser-Gupta, Christiana Gregoriou, Ann Heilmann, Adam Jaworski, Oliver Hensengerth, Helga Priska Mitterbacher, Peter Nix, Alice Bell, Paul Friedemann, Steffen Mussler, Stefan Maskiewicz, Oliver Stenschke, Albert Busch, Simone Winko and, not least, all students on the Leeds Hypertext Project, whose suggestions, criticism and support have been invaluable.

Introduction

We will not struggle against the line without also struggling against the web . . .
Resisting hypertext is by no means a simple matter.
(Stuart Moulthrop, 1995)

The twenty-first century is characterized by a complex situation with regard to media consumption and media-related behaviour in the developed world. On the one hand, since the advent of the World Wide Web as a popular medium in the early 1990s, there has been an enormous increase in hypermediality, visuality and aurality, which threatens to subvert the dominance of the written word in a process that J. D. Bolter describes as 'reverse ekphrasis' (2001).[1] On the other hand, book sales in the UK are said to be higher than ever before,[2] an upsurge which has partly been ascribed to the phenomenal success of J. K. Rowling's *Harry Potter* series since it was launched in 1997, as well as recent television programmes such as the BBC's *Big Read* and the *Richard and Judy* show's book club on Channel 4. Nevertheless, moral panic is spreading in view of the average time spent by Britons on reading, which now amounts to 5.3 hours per week, thus ranking fifth lowest in the world. This figure is pitched against an average weekly duration of 18 hours spent by British people watching television.[3] What seems to raise even more concern is the fact that as many as 40 per cent of Britons never read books at all, favouring, instead, leafing through newspapers and magazines and surfing the web. In fact, in 2002 British people spent on average seven minutes a day on the internet, and the numbers are rising constantly (*Daily Telegraph*, 27 May 2002).

Particular concern has been expressed by educationalists who fear that, as a result of the heightened amount of visuality found on television and the internet, literacy levels and imaginative skills, particularly among young users, may deteriorate and fall prey to an impassive submergence in the pictorial, the cinematographic, the pre-defined sequencing of images and sounds (Manuel, 2005). According to a recent report in the *Guardian*, 'one in five [British] 11-year-olds is failing to reach expected standards in reading' (3 June 2005), a dilemma that is considered serious enough to be tackled by the British government in its so-called national literacy strategy, which was launched in 1998 and is presently showing its first positive effects. Similarly, striking a provocatively sour note, American novelist, critic and hyperfiction author Robert Coover (1999) describes the (still) current state of affairs in the United States thus:

And even the word, the very stuff of literature, and indeed of all human thought, is under assault, giving ground daily to image-surfing, hypermedia, the linked icon. Indeed, the word itself is increasingly reduced to icon or caption. Some speak hopefully of the binding of word and image, many, perhaps also hopefully, of the displacement of word by image. There is a genuine fear – or hope – that our old language of the intellect, systematic discourse, and poetic metaphor may very soon be as foreign and esoteric as ancient Sumerian cuneiform tablets. (Coover, 1999)

Notwithstanding the optimistic outlook presented by the booming print literature market in Britain, Coover's endangerment hypothesis needs to be taken seriously.[4] As a matter of fact, as Miall and Dobson (rather disconcertingly) argue (2001):

> the reading of literary texts may simply seem rather dull in competition with the multimedia, virtual reality simulations that are now being rushed to market. How will literature fare in an environment where the computer medium has itself largely been appropriated and developed by commercial interests . . . ?

In the face of these commercialization, visualization and hypermedialization developments, literary scholars and educators alike find themselves confronted with major challenges: how can literature, the art of the written word, be promoted and taught in such a way as to make it relevant for an increasingly hypermedia-oriented readership? How can the rapidly evolving New Media be integrated in a university and school curriculum that still seeks to transmit classical literary competence? And finally, how can the notion of literary competence be re(de)fined to meet these new challenges and embrace rather than ignore or even resist those current trends?

With a view to providing answers to these questions, this book, which is aimed at scholars, instructors and students of literature, seeks to 'canonize', or help to canonize, literary hypertext, a specific form of contemporary literature that combines modern hypermedia with an at once 'traditional' and innovative approach to reading. By placing the written word at the forefront and conjoining it with other New Media arts, this kind of literature has the potential to counteract the endangerment of writing by the visualization tendencies of the modern media and to adapt writing and reading to the distinct medial and material qualities of the computer and the internet. As Theodor Holm Nelson, hypertext's grandfather and ever-euphoric visionary, puts it, a well-designed approach to hypertext reception, production and pedagogy will lead to:

> a return to literacy, a cure for television stupor, a new Renaissance of ideas and generalist understanding, a grand posterity that does not lose the details which are the final substance of everything. (Nelson, 1992)

Taking this enthusiastic outpour *cum grano salis* and taking into account all the major reservations and objections that have been brought forward against hypertext, I seek to arrive at a theoretical and practical approach that will 'prepare' this 'literary media genre' for canonization. In so doing, I will pay particular attention to hypertext's structural principles and the effects they have on reading and writing. In this respect, I will examine closely George Landow's (1992/1997) much-debated concept of the 'wreader' and use it as a recurring *leitmotif* to this study. It will become clear that the very process of reading hypertext does not in itself liberate, or 'empower', the reader. On the contrary, hypertext readers are far more inclined to feel restricted, or disempowered, in their decision-making processes, a situation which more often than not results in feelings of frustration. Having said that, the concept of the 'wreader' can indeed be sanctioned provided that readers are actually given a chance to participate in empowering, collaborative projects in which literary hypertext is read, discussed and created jointly rather than in isolation.

Bearing in mind that canonization processes are inextricably linked to changing educational policies and their underlying ideologies, I propagate the pedagogic use of literary hypertext (see Ensslin, 2004, 2005a, 2006), both exploratory (reception-oriented) and constructive (production-oriented). Based on theoretical, hermeneutic and empirical findings, I propose that literary hypertext harbours high epistemological and pedagogic potential, thus facilitating its canonization in a hypermedially conscious curriculum. Rather than undertaking an extensive examination of digital media in general, which has been done by theorists such as Aarseth (1997), Murray (1997) and Hayles (2002), I restrict myself to literary hypertext, as it may be considered *the* digital poetic form most akin to the book.

Unlike in Germany, Switzerland and the Americas, hypertextual forms of creative writing in the UK have been entering academic and public discourse only languidly, an observation which I will support (in Chapter 2) by empirical data collected from British press discourse and teachers' statements about their professional practice. Reasons for this inhibitive situation can only be given hypothetically, in terms of a general literary conservativism, which is grounded in a pervasive belief in prescriptive canonicity as exemplified by Harold Bloom's *The Western Canon* (1994) and that manifests itself in the National Curriculum, which has recently been reformed to address the needs of learners from different social and ethnic backgrounds, yet largely fails to encompass creative New Media phenomena such as literary hypertext as a nexus of written narrative and hypermedia aesthetics.

As previously mentioned, one of the major aims of this study is to investigate the concept of the literary canon and the process of canonization, and to apply them to the controversial and therefore easily marginalized literary medium of hypertext.[5] I will argue that literary (rather than scholarly or expository) hypertext requires a new, extended concept of both literature and textuality, which takes into account not only its 'marked' mediality, but a radically unconventional understanding of the reading process and the interaction between bottom-up and top-down processing. The dynamic nature of hypertext as discussed in this study will further translate into an 'alternative' hypertext canon, which is essentially grounded in the principles of early twentieth-century *avantgarde* canons. To reflect the globalizing tendencies of the web and, in its wake, of digital literature, this hypertext canon is bilingual, featuring works written in two dominant internet languages, English and German. Not all of these works were written or designed by *native speakers* of either language, which is yet another characteristic phenomenon of computer and web-based authoring.

Furthermore, to exemplify the interconnectedness of descriptivism and prescriptivism in canon formation, the hypertext canon has been selected on the basis of a number of conditions (a rule canon). To prove that hypertext is indeed 'worthy' (to flag up a value-ridden term which is frequently used by canon-makers, yet cannot be sustained without a solid evaluative basis) of establishing an alternative canon, which is seen to be a prerequisite of being integrated in the school (and university) curriculum, it needs to be shown that distinctive examples of this genre fulfil certain criteria that conform to aesthetic, academic, and educational standards. Those criteria include aspects of text production, reception, subject matter, and form. The resulting hypertext canon and the implications that can be drawn for the production of hypertext may serve aspiring writer-programmers as a set of good practice guidelines (Günther, 1987).

To help prospective teachers and novice readers of hypertext to find a working basis, the aforementioned 'canon' of hypertexts is based on a set of formal, conceptual, reception- and production-oriented criteria, which take into account all I shall have to say about the canon and its problematic position within modern literary education. The problematic status of value judgements, to which all attempts at suggesting canonization criteria – and in fact canons themselves – are subjected, will be discussed, and the catalogue of hypertexts will take into account the consequences drawn from these deliberations.

The fact that the psychological effects of reading hypertext documents tend to be characterized in terms of 'cognitive overhead' or 'getting lost in hyperspace' is not seen as an impediment but rather as a constitutive aesthetic attribute, which, paradoxically, enables learners to form a critical opinion of texts that seem to defy coherent forms of criticism and shared understanding. It will become evident that the didactic interplay of exploratory and constructive hypertext (Joyce, 1988/2002b) potentially sets free creative potential in learners as they are given responsibility for their own learning notwithstanding the risks brought about by the medium's intricate technology. The didactic applicability to a constructivist literary classroom will be further exemplified through a case study report describing the implementation and results of an empirical literary hypertext project. The results show how a hypermedially extended concept of literary competence can successfully be employed, particularly in an A-level or undergraduate curriculum. Following the principles of constructivist learning philosophy, 'successful' is understood from the learner's perspective, whose intrinsic motivation levels, autonomy and hypermedially extended 'literary competence' lie at the centre of pedagogic interest.

To introduce some essential terminology, 'hypertext', in the broadest sense, serves as an umbrella term for a distinct organizational principle, which interlinks documents, files and text chunks (lexias)[6] into an interactive, associative network (Nelson, 1984; Nielsen, 1990, 1996; Lang, 1998).[7] In this study, 'hypertext' is used in a more narrow sense, i.e. as a short form of 'literary hypertext', which is understood as a distinct genre of so-called 'New Media writing' and is imaginary in nature rather than expository, scholarly or factual. This concept of hypertext comprises all three traditional literary genres: fiction, verse, and various forms of dramatic discourse – often in combined form. As will be elaborated later, hypertexts have a nonlinear compositional structure and thus categorically deviate from other digitized forms of writing, often called 'paper under glass', as they are organized in a traditional, linear way and can be printed as such. Hypertext is by definition un-printable, for such an act of material linearization would disrupt its characteristic underlying macrostructure. Due to its *non*linear macrostructure, the hypertextual reading process is *multi*linear. In other words, there are multiple possible reading paths through a hypertext, which, due to the temporal and spatial sequentiality of decoding language, have to be transgressed in an essentially linear way, but which defy the macrostructural monolinearity and hierarchies of the majority of literary print media, as the order and selection of text units varies from reader to reader and from reading to reading. To subsume structural nonlinearity and receptive multilinearity under one umbrella term, I will generally refer to the *anti*linearity of hypertext, which is, in actual fact, short for 'anti-monolinearity'.[8]

(Literary) hypermedia is understood as a certain type of hypertext, which integrates and semantically interrelates other semiotic systems like image, sound, and film with script, without, however, depriving the work of its textual, in the sense of graphemic, basis. As Michael Joyce, one of the founding fathers of literary hypertext, puts it, 'nearly all hypertext systems involve other media' (1988/2002b: 40). This is true in particular for hypertexts created after the popularization of the World Wide Web in the early 1990s, and for this reason my understanding of hypertext is trans-semiotically inclusive and covers all forms of *literary* hypertext, hypermedia ('hypertext multimedia') and cybertext (where text becomes a programmed 'machine', taking control of the reading process). Each of these terms will be explained in greater depth in Chapter 1.

That said, my focus is on 'literature' in its traditional sense of writing or script (litteratura) rather than other forms of New Media art, which are primarily visually or aurally oriented and include genres such as digital film, radio and television, as well as purely 'visible' (Kac, 1996) forms of New Media poetry (e.g. holographic and video poetry). The emphasis on written text is not only justifiable from a pedagogic point of view that seeks to address problems of literacy and media behaviour, but is borne out by recent findings of the Poynter Project, based at Stanford University (Stanford Poynter Project, 1995–2005;

see Suter, 2000). The research team in question has examined the eye move-ment of subjects reading online newspapers. They found that the overwhelming majority of readers first and foremost concentrate on written text rather than images. Furthermore, 75 per cent of them read the entire length of an article, whereas readers of print newspapers break off far sooner.

Bearing these prerequisites in mind, I further exclude from my investiga-tion predominantly visual and cinematographic manifestations of Aarseth's 'cybertext', i.e. computer games, MUDs (Multi-User Dungeons), MOOs (Multi-User Dungeons, Object-Oriented)[9] and digitized film, regardless of their narratological disposition and immersive qualities.[10] The term 'cybertext' is used here for what I call 'third-generation hypertexts',[11] which are character-ized by a gradual transfer of control from user to machine, leaving the former increasingly powerless. I will discuss this phenomenon in detail in Chapter 1. Suffice it to reiterate at this stage that my understanding of 'cybertext' is centred on the verbal sign as it appears on the user interface rather than in the programming code. Nevertheless, cybertext embraces the potencies of the programmed machine, which, as we shall see, opens up innovative and enga-ging literary forms. Similarly, Nick Montfort's (2003) concept of 'interac-tive fiction', which largely encompasses narrative 'adventure' games, or 'text adventures'[12] in the tradition of the *Zork* trilogy of the late 1970s, and which frequently realizes poststructuralist labyrinthine imagery (e.g. *Myst*), will not be discussed at any great length. To single out a further component of growing significance across a wide range of academic fields (humanities, psychology, architecture, engineering etc.), I draw a line between what Bukatman (1994: 13) refers to as 'textual' and 'virtual reality' (VR), subsuming hypertext under the former, and phenomena of direct, real-time, physically controlled experience of feigned ontological totality under the latter.[13]

Inevitably, the productive liberties granted by the internet allow or even invite an amalgamation of virtual and textual realities. Nevertheless, it needs to be repeated that 'literary' relies on verbal decoding as a phenomenological and hermeneutic basis for cognitive and aesthetic effects. Such effects are bound to differ fundamentally from real-time experience, as verbal decoding creates a distance between text and readerly experience, which can only be bridged by imaginative pro-activity and therefore remains a crucial element of literary reception. Hence, instances of VR that emphasize visual and haptic experience cannot be included in this study.

I will further exclude so-called 'codeworks', or artworks that reflect the com-puter's intrinsic textuality, including ASCII art, recursion and programme code poetry (Cramer, 2001, 2004; Heibach, 2003). One certainly cannot ignore the fact that the computer is an essentially 'double-layered medium' (Wenz, 2001: 43 – my translation), which integrates the visible level of the user interface with the sub-level of the underlying electronic basis. Nevertheless, when it comes to questions of hypertext canonicity and the acquisition of hyper-media literacy, one cannot expect higher-than-average levels of computer lit-eracy. Furthermore, codeworks are generally categorized as 'net.art' rather than hypertext (Cramer, 2004), the former placing more emphasis on technological discourse than poetics and narrative. In a technophile environment, there is a permanent risk of losing a critical outlook on the ideological implications of the digital medium and its positivistic aestheticization. The 'aesthetic gain of digital literature' is permanently at stake, and it 'cannot be reduced to technology' (Block, 2004: 316).[14]

As previously indicated, the concept of hypertext itself and its subgenres tend to have fuzzy boundaries. They often display a mixture of multimodal (Kress and van Leeuwen, 2006) and transgeneric elements, such as an intertextual array of (written) text types (expository, documentary, narrative, lyrical, dramatic), and tend towards hybrid forms compounding written text with other media texts such as still and moving image (e.g. Stefan Maskiewicz's *Quadrego*, Zeitgenossens' *Yatoo*, Dorit Linke's *Der Apfel*), game, riddle or treasure hunt (e.g. Nika Bertram's *Der Kahuna Modus*, Romana Brunnauer's *Zwei Tote?*, M. D. Coverley's *Califia*).

I further distance myself from overspecified and therefore misleading catchall terms such as Howell's (1990) and Kuhlen's (1991) 'hyperfiction', as both authors understand it as an 'application of the non-linear principle of hypertext' (Kuhlen, 1991: 46) to hypertext literature in general rather than as one specific, narrative genre. The term 'hyperfiction' has frequently been used to denote pre-World Wide Web literary hypertexts in software programmes such as Apple's HyperCard and Eastgate's Storyspace.[15] The difficulty with delimiting the term thus is that commercial hypertexts of all genres are still written in specified hypertext software, mostly traded by Eastgate Systems. To abandon such producer-defined, commercially ideologized terminology, I will use the term 'hyperfiction' to describe specimens of a specific subgenre of hypertext, which places narrativity over dialogicity, prose over verse or rhyme, and shows (in its most radical form, the hypernovel) a tendency towards 'epic' length.

In 1988, hypertext pedagogue Michael Joyce first published his essay 'Siren Shapes: Exploratory and Constructive Hypertexts' (Joyce, 1988/2002b), which became the perhaps most frequently quoted reference in the area of hypertext pedagogy. In it, Joyce distinguishes between two major applications of hypertext as a learning tool. On the one hand, 'exploratory' uses focus on hypertext as 'a delivery or presentational technology' (*ibid.*: 41), looking at the ways in which readers, or 'audiences' (*ibid.*: 41), can control the transformation of an informational body into personalized knowledge structures according to their individual needs and predilections. This is facilitated through the possibility of choosing multiple navigational paths through a text and alternative visual representations of the macrostructure, as well as the opportunity to interact with and modify an existing work creatively. 'Constructive' uses, on the other hand, concentrate on the inventive, productive and participatory side of hypertext, using it as an analytical and synthetic tool for developing and assembling a body of information that learners, or rather 'scriptors' (*ibid.*: 42), map in alignment with their particular needs and interests.

In this approach, learning equals processing and, at the same time, transforming information in such a way as to make information one's own cognitive property. According to Joyce, hypertext thus models and visualizes learners' transformational knowledge.

Expanding Joyce's differentiation, Smith (1991) defines (pedagogic) hypertext, in the sense of an organizational, epistemological device, as 'a matter of negotiating between hypertext as information system and hypertext as facilitation' (quoted in DeWitt, 1999: 131), with the former corresponding to the notion of 'exploratory', and the latter to that of 'constructive'. Whereas in Smith's view, hypertext as an information system limits the user's freedom, foregrounding 'the system over the user' (DeWitt, 1999: 132), hypertext as a facilitating 'space' helps students to learn constructively, by 'mak[ing] relationships and construct[ing] meaning, [which are] activities that feed into and enrich other processes' (*ibid.*: 132), as well as by exploring existing material and knowledge structures. Smith thus emphasizes the pragmatic and enabling nature of paedagogic hypertext as a means of information retrieval and a versatile instrument for the construction of knowledge and skill.

Taking Joyce's binary concept of pedagogic hypertext as a starting point, this study is divided into two major parts, entitled 'Explorations' and 'Constructions'. These are preceded by an extended 'prologue' (Chapter 1), an introductory chapter that sets out the ontological, critical and aesthetic content of the subsequent study and outlines major Anglo-American and 'German' (in the sense of German, Swiss and Austrian) research into hypertext theory. Part 1 ('Explorations', Chapters 2 and 3) presents an exploratory approach to hypertext, which moves on from Joyce's conception insofar as it seeks to generate and explore a list of selected *literary* (rather than expository or critical) hypertexts in a hermeneutic fashion.[16] On the basis of current definitions of literature and the current discourse surrounding canon theory, the selection criteria for such an approximate 'canon' will be set out and explained in detail (Chapter 2). Of particular interest will be the question of why hypertext has, to date, not entered the National Curriculum of England and Wales, a process which would be seen as decisive evidence of a burgeoning canonicity status. To concretize those theoretical investigations, Chapter 3 suggests an 'alternative' canon of three 'generations' of hypertext, which is based on the criteria set out in Chapter 2.

Part 2 of this study ('Constructions', Chapters 4 and 5) takes up Joyce's idea of constructive hypertext pedagogy and applies it to a contemporary undergraduate literary classroom in Britain. Unlike Joyce, my approach uses collaborative, *creative* hypertext writing as the major tool for knowledge transformation, taking into account the need for creative expression, intrinsic motivation and individualized learning. To provide a theoretical foundation to this approach, Chapter 4 explores the central tenets of radical constructivism and their implications for the development of literary competence. Three major approaches to literary competence are discussed, whereupon a hypermedial expansion of current theories is suggested. Chapter 5, finally, presents the results of a case study in which, on the basis of action research, constructive hypertext was used in a hypermedia-extended, undergraduate literary class-room. Learning outcomes and student responses are discussed in the light of the aforementioned hypermedially extended concept of literary competence, and conclusions are drawn for didactic practice.

Chapters 1 to 4 are grounded in archival, software and internet research. At the time of writing, the hypertexts listed in Chapter 3 were either internet-based or came on data carriers such as CD-ROMs or floppy disks. To gain access to some of Eastgate's publications which are compatible with neither Windows nor Apple versions later than OS 9, a Macintosh computer had to be set up to allow an obsolete operation system to run on it. Chapter 5 reports, as previously mentioned, the findings of an empirical teaching project. These were – in alignment with the principles of action research – obtained, on the one hand, by means of learner logs, tape-recorded interviews and classroom activities, and, on the other, by a stylistic analysis of student writings.

Chapter 1

Hypertextual Ontologies

1   Nodes, Links and Networks

[H]ypertext is the grin of the Cheshire Cat. The cat is long dead and transmogrified. However, its simple yet tantalising grin permeates almost every aspect of computing – from home shopping to computer-supported distance learning, or support groups for the bereaved to interactive multi-player games.

(McAleese, 1999a: v)

This chapter is designed as an extended prologue to the study as a whole. It aims to summarize the major research into hypertextual ontologies and poetics undertaken so far by scholars around the world, with a view to providing a general introduction to the quiddities of hypertext. A variety of central approaches will be covered, including formal, generic, historical, production-oriented and reception-oriented approaches, and discussed critically, using examples of hypertexts in English and German. With a view to placing hypertext within a distinctly literary tradition, I will investigate it both synchronically, by means of a formal-generic approach, and diachronically, by providing an overview of the major literary and medial developments that have shaped hypertext before and since it came into being in the late 1980s. To summarize the prevailing aesthetic features of literary hypertext, the final section of this chapter seeks to approach a poetics of hypertext, converging previous attempts with some new ideas of my own.

The term 'hypertext' is a coinage of the twentieth century, yet the principles of multilinear reading, interrelating, annotating and cross-referencing, and indeed the link, on which hypertext is formally based, are over 1,000 years old. So-called proto-hypertexts can be traced as far back as the Middle Ages, when the first glosses (annotations) in the Jewish Talmud, the Bible, Canon law and medical texts appeared.[1] Moving further on in history, European Enlightenment scholars produced the first printed encyclopaedias. For example, Diderot and d'Alembert's *Encyclopédie* (1751–80), Samuel Johnson's *Dictionary* of 1755 and the first publication of the *Encyclopaedia Britannica* in 1768 by the Scotsmen Adam and Charles Black all represent early forms of hypertextual cross-referencing, or 'super-scribing' text in order to explain, elaborate and connect intertextually. As Bolter points out, 'in some scholarly medieval codices, the page became a web of text and interpretation, tradition and innovation'

(2001: 22). One early literary form of proto-hypertext mentioned by Bakhtin (1981) in his essay 'From the Prehistory of Novelistic Discourse' is the so-called medieval 'cento', which is Latin for 'patchwork'. It was a genre 'composed exclusively out of others' verse-lines and hemistichs' (Morris, 1994: 69). In other words, it emerged from a compilation of passages taken from works by great poets of the past. As will be shown in Chapter 3, hyperfictions such as Shelley Jackson's *Patchwork Girl* (1995) take this idea literally to create distinctly hypertextual characters, who are 'stitched together' from a variety of other characters, who are thus reincarnated as a new, composite 'cyborg'.

The Baroque Age, with its affinity to stylistic conceit, featured instances of labyrinthine poetry and so-called 'poetic machines' such as Georg Philipp Harsdörffer's *Wechselsatz* in *Poetischer Trichter* (1648–53) and Quirinius Kuhlmann's *Libes-Kuß* (1671). In the Romantic Period, the idea of the 'absolute book', influenced by Friedrich Schlegel's utopian ideal of a *progressive Universalpoesie*, elevated intertextual connectivity to a paradigm of a whole age. Examples of proto-hypertextual, antilinear fiction, the earliest of which emerged alongside the rise of the ultimately 'non-conformist' novel,[2] include Lawrence Sterne's *Tristram Shandy* (1760),[3] Jean Paul's footnote fiction (e.g. *Siebenkäs*, 1796/97; *Titan*, 1800–03), James Joyce's *Finnegans Wake* (1939), Marc Saporta's *Composition No. 1* (1961), Vladimir Nabokov's *Pale Fire* (1962), Julio Cortázar's *Rayuela* (*Hopscotch*, 1963), Arno Schmidt's *Zettels Traum* (1970) and Milorad Pavić's *The Dictionary of the Khazars* (1984).[4]

With regard to (digital) hypertext as a medially determined literary 'genre',[5] or 'hypertext proper' – which forms the focus of this study – let us continue with an investigation of the actual technological concept of hypertext, which, after all, forms the macrostructural foundation of the literary concept. The most widely acknowledged definitions have been suggested by Ted Nelson (whose first public use of the word 'hypertext' dates back to his 1965 lectures at Vassar College), Jakob Nielsen (1990), Paul Delany and George P. Landow (1991), and Jay David Bolter (2001). Essentially, the abstract idea of 'hypertext' is based on the rhizome metaphor (Deleuze and Guattari, 1987), characterized by a ramifying, horizontally organized root structure, which is, unlike arborescent structures, decentralized, i.e. there is no core, or 'trunk', and no visible hierarchy. Similarly, Nelson's ubiquitously quoted definition of hypertext classifies it as:

> non-sequential writing – text that branches and allows choices to the reader, best read at an interactive screen. As popularly conceived, this is a series of text chunks connected by links which offer the reader different pathways. (1984: 0/2)[6]

Evidently, Nelson's explanation combines issues of production, reception, mediality and textuality. It emphasizes hypertext's compositional nonlinearity, which allows a certain extent of freedom on the reader's side; its compulsive mediality and dependence on browser technology; and, tentatively, the narrative consequences of its abstract text-organizational principles. Due to its generic descriptiveness, this definition readily subsumes a wide range of hypertextual phenomena, even those that are only minimally antilinear.

Nielsen's rather more prescriptive yet partially obscuring definition picks up Nelson's concept of structural nonlinearity, casting somewhat more light on the reader's cognitive activities and emotive state during the reading process. Curiously enough, it seems to contravene the widely accepted view that hypertext readers have to cope with an unusually high cognitive load, and thus denies an essential part of the aesthetic challenges implied by the concept:

> Hypertext is non-sequential writing: a directed graph, where each node contains some amount of text or other information ... [T]rue hypertext should also make users feel that they can move *freely* through the information according to their own needs. This feeling is hard to define precisely but certainly implies short response times and low cognitive load when navigating. (Nielsen, 1990: 298 − emphasis in original)

A more refined, phenomenological attempt is made by Marie-Laure Ryan, who emphasizes the psychological effects of the reader's co-constructive, physically interactive reading activity as well as the problematic textuality of hypertext. She also points to the fact that the alleged freedom of the reader is only relative, as the ultimate decisions regarding choices of reading paths are made by the author (I shall discuss this dilemma in greater detail in Chapter 1.4):

> In hypertext, the prototypical form of interactive textuality (though by no means the most interactive), the reader determines the unfolding of the text by clicking on certain areas, the so-called hyperlinks, that bring to the screen other segments of text. Since every segment contains several such hyperlinks, every reading produces a different text, if by text one understands a particular set and sequence of signs scanned by the reader's eye. Whereas the reader of a standard print text constructs personalized interpretations out of an invariant semiotic base, the reader of an interactive text thus participates in the construction of the text as a visible display of signs. (Ryan, 2001: 5–6)

Bolter (2001) makes a major contribution to hypertext criticism not only in that he outlines the history of writing and the implications of its changing mediality and materiality (from print to hypertext technology), but in that he adds to the established script-based concept by elaborating the dimension of hypermedia (digitized sound, graphics and video), another term coined by Nelson. Bolter describes the widely observable increase in visuality, effected by the hypermediality of the contemporary web, in terms of 'reverse ekphrasis'. This concept inverts the long-established rhetorical device of 'ekphrasis' (the verbal instantiation of a concrete, visual object or piece of art), emphasizing instead the condensation of conceptual details into pictorial representation.

Bolter goes as far as to liken elaborated hypermediacy to 'a sort of popular *Gesamtkunstwerk*' (*ibid*.: 26), which, despite being a comprehensible thought, fails to take into account Wagner's distinct philosophical implications. These are grounded in his view of classical Greek drama as 'man's ultimate achievement, the self-expression of a whole people in its deepest and most noble aspect, a religious bonding ritual combining all the arts – notably poetry, music, and dance – in perfect synthesis' (Bridgham, 2000: 337).[7] A similar intention has never been formulated by hypertext writers or theorists, nor does the largely ludic, deconstructivist approach followed by most suggest a concomitant paradigm. Hence, I will refrain from exploring the Romantic notion of the *Gesamtkunstwerk* any further.

Bolter further introduces the notion of topographical writing, which he juxtaposes with conventional, hierarchical writing. Topographical writing, as its etymology suggests, broadly refers to spatial organization of writing, the mapping and charting of distinct textual elements and their multiple interconnections. The metaphor readily lends itself to electronic writing, particularly hypertext, which Bolter views as of a both visual and verbal nature. Hypertext, according to Bolter, 'is not the writing *of* a place, but rather a writing *with* places, spatially realized topics' (2001: 36 – my emphasis). Similarly, it is the hypertext author's responsibility to design a textual space, a 'story space', that contains the virtual totality of all potential realizations his or her fiction can take and into which the reader plunges arbitrarily, rather than embarking on a pre-defined, singular reading path.

Moving back in the history of electronic textuality, the concept of digital hypertext as a technological means to interconnect text elements was developed long before the introduction of the internet. In the 1960s, when ARPA (Advanced Research Projects Agency) and its MIT-based information technology scientists were in the process of developing ARPANET, the prototype of the internet, Theodor Nelson started to revisit Vannevar Bush's revolutionary idea of the *Memex* ('Memory Expander'), an information system designed for the connection and storage of as well as access to all documents and communications in the world, which Bush had first envisaged as early as the 1930s.[8] Nelson's main contribution, which has to date remained a merely visionary construct, was the application of Bush's idea to literature. Following an inclusive approach to literariness, i.e. panfictionalism, Nelson aimed to connect all literary works into a so-called 'docuverse', an abstract concept upon which the web is ultimately based and which Nelson wanted to concretize in a project named 'Xanadu'. The project still exists today, but the focus has shifted to developing a system which could not possibly be represented by paper-based technology. It is based on an intricate, horizontal rather than vertical, hierarchical organization of interlinked nodes, the last of which characterizes the pseudo-democratic arrangement of interdependent pages in HTML editors. This latest version of Xanadu, once completed, is intended to facilitate the inserting and referencing of quotations into any given text document.

Many of the techniques used in hypertext can be traced back to the literary experiments of the 'classical' modernist *avantgardes* of the early twentieth century, which piloted techniques such as montage, collage, serialization, intermediality, aleatorics, interactivity and collaborative writing (Heibach, 2003) and were emulated by US poststructuralist artists and writers in particular. Similarly, these techniques are by no means inventions of hypertext authors but have been re-applied to computer-generated literature, thus expanding and accelerating previously analogue forms of experimental writing. That said, as Gendolla and Schäfer (2001: 80) argue, the newly extended dimensions of inter-human and human-machine communication, facilitated through digital synchronous and a-synchronous networking, form a particularly prolific experimenting ground. This includes, for instance, the playful, creative exploration of devices otherwise known as spyware and spam (e.g. Holeton's *Figurski at Findhorn on Acid*) and the possibilities of secretive information transfer.

In electronic forms of writing, electronic data transmission replaces the material production and distribution of text, which allows for a synchronization of composition, editing and reading. Similarly, text production has to be seen in terms of a permanent process rather than a static result. Furthermore, the nature of electronic writing implies that 'documents are becoming applications' (Siegel, 1997: vii). In other words, 'web sites sound more like software. The truth is, many sites *are* like software' (Powell, 1999: 655). Electronic writing develops its own dynamics, which surfaces in ever-changing macroaesthetic challenges to the reader, who has to appropriate the idiosyncratic technological and structural implications of every single textual phenomenon before he or she can embark on the actual reading experience. Electronic literature physically interacts with the reader, 'let[ting] words on the loose' (M.-L. Ryan, 1999: 1), thus revealing the processes of writing to the reader.

As anticipated by the poststructuralist metaphors of link, node and network,[9] which are in a state of constant flux, hypertext may be characterized in terms of interconnected granularity (McAleese, 1990), which is defined in terms of chunk-sized information units, 'chunks of bytes' (Nelson, 1984), 'episodes' (Howell, 1990: 139), or, most commonly, 'nodes'. According to Conklin (1987) and Snyder (1997), nodes do not equate paragraphs. They are separate, self-contained units that do not offer seamless transitions but rather invite multiple progressivity. As a result, the reading process is multilinear and associative.[10] Each reading produces a different 'text'. Macrostructural sequentiality is replaced by networks of 'lexias' (a term coined by Barthes [1970/1987] and applied to hypertext by Landow [1992/1997]), of textual nodes, or 'units of reading' (Barthes, 1970/1987: 11–12), that – viewed superficially – represent Derrida's concept of decentralized form and meaning. Such networks of lexias, or 'webs', as they are commonly referred to, can be divided into hyperdocuments and hyperwebs (Storrer, 2002: 164). Whereas hyperdocuments, such as closed hypertexts (which are mostly not entirely closed, but allow varying degrees of reader contribution), are comparably small, comprehensive, self-contingent networks, hyperwebs like the World Wide Web itself are typically inexhaustible in size and outreach.

It has to be noted, however, that the direct, uncritical translation of Derrida's deconstruction tenets into hypertext criticism is a risky undertaking and cannot be fully verified. To mention just one fallacy, hypertexts are never entirely non-hierarchical and decentred. Although, seemingly, all nodes are equivalent, entry pages tend to be the same, i.e. readers are initially presented with the same lexia and possible reading paths. Similarly, some lexias tend to be more 'equal' than others in that they statistically recur more frequently, thus forming so-called 'loops', thereby signalling to the reader a higher-than-average degree of narrative, cognitive or aesthetic significance.

Links, or 'dynamic footnotes' (Heim, 1987: 162; Moulthrop, 1993: 76), have been widely described as hypertext's distinctive structural element (Simanowski, 2002c), insofar as they are realized as technical rather than purely editorial devices (as is the case with any proto-hypertexts) of navigation and interaction. They are not only elements of the text, they constitute it and often operate independently of any context. According to Harpold (1991) and Landow (1999), links bridge as well as maintain separation. As though he were meaning to deliver a theoretical basis to Shelley Jackson's neo-Frankensteinian *Patchwork Girl*, Harpold (1991) maintains that:

> Hypertexts are dismembered sorts of texts, marked by wounds at each irreducible turn of the narrative, and that reading these texts is a kind of ritual binding of the wounds, and an elevation of the fragmented corpus to a totemic object.

From a text-linguistic perspective, links are a cohesive means that constitute hyper-textual 'coherence' (Kuhlen, 1991; Storrer, 2002). Coherence is accentuated here because it seems to contradict the concept of literary hypertext, which deconstructs the traditional principles of closure, centrality and unified meaning. Nonetheless, coherence in hypertext is achieved in different ways than the conventional notion introduced by Halliday and Hasan (1976) suggests. Semantic coherence in hypertext arises from surface structures that seem to lack microstructural cohesion. The link as the central cohesive element replaces interlexial endophora (e.g. pronouns, synonyms and antonomasias which either point backwards – anaphorically – or forwards – cataphorically – in a text). Hence, hypertext readers construct coherence from their specific reading paths. They do so autonomously, i.e. largely without being aided by conventional, cohesive elements, and revisit their mental representations of the text whenever necessitated by contravening textual information.

Simanowski (2002c) distinguishes between the stylistics, semantics and psychology of the hyperlink, whereby semantic and psychological features need to be understood as concomitant factors. Stylistically, the link has the tripartite function of being part of the text (a sign), an index (a pointer) and, simultaneously, a stepping stone to another text (an action). As a proleptic microstructural figure, the link implies the existence of 'the other', which is particularly interesting if 'the other' does not correspond to the label by which it is indexed. This latter device is frequently employed by creative hypertext writers deliberately to flout readers' expectations and cause them to revise their previous constructs of textual meaning.

With regard to cognitive semantic features, Simanowski and other theorists maintain that hypertexts are at a risk of facilitating superficial, impatient reading, which may go as far as to a 'loss of thinking culture' (Rötzer, 1998: 19 – my translation), or, put rather less pointedly, a loss of the 'hermeneutic tradition of interpretation' (Tuman, 1992: 62). Drawing on Wirth (1997), Simanowski (2002c) further explains that a lack of link semantics results in carnivalization,[11] i.e. a 'delirium of possibilities' (Wirth, 1997: 319 – my translation) which may lead to irrational, erratic and 'abductive reading' (*ibid.*: 329 – my translation) and a loss of critical pondering for the sake of the simplistic, oppositional thinking often found in television talk shows. Further concern is voiced by Harpold (1991), who warns that efficiency and pleasure arising from seeking to bridge narrative gaps, which are understood as traumatic 'cuts', may lead to a 'fetishization' of the link, which, however, does not result in a satisfactory mending of those cuts.

To return to a previously mentioned issue, the most widely held view is that the presence of links presents readers with multiple navigational options, thus causing them to proceed in a multilinear fashion. This is, upon close examination, a simplification. Strictly speaking, we have to distinguish between three levels of relative (anti)linearity. First, the macrostructural level, or the underlying hypertext map or 'web', is organized in a non-sequential manner. Its various interconnections undermine structural linearity and, instead, provide the reader with a large number of possible reading paths. Second, the computer interface presents the reader with lexias that have to be read in a linear fashion, no matter how many links they display. Reading, in the sense of decoding linguistic signs, is temporally and spatially determined, and regardless of which pathway(s) the reader chooses, the reception process will invariably be sequential (from left to right, one verbal element following the other). Third, the product of the receptive process is the aesthetic object, a mental construct in the reader's imagination. Depending on how many readings have been undertaken, this aesthetic object may present itself as a flexible, ever-changing image, which mirrors the macro- and microstructure as perceived by the reader and which includes subjective impressions of antilinearity. Evidently, the higher the number of links and nodes, the greater the complexity of a hypertext's macrostructure. This complexity is heightened further by a deliberate lack of designated links, which, at first glance, seem intent upon offering the reader clarification, yet often fail to do so and, instead, introduce even more new concepts and structures. This strategy, as well as omitting content maps and other navigational aids, is frequently employed by literary hypertext authors to achieve certain aesthetic effects in the reader. In expository or scholarly hypertexts, by contrast, structural obscurity through deficient transparency is considered a weakness.

Kuhlen (1991) has been among the first to attempt a taxonomy of hyperlinks, which broadly divides them into referential (not explicitly specified, i.e. purely associative) and specified ('typisierte') links. 'Specified' here stands for the demarcation of various semantic relations (e.g. hierarchical, equivalent) between lexias, which can be realized by links. As Kuhlen himself concedes, however, the major problem with his taxonomy is that many hypertext systems, particularly literary hypertexts, rely solely or mainly on referential linking. Therefore, with regard to literary hypertexts a far more elaborate distinction between various types of referential links is required. Furthermore, Kuhlen induces his taxonomy from a specific type of offline hypertext systems that have become obsolete or, for that matter, do not exist any longer. He also aims to find names for link buttons with a view to facilitating navigation. In so doing, he undermines essential aesthetic criteria of literary hypertext, which rely on macrostructural obscurity. His taxonomy may thus be considered inapplicable to literary hypertext.

To cast light onto the 'impenetrable tangle or arbitrary morass' that is often seen to constitute hypertext's macrostructure, Bernstein (1998) induces a number of linking 'patterns', mainly from examples of *literary* hypertext, which he considers less short-lived than scholarly or journalistic hypertexts. Those patterns are named with the aim of helping readers to understand, analyse and describe hypertextual phenomena: 'The problem is not that the hypertexts lack structure but rather that we lack words to describe it' (*ibid.*). Bernstein suggests the following linking types, which often co-occur in a hypertext:

Dynamic links are changeable insofar as their appearance is contingent on the reader's preceding interactions, and individual reading paths alter depending on which lexias have already been visited. Dynamic links frequently occur in first-generation hypertexts, e.g. in Michael Joyce's *afternoon, a story*. *Cycles* or cyclical repetitions are loops that take the reader back to a previously visited lexia. A subcategory of the cycle is the *Joyce's Cycle*, which also occurs in *afternoon, a story* (e.g. [*I want to say*]).[12] It automatically changes the reading path upon re-visiting a lexia, thus causing the reader not to return yet another time. The *Douglas's Cycle*, on the other hand, does not offer a way out of the respective section and thus marks closure or exhaustion. It is derived from Jane Yellowlees Douglas's *I Have Said Nothing*, which makes ample use of this linking technique. Cycles that mutually interconnect and can be switched to and fro by the reader are called *contours*. They can be found in some sections of Shelley Jackson's *Patchwork Girl*, e.g. 'A journal', where the reader is repeatedly made to return to the same body map and embark on various interconnecting loops describing and literally piecing together the monster's constituent organs. *Counterpoint* structures are discursive, consisting of dialogic, antithetical elements such as theme and response, question and answer, as can be found in Cathy Marshall and Judy Malloy's *Forward Anywhere*, or present and past, as exemplified by Douglas's *I Have Said Nothing*. *Mirrorworlds* add a second narrative or intertextual level, reflecting on and parodying the main point of view of the main 'story'. John McDaid's *Uncle Buddy's Phantom Funhouse*, for instance, consists of two 'houses', i.e. narrative levels, one of which represents a realistic archive of documents, whereas the other, called 'Auntie Em's Haunt House', symbolizes a fantastic world, which parodies the world of the reader and the principal, yet elusive and absent, character, Newkirk. Similarly, Bill Bly's *We Descend* intermingles various intertextual levels, as it combines the diary entries of a scholar with documents from his text archive, thus forming a highly fragmented, interrelated set of interwoven plots and degrees of realism. A *tangle* represents, as its name suggests, a playful approach, as the sheer number of links and lack of guidance deliberately disorient the reader. As in Carolyn Guyer's *Quibbling* and Jacques Servin's *BEAST*, confusion is used as an awareness-raising aesthetic effect, to draw attention to subtextual or intertextual implications. *Sieves* are understood as decision trees, which direct the reader to certain episodes. Whereas Gavin Inglis's *Same Day Test* presents a straightforward example of mostly binary sieves, Ruth Nestvold's *Cutting Edges, Or, A Web of Women* mingles plot decisions with character decisions, thus creating a complex, multi-perspectival approach to plot development. A *montage* presents the reader with several different writing spaces, or superimposed windows, which appear simultaneously and thus suggest a collocational, often transsemiotic meaning, as is exemplified by M. D. Coverley's *Califia* and Jacques Servin's *BEAST*. *Neighborhoods* are lexias which share common visual or navigational features so as to make them seem more closely connected than the link may suggest. As the example of Deena Larsen's *Marble Springs* shows, such conceptual proximity is often enhanced by metaphoric site maps which establish spatial consciousness and orientation in the reader. *Split/Join* patterns are used to alter the sequence of lexias according to reader interaction. This technique connects and disconnects sections in a way similar to interactive narratives, such as text adventures, thus causing multiple branching, or splitting, storylines that follow a coherent logic and eventually bring the reader back to a central core (joining). Dorit Linke's *Der Apfel* (2002), for instance, ends on a straightforward, tripartite version of the split/join pattern that gives the reader three equally unsatisfactory endings to choose from. *Missing links* are used to defy the reader's expectations in that they simulate their own existence and are often constructs of wishful thinking in the reader's imagination. They represent elements of intentionally withheld information and are thus cognates of traditionally verbal stylistic devices like ellipses and allusions. Bill Bly's *We Descend* uses missing links as its major stylistic and narrative element, as it is intent upon cutting off storylines at the most precarious and suspenseful moments, leaving the solution of the mysteries to the immersed reader's imagination. Closely related to missing links are *feints*, which operate similarly to flashforwards in traditional fiction. They proleptically suggest future navigational possibilities without, however, giving the reader immediate access to them. Nika Bertram's *Der Kahuna Modus* (2002), for instance, promises readers to reach Kahuna level 3, to win Ary's (a punk lady's) heart permanently, and to defend it against the 'Big Nasty'. Evidently, feints fulfil a far more intricate function than flashforwards in linear narrative, as they send readers on a conceptual quest for information they may never happen to retrieve, due to their individual choices of reading paths. Examples of hypertext maps used as *navigational feints* are Stuart Moulthrop's *Victory Garden* and Stephanie Strickland's *True North*.

Clearly, Bernstein's complex taxonomy of links is far more applicable to literary hypertext than Kuhlen's, yet equally self-evidently it calls out for continual updating. Hyper-poetic forms evolve in the same rapid way as web technology does, and any theory on linking types has to take heed of the radical changes brought about by those developments. No account has, for instance, been given yet of innovative software applications like Stefan Schemat's Hyper Trance Fiction Matrix, which activates (hidden) links according to users' breathing intensity in Kate Pullinger's *The Breathing Wall*. Nor has Bernstein, or in fact any other hyperlink taxonomist, yet integrated the intricate navigational implications of cybertext and the complexities of pre-programmed, synchronous text production by the 'text machine' (Aarseth, 1997: 21). To further outline recent developments in hypertext creativity vis à vis earlier 'generations' of hypertext, the following section will take a quasi-diachronic look at hypertextual forms and developments and focus specifically on changing aspects of mediality.

2 New Media Writing – Hypertext – Hypermedia – Cybertext: Aspects of Mediality

[The poet] must be quite aware of the obvious fact that art never improves, but that the material of art is never quite the same.

. . .

for my meaning is, that the poet has, not a 'personality' to express, but a particular medium, which is only a medium and not a personality, in which impressions and experiences combine in peculiar and unexpected ways.
(Eliot, 'Tradition and the Individual Talent': 51/56)

The following section will examine hypertextual developments diachronically. It will revisit the terminology question and investigate in detail aspects of mediality which are constitutive of various 'generations' of hypertext, as I shall refer to the temporally overlapping techno-historical stages of this literary media genre. It will become clear that the progress of technological developments does alter the genre in a techno-methodical rather than qualitative-evaluative way, as an ever-increasing diversity of artistic tools and methods is becoming available for writers to experiment with and to change the notions of language, text and literature accordingly.

To embrace the diversity of subgenres and concrete manifestations of digital literature, the Nottingham-based digital writers' community TrAce/Alt-X introduced the umbrella term 'New Media Writing' in 2000. The beauty of the term is its encouraging openness, inviting writers to express themselves in whatever creative way they may come up with for the digital medium. However, as Simanowski rightly observes, the term does not specify any aesthetic criteria and is therefore of little use for a critical approach (2002b: 21). In an interview, Bernstein further explains that ' "New Media" is a marketing term, and it's essentially meaningless. In general, "new media" encompasses hypertext along with all the other electronic media' (Carr, 1999). For these reasons, I will refrain from using 'New Media' and, *in lieu*, adhere to more specific terms and concepts that pay heed to the microstructural and macrostructural features of literary text, which, after all, has to be read by ways of lexical and syntactic decoding. Thus, in analogy to technological advances and aesthetic effects relating to them, three generations of hypertext are distinguishable: hypertext, hypermedia and cybertext.[13] The following definitions are based on methodological, semiotic and the resulting aesthetic criteria, rather than technological specifications. I will thus outline the central tools used by writer-programmers of all three generations, without, however, incorporating them in any ensuing literary analysis (see Chapter 3).

Hypertext refers to a largely script-based form of interactive computer-based literature, translating previously linear forms of writing into a technologically nonlinear format and thereby instigating multilinear reading processes. The crucial structural and aesthetic component of hypertext is the hyperlink, which opens up to the reader various navigational possibilities. Some theorists refer to the earliest specimens of hypertext as 'hyperfictions', thus failing to include script- and window-based hyperpoetry and hyperdrama, which started to be written virtually at the same time. The first hypertexts were written by North American literary scholars, with the intention to demonstrate hypertext's potential to implement and thus verify central tenets of poststructuralism (e.g. the death of the author, the decentralization of textual meaning and coherence, the rhizome metaphor, antilinearity, and the notion of the text chunk called 'lexia', which was coined by Barthes [1970/1987]). Therefore, it is not surprising that some early works emphasize, if not exaggerate, the theoretical component, neglecting the aesthetic effects necessary to draw a wide, non-academic readership.

Pictorial devices are employed sparsely if at all in prototypical hypertext, which emphasizes the kinship to conventional print literature. Typically, pictographic elements are limited to navigation maps and desktop icons (e.g. Deena Larsen's *Marble Springs* and Stuart Moulthrop's *Victory Garden*), which can represent additional layers of metaphorical meaning (e.g. the 'brain map' and 'body map' in Shelley Jackson's *Patchwork Girl*). Other frequently quoted examples are Michael Joyce's *afternoon, a story*, Carolyn Guyer's *Quibbling*, Adrienne Eisen's *Six Sex Scenes*, Judy Malloy and Cathy Marshall's *Forward Anywhere* and Gavin Inglis's *Same Day Test*.

Early exemplars were mostly edited and received in pre-World Wide Web programmes such as NoteCards, HyperCard, GUIDE,[14] Intermedia and Storyspace, which, to this day, remains Eastgate's major authoring and editing tool. More recent hypertexts, however, can also be found on the internet. Once HTML started to be used as the major text editing tool, the gap between hypertext and hypermedia narrowed because the use of hypertext mark-up languages not only facilitates but invites the inclusion of multiple semiotic systems. The underlying programming code, which forms the 'deep structure' of a hypertext linguistically, encodes the 'surface structure' of a hypertext, which includes any other paratextual or hypertextual features such as font design, paragraphing, backgrounds and hyperlinks. In that sense, hypertext is an essentially plural concept, not only because it implies, in its most radical form, an infinity of reading paths and, as a result, textual meanings, but because its textuality implies, on the interface level, trans-semiotic openness.

Hypermedia, short for 'hypertext multimedia' (Nielsen, 1990), is, like 'hypertext', a Nelsonian coinage. Its evolution was boosted by the 1993 invention of *Mosaic*, the world's first graphic browser and, following in its wake, the popularization of the World Wide Web with HTML, its major programming language. The key achievement of HTML as a standardized mark-up language was its propensity to create a variety of different semiotic systems, previously analogue, i.e. separated in terms of mediality and materiality, on the basis of a unified, text-based programming code. These semiotic systems comprise text, graphics, digitized speech, audio files, pictographic and photographic images, animation and film.[15]

Produced by means of HTML, XML, JavaScript, Flash and Shockwave programming, hypermedia is characterized by a variety of pastiche and collage techniques. In these, interactivity emerges through technologically manifested intermediality and, in the case of collaborative writing projects, through direct reader interaction and authorial participation via text submissions to the webpage in question, i.e. by writing in specially provided text windows and clicking 'submit' buttons to integrate contributions with already existing text networks.

When analysing hypermedia documents (to a greater extent than first- or third-generation hypertexts), semiotic theories have to be taken into account as they provide a basis for interpreting the intertextual potentialities of such documents. In other words, lexias have to be interpreted in terms of how scripted text and other semiotic systems interact to create (additional) extra- or intertextual meaning. Charles Sanders Peirce's semiotic theory (see Selden, 1985, for a summary) lends itself aptly to such analytical questions. His distinction between symbol, icon and index (or symptom) can be applied to hypermedia as follows.

Peirce's starting point is that intertextuality, which includes all semiotic systems, is based on the assumption that authors and readers share 'culturally constructed systems of meaning, based on shared experiences with the world's texts' (McKillop and Myers, 1999: 67). According to the tenets of reader response theory, individual differences make for diverging readings, although some readings seem more likely to be shared by members of a particular speech community. With respect to hypermedia, authors employ images, animation, film and sound to create additional layers of meaning, which correlate to textual meaning in various ways. The most frequent use of the media is iconic, which means that, for instance, images are used to 'mirror or reproduce isomorphically the meaning of another sign' (*ibid.*: 80).

Second, indexical meaning is constructed via images – to use our first example again – which share elements of meaning with the text yet contain idiosyncratic semantic features that move the meaning of the text beyond its original scope. Finally, media are used symbolically if they do not share any semantic features with the text and, thus, create layers of meaning beyond the conventional implications of both signs. The analyses in Chapter 3 will exemplify specific uses of Peirce's tripartite distinction. It will demonstrate, among other things, that hypermedia authors do not generally restrict themselves to one particular use of non-verbal signs.

From an aesthetic point of view, hypermedia readers are confronted not only with interlinked text lexias but especially image-text, image-image and text-image links, as well as drag-and-drop mechanisms. As opposed to first-generation hypertexts, which use images mainly as illustrative or decorative means, hypermedia writings form an internally organic, intertextual, intermedial and intermodal (Heibach, 2003; Constantinou, 2005) whole. Prototypical examples are concrete digital poems such as Bastian Böttcher's *looppool* (1997), Ursula Menzer and Sabine Orth's *Er/Sie* (2001), Tone Avenstoup and Robert Lippok's *marbel + matrikel* (2002) and Judd Morrissey and Lori Talley's *My Name Is Captain, Captain* (2002). Another major phenomenon is what I have previously referred to as collaborative writing projects, which form an important part of this study and will be elaborated in the context of reading and authoring hypertext (Chapter 1.4)

As discussed in a previous section, let me flag up again a fallacy that has pervaded hypertext criticism with regard to hyper- and transmediality: the adoption and translation of Richard Wagner's concept of the *Gesamtkunstwerk* into a *Gesamtdatenwerk*, an integrated data network (Ascott, 1999), which, nonetheless, lacks any theoretical and philosophical foundation similar to that maintained by Wagner. Although serious hypermedia artists attempt to merge literature, art, theatre and philosophy, they by no means follow Wagner's major aims, to hark back to the (nationalistic) ideals of Greek tragedy and to represent common life on stage by means of an organic holistic artwork. Despite the progressive technologization, and, consequently, mechanization of life and the body (cf. Haraway's 'cyborg'), humanity continues to be largely determined by its physicality, which the virtual medium cannot achieve to represent convincingly.

Cybertext is a term coined by Espen Aarseth (1997), who sees hypertexts that are programmed in particular ways as autonomous 'text machines' that assume power over the reader by literally 'writing themselves' rather than presenting themselves as an existing textual product. The concept of cybertext is based on Aarseth's alternative model of textual communication (*ibid.*: 21, fig. 1), which places the 'text machine', a mechanical rather than metaphorical concept, at the centre of the communicative triangle. The text machine is symbolically surrounded by the (human) 'operator', the 'verbal sign' and the material 'medium' that disseminates the text. These three elements engage in a complex interplay with the text and each other, which results in a variety of different

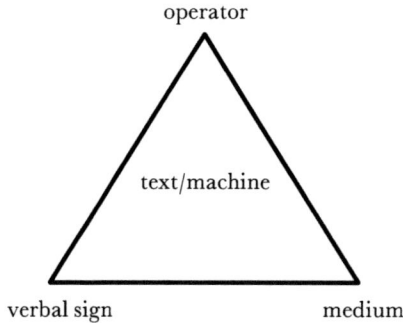

Figure 1 Aarseth's text machine

cybertextual subgenres, depending on which element is emphasized most strongly. What Aarseth aims to communicate is a distinct sense of performativity as conveyed by cybertexts, which renders the operator a constitutive yet relatively powerless element of (cyber)textual performance.

Interestingly, Aarseth omits two crucial elements of conventional communication models: first, the notion of reference, in the sense of Roman Jakobson's (1960) extralinguistic 'context', which would traditionally form an essential part of any communicative event, or even constitute the purpose of it. Second, the model disregards the crucial role of the author-programmer, who is ultimately responsible for the creation and 'behavioral' mechanisms of the text machine. One is inclined to assume that the author is contained within the operator concept. However, this poses the nagging dilemma of not being able to distinguish between the ultimately apotheotic function of the programmer and the reduced role of the user-player.

Aarseth (1997) defines cybertextual phenomena as 'texts that involve calculation in their production of scriptons' (75). As opposed to textons, which are essentially 'strings [of signs] as they exist in the text [code]' (*ibid*.: 62), scriptons are 'strings [of signs] as they appear to readers' (*ibid*.: 62). Underlying this are algorithmic text production processes, which automatically generate uncountable variants of a previously entered textual body. In cybertext, textons generate scriptons perceived and responded to by the reader, a process which, in its entirety, could be seen as a neo- or cyber-deistic concept, with the programmer 'creating' an organic system and, once it is finished, leaving it to its own mechanistic devices. Other than biological organisms, however, this mechanism is non-autopoietic insofar as it can only work provided that it is operated by a user. Aarseth thus shifts the focus of attention from the traditional triad of sender–message–receiver to the 'cybernetic intercourse between the various part(icipant)s in the textual machine' (*ibid*.: 22). In this conceptual framework, the medial triad of (idiomatic) code, (poetic) message and (physical) channel (Jakobson, 1960; see Chapter 1.5) act as equivalent interactive components of a neo-pragmatic concept of textual performance, which marginalizes semantic issues, emphasizing, *in lieu*, the multifarious interplay between the three major interactants of the text machine, which are quintessentially human, linguistic and material. From the reader's point of view, the pro- grammed code dominates the text visible on the interface and hence manipu- lates the reading process of its own accord. The aesthetic effect of this is that the reader loses control over the textual organism, which unfolds, once acti- vated, even without reader intervention.

The cybertext generation is relatively young and uses the latest achievements in hypermedia technology, whereas other, visionary devices, e.g. the 'emo- mouse' and acoustically and visually controlled interfaces, are still under development. Auer (2000) ventures as far as to say that, by virtue of such inno- vations, a more corporeal notion of interactivity, which directly responds to human emotions and physical conditions, may ultimately replace the hyperlink as the central aesthetic and structural feature of hypertext. As cybertext is still at an experimental stage – and will remain so for the time being – fewer repre- sentative examples are yet to be found than for the first and second generations. Prototypical specimens include Stuart Moulthrop's *Hegirascope* (1995/1997), Urs Schreiber's *Das Epos der Maschine* (1998) and Kate Pullinger's *Breathing Wall* (2004), which, among others, will be discussed in Chapter 3.

The three generations of hypertext reflect stages of text transforming 'into an intelligent object' (Heibach, 2004: 43; see also Glazier, 2004: 61). This is not to say that any hypertext phenomenon may be clearly categorized along genera- tional lines. The terms 'hypertext', 'hypermedia' and 'cybertext' represent ten- dencies rather than absolutes and have to be located on a continuum rather than in terms of abstract poles. As indicated previously, ever since the late 1980s, and to an increasing degree, the three generations have been overlapping and transgressing each other as well as other meanwhile digital media such as radio, film and television. We can thus conclude that, as opposed to analogue media such as traditional television, records, video and audio tapes, an end of hypertext, hypermedia or cybertext literature is not in sight and will not be in the foreseeable future.

3   Literary Genres and Hypertext

A new poetry for the next century must be developed in the new media, simply because the textual aspirations of the authors cannot be physically realized in print.
(Kac, 1996: 100)

But what does it mean to identify a 'main plot' if each character is associated with a fully developed story, and each of these stories is told in the performance space (albeit in different areas of that space) with the same attention and focus?
(Deemer, 1994)

We could say that there is no story at all; there are only readings.
(Bolter, 2001: 125)

So far, we have viewed hypertext from synchronic-formal and diachronic-evolutionary perspectives. To establish this literary media genre as a distinctly literary form, however, it needs to be pointed out that literary hypertext follows traditional generic conventions insofar as it can be divided into instances of hyperfiction, hyperdrama and hyperpoetry. Although hyperfiction has so far proved to be the most popular and prolific genre among writers, one must not neglect either practical or theoretical material surrounding the other two genres – particularly as regards hyperdrama, the most underresearched genre of the three.[16] In what follows, I will summarize critical, generic approaches to literary hypertext as well as outlining the prevailing formal elements of the three major genres mentioned above. Examples from all three generations of hypertext will provide further illustration.

Genre analytical approaches to hypertext can be divided into two general categories. The first category includes theories that set out to compare and contrast hypertext with established literary genres (e.g. Schnierer, 2000, 2001, 2003; Calvi, 2001). Schnierer (2000), for instance, asserts that the concept of hypertext resembles that of closet drama, thus emphasizing its non-performative yet still dramaturgical character. His thesis runs counter to many other approaches (e.g. Sandbothe, 1997), which accentuate the performative properties: originally of IRC (Internet Relay Chat), MUDs and MOOs, yet also increasingly identifiable in recent forms of hypermedia and cybertext (e.g. Aarseth, 1997; Wirth, 2000; Simanowski, 2001c).[17] Having said that, with regard to the reader-stage in terms of reader–interface relationship, one may rather speak of forms of *interactive* drama with a one-man audience, which involves reading, watching and partaking in a similar way as, for instance, Elizabethan theatre audiences did (although collectively and vocally). With this in mind, Suter understands the reader as a 'performer' (2000), who takes an active role not only in the imaginary space created, but physically, by interacting with the text on screen.

In his examination of hypertext poems, Schnierer (2003) emphasizes that hyperpoetry is 'not a new category *sui generis*' (97), but essentially unrhymed, free-verse 'poetry that has hypertextual features' (*ibid.*: 93), with 'hypertextual features' relating to the nonlinearity of organization and the multilinearity of reading, which were already exemplified by proto-hyperpoems by Tristan Tzara and Raymond Queneau. Such poetry often appears in collections and cycles, often lacks editorial control and emphasizes typographical design – much like concrete poetry, incidentally. Schnierer further postulates 'the homology of hyperpoetry with oral poetry' (*ibid.*: 98), such as folk songs, ballads, dub poetry and rap, on the basis of its resistance of closure. Oral poetry changes its shape with every 'reading', and thus combines 'the fixed with the optional' (*ibid.*: 98). In sum, Schnierer makes the point that 'hyperpoetry seeks to set itself apart not from "old" poetry, but from hyperprose' (*ibid.*: 97), which has so far obtained the most critical and creative attention of all hypertext genres.

A second strand of generic approaches has emphasized the unique nature of hypertext, which cannot be likened to any other form of literature and thus calls out for a new form of criticism that takes into consideration the changed conditions of mediality. In this second category, there is fundamental disagreement as to whether or not this necessitates an entirely new form of criticism. Landow (1992/1997), for example, speaks of a 'convergence' between hypertext and poststructuralist criticism, assuming a disposition of playfulness and deconstruction. Schnierer (2003) argues against this, highlighting the affinity especially of hyperpoetry with modernist criticism, which is grounded in 'a seriousness of purpose' (99) and the 'dominance of poeticity over the less specific concept of textuality' (*ibid.*: 92).

Aarseth (1997), Hayles (2002) and Heibach (2003), on the other hand, call out for an entirely new dialectics and format of criticism, which takes into account the mediality of the computer and the delinearization of scholarly research. To illustrate her point, Hayles manipulates the usual sequence of a scholarly book in *Writing Machines* as well as playfully varying typescript in such a way as to make it appear animated and in flux. On a more moderate level, Heibach (2003) includes a CD-ROM, which presents her major tenets in the format of a hypertext. Such attempts at emulating hypertext in print are well intended yet do not contribute greatly to established research methods, which can only be successful if they continue to be linear (in the case of printed sources) or antilinear (in the case of digitized, scholarly hypertext). As research into the psychology of learning has shown (see Chapter 5.1), information has to be communicated in a serialized fashion in order to achieve a maximum of conceptual intake, and hypertext critics will have to continue to present their research in as linear a way as possible – at least as far as their print publications are concerned – to make their voices heard, particularly among other, less hypertextually inclined members of academia.

With this in mind, I take the view that hypertext does not require a new form of criticism, but rather an extended set of analytical criteria, which result from its augmented sense of mediality. I therefore argue that Goethe's traditional tripartite categorization of 'natural forms of poetry' (as explicated in *Notes and Essays on the 'West-Eastern Divan'* of 1819), 'that which narrates clearly, that which is enthusiastically excited, and that which is personally acting epic, lyric, and drama' (187), can be retained for hypertext literature, and I will refer to them as hyperfiction, hyperpoetry and hyperdrama.

Clearly, the 'personal' aspect of drama as explained by Goethe needs to be modified, for *hyperdrama*, unlike proto-hyperdrama, defies the theatrical stage and all that comes along with it (e.g. dramatis personae played by 'real' actors, props and auditoria) without, however, giving up its distinctly dialogic discourse, its paratextual features (e.g. stage directions) and scenic macrostructure. Proto-hyperdramas are dramas that are performed on a real stage and whose dramaturgic conception allows audience members to follow the characters *ad libitum*, a principle which subverts established concepts such as discrepancy of knowledge, main plot, subplot, principal and minor character (Schnierer, 2000), mainly by introducing a 'realistic' split/join structure (Bernstein, 1998; Schnierer, 2001: 146).

The most prolific British proto-hyperdramatist is Alan Ayckbourn, whose *The Norman Conquests* (1973) and *House and Garden* (2000) can be performed consecutively, as traditional, single-stage dramas, or synchronically, either with two separate auditoria or on an open stage, which allows the audience to roam freely.[18] Second, there is digital hyperdrama, or just hyperdrama, as I will call it. The term was coined by hyperdramatist and theorist Charles Deemer, who understands 'traditional drama as a special case of hyperdrama' ('The New Hyperdrama'), because of its monoperspectival approach.

Deemer's early works include *Chateau de mort* (1986) and its much later sequel, *The Bride of Edgefield* (1996b). Deemer calls them proto-hyperdramas, mainly because they were created in the early 1980s with the help of 'Iris', a DOS-hypertext programme. In our terminology, however, they are hypertexts proper, as they were written for the computer. More recent hyperdramas by Deemer are *The Seagull* (a hyperdramatic adaptation of Chekhov's play, also available in print, 2004) and *The Last Song of Violeta Parra* (1996a), which I will look at in greater detail in Chapter 3.1. Tautologically or not, hyperdrama lends itself particularly well to performance-based approaches to hypertext criticism (e.g. Douglas, 1993; Simanowski, 1999a), as the interface serves as a two-dimensional, metaphorical stage, with the reader acting as a director or a mobile audience member in Ayckbourn's 'realistic' tradition. Hyperdramas are further distinguished by conciseness and – interestingly – at least one of the three Aristotelian unities (action, time and space). Other dialogue-based, approximate albeit not explicitly denominated examples of hyperdrama include Judy Malloy and Cathy Marshall's artistic interlocution, *Forward Anywhere*, which consists of a dialogue between the two writers about their creative process; Romana Brunnauer's dialogic mystery, *Zwei Tote?* (2002), which gives the reader clues by means of interpersonal encounters; Stefan Maskiewicz's 'dialogic soliloquy', *Quadrego*, in which a girl named 'Iris', who suffers from Multiple Personality Disorder, talks to her three *alter egos*; and Christy Sheffield Sanford's hyper-metadrama, *Safara in the Beginning* (1996), which Schnierer (2000: 544) refers to as 'a closet drama within the closet drama', as it features fragments of a play, or a film script, within the actual (narrative) hypertext.

To add to my earlier explications about *hyperpoetry* and its forerunners, concrete and experimental poetry, it has to be said that this particular hypertext genre is perhaps the most creative and trans-artistic (in the sense of multimodal and intermedial) of all hypertext genres. Not only does it tend to exhibit elements of nomadism (incorporating various languages and sign systems), flux (representing movement rather than stasis) and medial self-reflexivity (see Block *et al.*, 2004), it ventures out into the spheres of other arts such as painting, film and music, thus leading the reader away from verbal narrative to a multisensory textual experience. Evidently, this kind of verbal art, which I still refer to as literature, is most common and also most effective in the paradigms of hypermedia and, to a lesser extent, cybertext, mostly because editing software such as flash technology allows animation, thus evoking the principles of kinetic poetry. As Schnierer (2003) points out, hyperpoetry in the narrow sense of first-generation hyperpoetry 'has consistently been less varied and experimental than hyperfiction' (94), mainly because first-generation hypertext yields the most interesting aesthetic effects in relation to the narrative opportunities it opens up to writers and readers alike. That said, there is a tradition of first-generation hyperpoetry which uses the link as its major organization principle, rather than experimenting with new technological developments. Among its major representatives are Jim Rosenberg (*Diagrams*, 1968–99), Cathy Mac (*Unnatural Habitats*, 1994), Tim McLaughlin (*Notes toward Absolute Zero*, 1995), Stephanie Strickland (*True North*, 1997) and Robert Kendall (e.g. *The Seasons* cycle, 1999–2000).

Hypermedia poetry, or digital concrete poetry (as many poets refer to their work), includes, for instance, Ursula Menzer and Sabine Orth's kine-lexical experiment *Er/Sie* (2001), Zeitgenossen's audio-geometric roll-over poem, *Yatoo* (2001) and Judd Morrissey and Lori Talley's procedural shape poem *My Name Is Captain, Captain* (2002). Deena Larsen's narrative poem *Marble Springs* (1993) and Urs Schreiber's 'techno-epic' *Das Epos der Maschine* (1998) are generic cross-overs, incorporating narrative and verse. Along with Stuart Moulthrop's ever-changing poem *Hegirascope* (1995/1997), Urs Schreiber's *Epos der Maschine* is also one of the few representative examples of cyberpoetry I have encountered so far.

Hyperfiction, as understood in this study, significantly deviates from Heibach's (2001) concept, which excludes all forms of fictional hypertext that are neither purely text-based nor closed in the sense of 'complete' and 'non-modifiable or extendable'. Contemporary web editors allow hypertext authors to include in their hyperfictions a varying degree of visuality, which is used to add further semiotic layers of meaning without, however, reducing the written word to a mere servant of the image. According to my definition of 'hyperfiction', the genre ends where the visual starts to dominate and deprive the textual of its semiotic potential.

As opposed to hyperpoetry and hyperdrama, hyperfiction shares with print fiction its conventionally narrative element. The experimental potential of the medium with its nonlinear structures, however, allows authors to play with changing points of view. As a result, the readers have to continually (re-)create in their minds a network of narrating figures (cf. Bell, forthcoming). In analogy to print fiction, I distinguish between extensive and concise forms of hyperfiction. Hypernovels, on the one hand, are characterized by a large repository of characters, long reading duration, and plot structures that defy singular development.[19] Macrostructurally, they comprise a large number of lexias, which may, in totality, reach novelistic extensions. Furthermore, they are intricately interlinked, featuring loops and other cyclical elements which cause readers to return to previously visited segments. Among the most often quoted hypernovels are Michael Joyce's *afternoon, a story* (1987/1990), Stuart Moulthrop's *Victory Garden* (1991), John McDaid's *Uncle Buddy's Phantom Funhouse* (1992), Shelley Jackson's *Patchwork Girl* (1995), Mark Amerika's *Grammatron* (1996), Bill Bly's *We Descend* (1997) and M. D. Coverley's *Califia* (2000).

Hyper-short-fictions, on the other hand, tend to exhibit a relatively low number of lexias, possible plotlines, loops, characters, narrative perspectives and spatial arrangements. They often appear as cycles or compilations of inter-woven character studies or plots and are usually readable within a maximum of a few hours, in other words 'at one sitting', as Edgar Allan Poe explained in his review of Nathaniel Hawthorne's *Twice Told Tales* (1842). With regard to hypertext, however, Poe's definition has to be qualified more than it may have to be in the case of any conventional, linear short narrative, as hypertext by definition defies the idea of 'one sitting' and, instead, calls out for continual revisitation. By the same token, Poe's claim that a short story should have 'a unity of impression, of totality and of single effect' cannot be sustained for hyper-short-fictions, which thrive on precisely the opposite: a disunity of impression, segmentation and multiple effects upon each revisitation. I will further expound this idea in Chapter 1.5. Suffice it to note at this stage that hyper-short-fiction may in the future, due to its user-friendly approach (i.e. brevity, succinctness and receptive 'manageability'), exceed hypernovels in popularity with a broad rather than academic readership (see Ryan, 2000). Examples of hyper-short-fiction include Gavin Inglis's *Same Day Test* (1999), Deena Larsen's *Samplers: Nine Vicious Little Hypertexts* (2000) and Rob Swigart's *Down Time* (2000).

As a rule of thumb induced from concrete examples, the concept of literary hypertext is ultimately grounded in the three traditional literary genres as described by Goethe. By the same token, hypertext by its very own nature embraces intertextuality in such a way as to transgress and/or merge genre boundaries (to varying degrees), a fact which, in many cases, prevents clear-cut genre categorization. This observation ties in with the diachronic approach taken in the previous section, which came to a similar conclusion with regard to blurring 'generation' boundaries. The textual analyses in Chapter 3 will further exemplify the ways in which such hybridities may take shape. Before turning from critical theory to practice, however, I shall move on to another essential aspect of hypertextual communication and examine the contingent roles of author and reader in the light of hypertext's idiosyncratic structuring principles.

4   Reading and Authoring Hypertext – A Role Change?

> *You read the way you always have, with touch and look, in a stream or in bursts, in a ritual,*
> *a rhythm, or a reverie or as you like it.*
> *(Joyce, Twilight, a Symphony [Reading Storyspaces])*

A plethora of hypertext theories and research have gone into issues surrounding the reception and production of hypertext or, more specifically, the ways in which, as a structural organization principle, it shapes processes of authoring and reading. Similarly, the roles of author and reader have often been perceived to be reversed, mostly as a result of the reader's relative freedom of choice between different reading paths and the alleged concomitant 'disempowerment' of the author. With a view to offering a more realistic outlook, this section will reveal various (mis-)conceptions regarding hypertext authors and users, including the controversial Landowian concept of the 'wreader'.

As pointed out earlier in this chapter, the distinctive interlinking structure of hypertext causes the reader to choose different pathways every time he or she re-enters a textual network. Inevitably, the key effect of navigating through or browsing a text that undermines a centralized plotline is that each reading results in at least one, if not many different textual meanings depending on how coherently each path is structured. With regard to how this kind of reading diverges from reading conventional linear texts, McAleese (1999b: 6) highlights browsing and navigating as the two major hypertextual reading strategies:

> There are two states: browsing is where an idea is followed using the linking mechanism of the hypertext elements (eg cards, windows, nodes); navigation involves the use of a graphic aid such as a browser or map to show an overview representation of the nodes and links.

As a matter of fact, most literary hypertexts are read in terms of browsing, and even those few which provide graphic overviews such as map views and (tree) hierarchies often deceive the readers' navigational expectations in such a way as to give them the impression of navigating where they are in fact browsing pseudo-navigational structures, as is done by Stuart Moulthrop in *Victory Garden*. Counter-examples defying navigational confusion include Deena Larsen's *Marble Springs* and Andreas Luis Seyerlein's *Callas Box* (2002), where symbolic or cartographic map views keep their promise of directing readers to where they are planning to go. Due to the fact that navigating literary hypertext mostly equals browsing – navigational aids are often employed as deliberate orientational fallacies – the terms 'browsing' and 'navigating' are used interchangeably in this study.

Particularly in early hypertext criticism, largely centred at Brown University, Roland Barthes' postulation of a 'dead author' dominated scholarly discourse. George Landow, Jay David Bolter and Robert Coover, the most prominent pioneers of hypertext theory, see Barthes' concepts cogently implemented by hypertext practice. In a 1992 essay, Bolter first proclaimed hypertext as 'a vindication of postmodern literary theory' (24). In the same year, Coover published his famous article, 'The End of Books', in the *New York Times Book Review*, in which he declared that 'hypertext presents a radically divergent technology, interactive and polyvocal, favoring a plurality of discourses over definitive utterance and freeing the reader from domination by the author' (Coover, 1992: 24–5). In his frequently quoted 'convergence thesis', Landow (1992/1997, 1994) systematized this claim, maintaining that hypertext was the testing ground, if not embodiment, of poststructuralist literary theory, as 'critical theory promises to theorize hypertext and hypertext promises to embody and thereby test aspects of theory, particularly those concerning textuality, narrative and the roles or functions of reader and writer' (1992/1997: 2). According to Landow, due to hypertext's distinctly 'poststructuralist' characteristics, such as textual openness, intertextuality, multivocality, decentering, and rhizomatic, nonlinear structures, one significant effect of its linking structure is a 'reconfigured', 'empowered' reader. Such a 'wreader', asserts Landow, takes full responsibility not only for the sequence of events but also, as a result, for the text itself in its structural and semantic totality.[20]

As indicated previously, Landow's, Bolter's and Coover's enthusiastic tenet, which ultimately goes back to Bush's and Nelson's visions of all-empowering, digital information networks, has rightly been met with a lot of criticism (e.g. Löser, 1999; Simanowski, 1999b, 2004; Winko, 1999; Auer, 2000; Rau, 2000a; Gendolla and Schäfer, 2001; Ryan, 2001; Glazier, 2002). Critiques are mostly directed at the theory's inclination towards pragmatic simplification of complex, abstract philosophical concepts, as well as self-righteous, ideologically-charged academic spin. Essentially, Barthes' (1968/1977c, 1970/1987) concept of the dead author is that of a 'socially and historically constituted subject' (Keep *et al.*, 1993–2000). Barthes' view is Marxist and anti-Hegelian in that man is considered a product of history and previous literatures, not vice versa. He aims to liberate language from its producer and medium. In assuming a 'dead' author, he refers to authorship in terms of originality and creativity. He departs from the traditional, idealistic view of an autonomous author, favouring, instead, that of the author as object of discourse. In other words, the 'death of the author' is not to be taken literally, in terms of an author who no longer produces a text and has therefore lost his or her authoritative control over textual meaning. It is rather to be understood as a subversion of logocentrism and the Romantic notion of the author as a godlike creator of reality for the sake of a new, all-embracing concept of text. Similarly, in his critique of Landow, Simanowski (2004) goes as far as to talk of a 'banalization' (80) of lost authorship in terms of reversed hierarchies, and of a 'betrayal of discourse theory' (81).

Barthes and Foucault regard the reader as empowered (in the sense of writerly vs readerly text) in terms of being at liberty to form personal connotations and associations. In a hypertext environment, however, this freedom is considerably restrained given the existence of manifest, technically implemented hyperlinks, which rather prevent creativity. Freedom, as Simanowski rightly argues, therefore only happens on a combinatory, not on a connotative level (1999b: 3), which results in associative restraint. As a matter of fact, links have a delimiting rather than empowering function, an effect which is further increased when it comes to cybertext, where a considerable amount of control is transferred from reader, or operator, to programme code. With this in mind, Simanowski turns Landow's thesis on its head by proposing that 'it is perhaps more appropriate to announce the death of the *reader*' (2004: 81 – emphasis in original). This, arguably, is as equally a hyperbolic claim as that of the dead author, but captures *in nuce* the restrictive effects that hypertexts can entail. Trying to find more germane reader metaphors, Simanowski (*ibid.*) suggests those of an 'unsettled traveller', or an 'observer' of increasingly pictorial representation. He rightly adds that the only feasible contexts where the roles of reader and author may legitimately be merged and/or confused are collaborative writing projects.[21] Such joint ventures, which Heibach refers to as instantiations of 'human-machine-human oscillation' (2001: 38),[22] hark back to collective composition procedures in the Middle Ages and the Baroque Age, scribal, handwritten newspapers in sixteenth and seventeenth century England, as well as joint ventures in the Romantic Period, Dadaism and Surrealism. In this respect, collective writing is by no means a novel form of literary creativity. Nonetheless, unlike literary hypertext as a whole, it may be considered the epitome of postmodern authorship – serving as an alternative, pluralistic concept to the deconstructed, 'dead author'. Evidently, the omnipotent hypermedia author, the 'uomo universale' (Auer, 2000), or Murray's 'new kind of storyteller ... who is half hacker, half bard' (Murray, 1997: 9), is a hypothetical, idealizing construct, as much as Landow's 'empowered wreader' is. However, along with Stefan Maskiewicz, we may anticipate that digital literature, like other media, will increasingly have to be produced by authoring teams rather than individuals, as cross-disciplinary creativity, combined with sophisticated programming skills, cannot be realized by the majority of aspiring authors (Simanowski, 2001d). In this respect, the internet's inherent dialogism, which theoretically implies and practically invites the multiple interchange between individuals of various creative and technological disciplines, is indeed a valid concept, which ties in with a thus modified concept of the 'wreader'.

Generally speaking, as far as the 'culinary'[23] flow of reading and artistic perception are concerned, guided forms of reader interaction support aesthetic appreciation. As groups of people combine their expertise in programming, writing, and web design, collective efforts are likely to achieve a maximum cognitive and emotional effect in the user. As Simanowski (2004) observes, collaborative writing projects draw their attraction from a social aesthetics in that they thematize the dynamics of web-based communication and the creative interplay that evolves between individual writers who proliferate even without face-to-face contact. That said, the real draw resides within the process rather than the product of collaborative writing, as participants watch their creative object grow while adding their contributions in response to each other.

As Gendolla and Schäfer (2001) put it, the novelty of digitized collective writing is its global reach. Mutual authorial and editorial activities include exchanging ideas, peer review and mutual complementation, as it is done on hosted websites such as *Berliner Zimmer*,[24] *Webgespräch*[25] and *Literatur-Café*.[26] Readers can participate, for instance, in completing Guido Grigat's 'collective memory' in *23:40* (1997), in associative bilingual poetry networks like Alvar Freude and Dragan Espenschied's *Assoziations-Blaster* (1999/2000) and in participatory novel-writing such as Curt Siffert's *StorySprawl* (1998) and Claudia Klinger's *Beim Bäcker* (2000). For those 'wreaders' with a more serious, professional or academic approach there are online journals, such as Kristine Blair and Lanette Cradle's *Computers and Composition Online*,[27] Roberto Simanowski's *dichtung-digital*,[28] and Heiko Idensen's *HYPERdis*.[29]

Author teams such as Bihler, Oßwald and Drescher, Judd Morrissey and Lory Talley, as well as Kate Pullinger, Stefan Schemat and Babel, benefit from individual specializations and distribute tasks according to skill. For example, for *The Breathing Wall* (2004), Kate Pullinger wrote a hypertext-based blend between psychogramme and gothic detective-mystery, which is driven by Stefan Schemat's innovative 'breath recognition' technology and based upon Babel's underlying hypertext structures. The result, a complex audiovisual reading, breathing and listening experience, has been such a success with readers that the co-authors have started developing a second version. I shall discuss *The Breathing Wall* in full detail in Chapter 3.3.

Examples of potential reader co-authorship in closed hypertext are Michael Joyce's *afternoon, a story* (1987/1990) and Rob Swigart's *Down Time* (2000), which offer readers the opportunity to write comments into text boxes, either in response to questions asked in the text or as annotations to the text. These text boxes, however, prevent any further linking, thus stopping the reader from becoming a genuine 'wreader' in the sense of actual co-authorship. In other words, the fact that most commercially traded hypertexts-on-datacarriers are offline media, forms of collective authorship, which would include the reading public in its entirety, are infeasible. Clearly, due to meanwhile highly sophisticated, interactive components of browser technology, examples of more 'democratically' collaborative writing projects are far more frequent in second-generation hypermedia (see also, for instance, Christian, 1996; Hasecke, 1997; Meetfactory, 1998; Ganymed and Nexo of Kystone, 2001).

In sum, it can be said that, taking into account any reservations relating to convergence theory in general, participants in collaborative writing projects come closest to Landow's 'wreader' concept. Clearly, readers of individually read hypertexts do not have the alleged liberty to author – either physically or metaphorically – their own story. In fact, the majority of mono-receptive and -productive hypertexts draw a clear distinction between the roles of the author-programmer and the reader, with their only common ground being the embeddedness in a computer system (see Bootz's 'systemic approach', 2004). Finally, with respect to the development from text through hypertext to hyper-media and cybertext, readers adopt different functions, depending on the nature of the media text they are confronted with. With regard to participatory hyper*media* collaborations, one may well speak of a 'wreader'. Contrarily, most first-generation hyper*texts*, which are read rather than written, do not allow readers to perform truly authorial activities. 'User' and 'player' are in fact the most appropriate words to be used in applications where representation and reception prevail and where readers at most 'play' certain pictorial characters rather than creating mental images from verbally encoded text (e.g. in MOOs, MUDs, interactive narratives and computer games). Finally, with respect to the most innovative and experimental forms of hypertext technology, new terms need to be introduced, which reflect the reader's receptive and/or productive activities, such as 'breather' in the case of Pullinger's so far unique *Breathing Wall*.

5   Towards Hypertext Poetics

Aesthetic use of hyperlinks, browsers, and the structure of the Internet, as well as participatory and collaborative projects and programs refer to cultural changes in global society, networked in terms of technology and data. They might be confusing to recipients, but thereby encourage critical and productive reflection.
(Block et al., 2004: 35)

To round off this extended ontological prologue, I will, in what follows, summarize the major aesthetic principles of literary hypertext, with a view to approaching a poetics of hypertext. In doing so, I will seek to cover generic aspects that concern hypertext as a distinctive literary media genre, and are thus valid for all three 'literary' genres as outlined in Chapter 1.3: hyperdrama, hyperpoetry and hyperfiction. Poetics is a discipline within philosophical aesthetics that engages with subjective matters of taste, beauty and pleasure. I will therefore begin by taking a particularly close look at typical aspects of hypertext *perception* and their effects on the reader, and draw conclusions for reader attitudes required to approach this unconventional literary media genre without being rejected by its characteristic unconventionalities. Moving on from there, I will further explore the question of what constitutes a poetics of hypertext and to what extent common features exist across all three major genres, hyperfiction, hyperdrama and hyperpoetry. As well as drawing on theories proposed by other hypertext theorists, I will propose my own approach, which is grounded in the principles of reader-response criticism. I will refer to it as aesthetics of revis(itat)ion (revisitation and revision), which applies in particular to complex rather than simplex hypertexts of all three generations and may be understood in terms of an augmented version of the hermeneutical circle.[30]

There is consensus that the arts owe their educative potential to their 'ability to shock and inspire, to change vision, ideas and feelings' (Stibbs, 1998: 201). Broadly speaking, literature's purpose is to raise consciousness in the reader. It does so through cognitive stimuli and aesthetic effects, which arouse varying degrees of surprise, or 'alienation' (Shklovsky, 1988).[31] Surprise may occur in various ways: cognitively, by confronting the reader, for instance, with controversial issues, previously unknown facts, or new insights into familiar or foreign cultures; and formally, by presenting the reader with unexpected stylistic means, such as dialectal varieties, particular uses of imagery, elision or repetition. Such stylistic techniques invite readers to reflect on standard(ized) uses of language, which are usually taken for granted.

In hypertext, surprise levels, especially for the 'wreading' novice, are manifold. Upon encountering this hypermedia alternative to print literature, the first-time reader is most likely to be taken aback by the 'marked' materiality of the medium. At a more experienced level, hypertext readers are faced with a whole variety of 'surprising' experiences that may, at first glance, seem rather daunting. Due to navigational opacity and a deliberate lack of conventional cohesive strategies (Kuhlen, 1991), feelings of frustration (e.g. 'lost in hyperspace') are constitutive to the hypertext reading process. They are caused by what Harpold (1991) calls 'the accidents of reading a hypertext (changing your destination, forgetting your point of departure, or getting lost along the way)'. Hence, such effects contribute to an 'aesthetic of frustration', which arises from disillusionment of otherwise 'classical reading modalities' (Bootz, 2004: 111).

Kuhlen (1991) identifies three major types of hypertext perception and the characteristic aesthetic effects they evoke in the reader. Particularly when reading *literary* as opposed to expository or scholarly hypertext, readers browse either randomly, associatively or purposefully. A side effect of *random* in the sense of aimless or 'question-less' browsing is the continuation rather than satisfaction of what Belkin *et al.* (1982) call an 'anomalous state of knowledge' (i.e. a need for information that is often unspecified or even unconscious) and which is also referred to as 'cognitive overhead' by Conklin (1987: 40) and Kuhlen (1991: viii). It is a condition that may be circumscribed as some kind of aesthetic stalemate, as readers virtually 'wait' for rather than work their way towards specific information or, for that matter, an unfolding of plot. One instance of (unpleasant) surprise resulting from such an attitude may be the observation that hypertext simply does not support the familiar, linear 'spoon-feeding' of information but rather requires conceptual and physical cooperation on the part of the reader, who permanently needs to question his or her search strategy in quest for, if necessary, alternative ways of searching. *Associative* browsing occurs if the reader chooses links according to the degree to which they appeal to his or her aesthetic or cognitive curiosity, which may be paraphrased as a somewhat erotic drive to permeate two-dimensional surface structures in a quest for deeper understanding. Although the anticipation of surprise and novelty may be considerable upon addressing a hypertext in this way, the main risk inherent in such an approach is the loss of suspense and attention resulting from the ultimate awareness of being 'lost in hyperspace'. Finally, if readers browse *purposefully*, i.e. with a set of burning questions in mind, their reading will be more selective and possibly more 'successful' (in the sense of yielding more relevant information) than with the aforementioned browsing methods. Another side-effect that typically occurs, however, even with purposeful readers, is that of 'serendipity' (*ibid.*: 129), which means that readers are likely to be distracted by any aspect of the plot which they did not originally intend to follow up yet which suddenly seems 'surprisingly' more fascinating than the originally pursued aim of reading. Consequently, the reading experience may yield a considerable amount of information, which does, however, not (entirely) meet the targets set by the reader upon entering the hypertext.

Taking into account that phenomena like 'cognitive overhead', 'lost in hyperspace'and 'serendipity' are encountered by hypertext readers in general, one is inclined to suspect that they are functionalized by writers of literary hypertext to shape the process of reading and its aesthetic effects in various idiosyncratic ways. In this respect, effects like 'confusion' and 'disorientation' ought to be seen less as inhibitory features than as distinctive varieties of suspense — if understood in an unconventionally challenging sense of 'uncertainty, anticipation and curiosity' (Cuddon, 1999: 883). Clearly, confusion and disorientation can only reasonably be coped with if they are recognized as characteristic features of hypertext and processed creatively by readers. To a greater extent than readers of traditionally linear texts, which are structurally 'un-marked' in the sense of not challenging the reader's macrostructural expectations, hypertext readers are urged to think about linking and other organizational strategies to approximate an overall picture of the text in front of them. This approximation process involves a set of interwoven sub-processes of continual semantic construction, deconstruction and reconstruction.

So far, a number of attempts to define hypertext aesthetics or poetics have been undertaken, in particular with regard to e-poetry (Glazier, 2002; Block *et al.*, 2004), hypermedia (Calvi, 2001) and hyperfiction (Simanowski, 1999a). Placing e-poetry firmly within the traditions of concrete poetry, installations of interactive media art and cubism, Block *et al.* (2004) put forward a catalogue of five distinctive attributes that, in their view, constitute the aesthetics of digital poetry, yet may be transferred to hypertext in general, particularly second-generation hypermedia.[32] These features include hypermediality, interactivity, networking, processurality and medial self-reference. Hypermediality is derived from the concept of hypermedia (hypertext multimedia), which combines the idea of textual webs with the digitization of formerly analogue multimedia and their joint and mutually supplementary creation of intersemiotic meaning. Semiotically, hypermediality translates onto multimodality and intersemioticity, i.e. the meaningful interplay of diverse semiotic systems (e.g. language, script, sound, music, image, animation and film). Interactivity and networking are mutually interdependent concepts. Block *et al.* use the former in a dual sense: first, in terms of an interchange between human being and machine, between user and computer, which, due to its contingency upon situational and psychological circumstances, results in highly personalized, unrepeatable aesthetic experiences. Second, interactivity refers to the poetically creative, synchronous and asynchronous forms of online communication between different users within a computer network, which is inextricably connected to the element of interpersonal and intertextual networking. Interactivity is essentially caused by the analogy and the dialogue between user and computer (Block, 2001: 107). Vertical design, i.e. organizing nodes in hierarchies as well as programming code in lines, only applies to holistic visualizations such as webviews and sub-interface phenomena. Due to the fact that the computer screen is bi-dimensional, users can only read one lexia at a time even in so-called counterpoint hypertexts (see Bernstein, 1998). As a result, all documents within a hypertextual network are received horizontally, i.e. in any preferred sequence.

The networking component is prominent in web-based collaborative creative writing projects such as Alvar Freude and Dragan Espenschied's *Assoziations-Blaster*, which invites users to contribute texts, particularly poetry, in association with given keywords. Evidently, this particular component only became feasible with the advent of the World Wide Web and the innovations it brought about with regard to verbal and non-verbal communication.

Processurality refers to the interest expressed by hypertext writers in the processes of the 'work in movement', the 'open work', as Eco (1989) calls it. Processurality has often been used as a programmatic term by writers of concrete and digital poetry alike (Mon *et al.*, 1960), referring to the reader's or user's physical and mental contribution to the construction of an essentially incomplete and infinitely extendible text, as well as the dynamic nature of linguistic or semiotic processes in a more general sense (Block *et al.*, 2004: 27/29). Second-generation hypermedia in particular add to these a distinct sense of kinetic, pictorial processurality, as it incorporates filmic and animated elements of script, image and photographic material.

Finally, medial self-reference, or medial reflexivity (as I am more inclined to name it), is another defining characteristic of hypertext. On the one hand, the concept is grounded in the computer's subsumption of text production, storage, editing, publication and reception into one medium. On the other hand, it is closely related to the 'McLuhan equation': 'the medium is the message' (McLuhan and Zingrone, 1995: 151). McLuhan (1964), widely regarded as the founding father of Media Studies, sees the medium as an extension of the human body and mind, which encloses material media (e.g. the book, the cinema screen and the computer) as well as language, as it projects thoughts into other people's minds. In McLuhan's view, the concept of the medium as an extension captures the considerable social and personal consequences of new technologies and therefore must be taken into account in any media theory. In other words, the focus should not be on the immediately obvious, material aspects but the social and infra-structural changes implied by the medium in question.

Hypertext implies a tripartite concept of the 'medium', namely the materiality of message, code *and* contact (channel), and their related poetic, metalingual and phatic functions, to use Jakobson's terminology (1960). It is the emphasis on the phatic function in particular which distinguishes hypertext from other forms of writing, which take the unmarked medium − the book − for granted. Hypertext, by contrast, takes place in a marked medium, which therefore needs to be thematized and explored creatively. One weakness of Jakobson's theory is its failure to distinguish clearly between 'physical channel and psychological connection' (*ibid.*: 353), as he refers to both as 'contact', whose function is to enable addresser and addressee to enter and stay in communication. However, physical channel and psychological connection are two fundamentally different concepts, which should be divided into two separate factors within any communicative model. Medial reflexivity primarily draws on the physical side of Jakobson's concept of contact. Message and code, on the other hand, are particularly significant for hyperpoetry, which is indebted to the metalinguistic traditions of concrete poetry and focuses on the message in the sense of the poetic use of language, i.e. 'the message for its own sake' (*ibid.*: 356).

Glazier's (2002) contribution to a poetics of hyperpoetry is his concept of '*occlusion*, or an aberration of the eye, literally and homophonously' (37, *emphasis in original*). He contends that digital poetics transforms the 'eye'/'I', which is in fact what he means by 'homophonous aberration', as well as the physicality of reading, in the sense of motoric processes of the reader's eyes and hands. Glazier further lists searchability, transmissibility,[33] virtual non-existence of physical size (as opposed to the spatial extensions of print media), anti-textuality (which implies the inherent possibility of error messages and other frequently encountered impediments to reading) and proneness to manipulation as distinctive features of web-based textuality. Importantly, Glazier mentions the narrative versatility of the link, which, *per se*, forms only potentially a part of the narrative: 'Once a link has been taken, it is no longer a link but a constituted part of the already traveled narrative; the link loses its potentiality, but in doing so, it opens up the possibility of other links' (35).

In her paper 'Hypertext and Comics: Towards an Aesthetics of Hypertext' (2001), Calvi focuses on pictorial narrativity as the interface between hypertext (especially hypermedia) and comics. She argues that hypertext should not be viewed mainly in terms of link typologies. Rather, it may benefit from the rhetoric models of comic art, which she describes in terms of complexity, changing point of view and frame composition. Similarly, for hypertext analysis, Calvi advocates the inclusion of non-narrative elements (e.g. background features of lexias, images, text layout and its interactions with nodes) for greater hermeneutical depth.

Highlighting the vital fact that hypertext depends on spatial conceptions that differ greatly from conventional, print-based narrative, Bukatman (1994) introduces the term 'rhetoric of spatiality' (13) to describe one major aspect of hypertext aesthetics and discourse. In so doing, Bukatman draws on Bolter's (1991) concept of topographical writing, which is verbal and visual at the same time, as it arranges textual units topographically and in multidimensional hyperspace.

One of the most generic approaches to establishing a poetics of hypertext is taken by Simanowski (1999), who mentions six defining aesthetic criteria: multimediality, technological aesthetic, performance, navigation, hyperlink semantics and computer screen aesthetic. Multimediality, which in a later paper (2001a) he changes to intermediality (emphasizing the meaningful interplay between various media), requires multimedia competence in the author and therefore calls out for creative joint ventures among experts of various relevant disciplines. An aesthetic problem inherent in multimediality is what Simanowski refers to as the problem of redundancy, which occurs if several semiotic layers perform the same semantic function. Clearly, exact synonymity across semiotic systems is virtually impossible, and Simanowski's concern can be qualified insofar as every semantic component may evoke different connotations or even denotations in the reader. Technological aesthetic, which must not be confused with Block *et al.*'s (2004) concept of medial reflexivity, also implies the joining of forces between creative writers and programmers, which is always at a risk of becoming too technology-centred. Importantly, on the reader's side a similar set of techno-poetic skills is required in order to guarantee textual appreciation that goes beyond what can be seen on the user interface and takes into account aspects of production and dissemination, as well as the ability to interact with a hypertext system effectively (see Chapter 4). Simanowski's concept of performance, or 'Inszenierung' ('enactment') as he calls it in a later paper (2001a), denotes the performativity of hypertext reception, which is inextricably bound to the moment of reception itself and can therefore only reasonably be explained in terms of an intrinsic approach, coupled with reader-response theory (the latter is neglected by Simanowski). Navigation requires the reader to interact physically with the text, thus shaping its very structure and subverting traditional authorial intentionality, as well as conventional structural components like climax, epiphany and resolution.

Hyperlink semantics forms, according to Simanowski (1999b: 1), the central aesthetic component and production-aesthetic challenge of hypertext, as it determines the degree of both freedom and restriction facing hypertext readers. Links carry a high amount of semantic information about the relationships between the lexias they connect, as well as their own function as navigational elements. Links are labelled in different ways, connecting units of different sizes and semiotic categories, indicating diverse directions and varying greatly in terms of accessibility, visuality, operability and transparency.

Finally, computer screen aesthetic takes into account the receptive qualities of the digital medium. The dictates of user-friendliness demand that author-programmers follow certain editorial principles, such as a minimal scrolling effort, maximally sharp visual contrasts and the use of specific font types and sizes. Similarly, the question of how the screen is to be filled to grant a maximum of aesthetic effect is one of the prevailing issues facing hypertext authors and, of course, highly contiguous with personal and 'cultural' taste.[34]

Having outlined some major theoretical approaches to hypertext poetics taken so far, I would like to come back to the issue of surprise and how it operates as a major effect in hypertext literature. Taking the viewpoint of reader-response criticism, let us consider, first and foremost, Hans Robert Jauss's aesthetics of reception (1982). In it, he differentiates between affirmative and critical literature. The latter is, according to Jauss, of higher aesthetic value than the former, because it changes the horizon of expectations in readers, i.e. his or her specific set of assumptions at a particular moment in time.[35] Put in simple terms, a text ought to 'surprise' readers by ways of altering their horizons of expectations, macroaesthetically (in terms of the work as a whole, bearing in mind its materiality and mediality) as well as

microaesthetically (in terms of its intrinsic, macrostructural and microstructural features, which I will discuss shortly). Hypertext newcomers, for instance,
are surprised primarily on a macroaesthetic level. They are unfamiliar with the
media genre itself, including all its material and conceptual implications.
Hence, they first of all need to accept it as a working alternative to substantially
more linear, physically palpable print forms. To put it more plainly, readers, or
users, find themselves placed in front of a comparably static computer,
equipped with a mouse and a keyboard, reading from a two-dimensional
screen, scrolling, clicking and typing, instead of holding a three-dimensional
book in their hands which, among many other things, they can take wherever
they want, leaf through, bookmark manually and write into.

The microaesthetic level relates to specific attributes of the 'text' itself, such
as its specific organizational structure, its linguistic and tonal intricacies, as well
as its denotative and connotative ambiguities (see Empson, 1930). Viewing this
element again from the reader's perspective, we have to see not only aesthetic
but in fact any kind of text as 'testing ground' for the human mind on its quest
for meaning. Literary texts elicit conceptual partaking on the part of the reader,
who needs to fill in, or concretize, the semantic gaps left open individually as he
or she permeates the text. By the same token, readers perceive particular levels
of indeterminacy when reading a text, which may be described in terms of
varying degrees of conceptual complexity. Through interacting with the text,
readers manage to compensate for these complexities (e.g. Iser, 1971, 1978).
Clearly, microaesthetic decisions on the part of the reader, such as the choice
of the reading path and the length of time spent on processing structural and
conceptual information given by a lexia, require a certain extent of previous
textual, or, in our case, hypertextual reading experience, which will enable
them to discern aspects of the writers' idiosyncrasy and particular approaches
to the medium and the literary opportunities it opens up.

Taking a closer look at the microaesthetic level, two subordinate categories
can be identified. I shall refer to them as 'macrostructural' and 'microstructural'. The macrostructural level comprises textual features such as coherence
relations between textual macro-units (e.g. chapters, stanzas, paragraphs and
lexias), as well as − especially in fiction and drama − macro-exegetic issues
such as characterization strategies, character and plot development, narrative
points of view, and spatial relationships. The actual *poetic*, in the sense of linguistic, divergences between texts occur at a microstructural, subtextual level.
Strictly speaking, this microstylistic 'foregrounding' comprises all structural
aspects of language, such as phonology, graphology, morphology, lexicology,
syntax, but also suprasegmental, textual features. Traditionally, however, sty-
listicians have mostly looked at the subtextual level, such as denotative and
connotative ambiguity and density, ellipses, modality, transitivity, imagery
and figures of speech (conceit, if used in stylistic exaggeration), sound patterns,
metre, rhyme and rhythm (Shklovsky, 1988; see also Toolan, 1998). By the
same token, poetry has traditionally been considered the epitome of stylistic
foregrounding, mostly because of its heightened emotive and mnemonic effects,

and, *nota bene*, succinctness. As we will see later on in this book, succinctness is one of the principal demands expressed by hypertextual 'prescriptivists' like Ryan (2000).

With regard to hypertext, the aforementioned list of microstructural devices does not need to be replaced but rather supplemented with features specific to this media genre, on both a microstructural (flash buttons and other interactive devices, link labels, text layout, drag and drop mechanisms, text boxes etc.) and, perhaps more significantly, a macrostructural level (e.g. linking strategies, trans-semiotic interplay, pre-defined paths, loops and digressions). With respect to the purposeful implementation of aesthetic effects in *literary* hypertext, I am inclined to disagree with Storrer's (2002) assumption that we do not require a new concept of textuality for describing hypertext. Storrer essentially describes expository hypertexts, whose authors make strategic use of alternative cohesive devices such as structure overviews, global and local context cues, flexible hypertrails and other reading aids. These devices conform to the 'just-in-time principle' and the principle of user-friendly, 'intelligent hyperdocuments' that help the reader navigate through a hypertext with a view to facilitating rather than distorting coherent, minimally ambiguous understanding. Storrer further argues that individual lexias are internally coherent, because they follow conventional cohesive principles (endophora). This generalization, as a rule, does not translate one-to-one into literary hypertext, which often deconstructs textual coherence even on an intralexial level.

Viewed from Storrer's perspective, hypertextuality seems to rely fundamentally on text linguistic features, which allow readers to read a text bottom-up (working from its micro- and macrostructural levels towards a general understanding) and top-down (employing their pre-existing knowledge of the world and textual expectations to make sense of what they read). One specific aesthetic feature of *literary* hypertext is, however, that it takes conventional bottom-up and top-down processing *ad absurdum*. It does so by disrupting the meaningful interplay between the two processes, permanently playing them off against each other. As a result, readers are forced to revise their temporary mental model of a text incessantly, to maintain several alternatives simultaneously, weigh them up, *revise* and refine them, question them and essentially *revisit* their own readings perpetually. This complex process is what I understand by an aesthetics of revis(itat)ion, which is specific to literary hypertext and needs to be accepted as a prerequisite for reading this kind of literature.

Likewise, closure and completion are not to be sought in a manner comparable to conventional print literature. Michael Joyce comments in *afternoon* that 'closure is, as in any fiction, a suspect quality, although here it is made manifest' [*work in progress*]. Instead, readers are faced with the fact that their aesthetic objects are indeed temporary mental constructs, which are bound to be revised fundamentally upon embarking on a different pathway. Having said that, not all hypertexts are subject to revisitation to the same degree. In particular, those that have a linear story at their centre (e.g. *Patchwork Girl*; *The Breathing Wall*) bear close resemblance to literature in print, and therefore call out less strongly for revisitation than other, completely de-linearized hypertexts (e.g. *Victory Garden, Hegirascope*). Hence, the concept of continual revis(itat)ion itself needs to be understood as a continuum rather than an absolute property.

In putting forward an aesthetics of revis(itat)ion, I am further alluding to William Hazlitt's essay *On Going on a Journey* (1822/2002), in which he suggests that intellectual travel is 'one of the pleasantest things in the world', thereby referring not only to the final destination but, rather, to the procedural, essentially infinite aspect of travelling in search of greater knowledge. And indeed, owing to the essentially unfinished nature of hypertext reception, the aesthetic object in the wandering reader's mind is in a permanent process of formation and re-formation. Harpold calls this teleological fallacy the 'principle of deferral' (1991), which is characterized by the continuous state of 'not being there yet'.

One may be inclined to think that the mere awareness that, no matter how much time has been spent reading a hypertext, there are still more lexias to read, which may categorically transform the mental concept(s) formed so far, precludes the possibility of ever arriving at a satisfactory conclusion. However, this is not the case: committed hypertext readers tend to arrive at a stage where they are able to stop revis(it)ing the text and their readings because their conceptual curiosity seems 'saturated'.

Similarly, likening this aesthetic effect to cheating readers out of a happy ending (Douglas, 1994; Simanowski, 1999b) risks a distortion of facts. After all, hardly any 'realistic' work of (sociocritical) world literature since the nineteenth century has ventured to delude the reader into believing that a restored body politick is an authentic concept. Likewise, the final 'release of (previously withheld) knowledge' (or information), as Simanowski (1999b) calls it, has frequently been denied in world literature ever since the dawn of literary modernism. Even in much earlier literary works, such as *Tristram Shandy*, we can see a predilection among some authors to experiment with and contravene conventions of closure. Far more compelling seems, in this regard, Simanowski's 'aesthetic of dissonance' (*ibid.* – my translation), which captures the disconcerting effects on the reader and is, paradoxically, achieved by an optimum of technological harmony.

Finally, a poetics of hypertext must take account of the fact that a great number of the so-called 'essentials' of hypertext are indeed not new. The concepts of interactivity, intertextuality, trans-semioticity and synaesthesia are, to varying degrees, implied by the very idea of literature itself. The crucial novelty is their alteration through the computer medium (Heibach, 2004). It is therefore compelling to repeat that the actual idiosyncrasy of hypertext is its ontological and aesthetic dependence on the medium, with its vast amount of functionalities, applications and navigational possibilities (which include the link as a decisive, yet not its sole structural novelty). As a result, every single hypertext confronts the reader with a new epistemological challenge, a phenomenon that is largely foreign to book consumption. The uncertainty as to how to use or appropriate the text in the first instance is in fact similar to using a new software package for the first time. This macroaesthetic expectation is unprecedented and does not find its equal in the book, whose technology and navigational principles have been unchanged since the invention of the printing press.

It is therefore not surprising that authors of first-generation hypertext in particular – who see themselves as pioneers of the genre – provide user manuals and system requirements similar to software packages and complex technological appliances. Similarly, hypertexts written in specialized editors such as Storyspace and HyperCard are most demanding and take techno-friendly readers with academic standards and critical knowledge for granted. Richard Holeton, for instance, introduces his *Figurski at Findhorn on Acid* (2001) with a methodological address to the reader. His instructions merge the functional, impersonal style of a technical writer with a hint of personalized authorial narrative, presented as unidirectional discourse between author and reader:

> **Directions**. If you haven't already done so, **set the resolution** of your display screen to 1024 × 768 if that setting is available to you (Start menu > Settings > Control Panel > Display > Settings tab > Screen area to 1024 × 768) and **maximize the Storyspace window** ... so that it fills your display screen. You have several options, explained below, for navigating the hypertext. **If you are new to Storyspace**, you may wish to experiment with one method at a time, returning to this space as needed to review the other options. [*Introduction* – emphasis in original]

Text here appears as a system, as a software package wrapped, as it were, in a Storyspace environment, which has to be 'learned' before it can begin to yield aesthetic pleasure. Furthermore, navigational skills are required for reading hypertext, and increasingly so as the reader develops a distinctive 'hyper-literary', hypermedia competence (see Chapter 4). Ironically, it is precisely the element of conventional 'literary pleasure' which is systematically undermined by many hypertext writers, who set out to prevent rather than facilitate a culinary, consumerist attitude in the reader.

Having explained in detail what the major aesthetic criteria of hypertext are, I will now turn to the actual body of this study: the binary principle of explorative and constructive hypertext, which is seen as a prerequisite to canonizing this hitherto marginalized literary media genre. Moving on to somewhat more general literary concepts, the next chapter will explore to what extent the aesthetic considerations undertaken in this section tie in with a hypermedially extended concept of literature *per se*. This will then form the basis of a discussion surrounding general prerequisites and, more specifically, hypertext's potential for canonization. By the same token, the following chapter will provide a theoretical basis for the construction of a hypermedially extended concept of literary *competence*, which will be the focus of the final chapter of this book.

Chapter 2

Hypertext and the Question of Canonicity

1   Concepts of Literature

I would like to take the position that hypertext is fundamentally traditional and in the
mainstream of literature.
(Nelson, 1984: 1/17)

Literary educators make curricular and methodological decisions on the basis of
contemporary notions of literariness. Such notions also help to delimit literary
studies from related subject areas such as philosophy, the visual arts, history
and computer science, which is, in itself, an object of unlimited controversy
among critics. Hence, in order to arrive at a widening understanding of literature in the twenty-first century and of its medial innovations, it is necessary,
first of all, to take a look at existing concepts and theories of literature.[1] Theorists
throughout the centuries have adopted a variety of perspectives, which are
outlined in this chapter. As a basis for understanding hypertext literariness,
notions of aesthetic procedurality will be of particular interest.

To start with, one of the major concerns seems to be the poststructuralist claim
of panfictionalism (Willems, 2000: 217–67), which maintains that virtually
everything is fiction: not only written texts of all kinds, but reality in itself (cf.
Lyotard's 'grand narrative' or 'master narrative', Barthes' 'myths' or DeMan's
fuzzy boundaries between primary and secondary literature [1983: viii]). This
has caused an essential need for literary studies to stress its idiosyncratic, legitimate status and define itself in opposition to disciplines dealing with clearly
non-fictional in the sense of non-imaginary objects. Be that as it may, there is
overall agreement that 'literature' very much depends on contemporary manifestations of what is understood as such, and therefore defies any exhaustive
definition. This may be a painful observation, yet has to be seen as constitutive
for understanding the very discipline of literary theory and criticism.

In terms of perspectives taken towards literary concepts, the following categories can be identified. First, there are referential approaches, pertaining to
ideas of (1) mimesis (e.g. Plato's understanding of the poet as imitator of
things as they appear in *Republic*, Aristotle's concept of imitating human action
in *Poetics*, Pope's idea of emulating ancient Greek and Roman poets in *Imitations*
of Horace [1737], and Wimsatt's [1978] notion of the mirror as a literary metaphor); (2) imaginariness in the sense of non-factuality (e.g. Wellek and Warren,

1956); and (3) semantic content (Lyas, 1969; Beardsley, 1973; Matthews, 1978) – this 'school' of critics emphasizes the connotational density of literary and poetic language, as well as the difference between meaning and proposition in literature. Pragmatists (4), on the other hand, look at the way literature is used in context, in other words literature's illocutionary forces and its applicability to Speech Act Theory (Ohmann, 1971; Beardsley, 1973). Referential definitions emphasize the object of literature, i.e. its 'symbolical' (Bühler, 1934), extralinguistic meaning. Referentialists look at literature's mimetic function and in what particular ways it depicts, imitates or indeed deviates from 'reality'. The crucial problem with this approach is, of course, the very notion of 'real', which varies from reader to reader and thus cannot be understood as a universal.

Second, the figure of the author has been of major importance ever since the emergence of the individual as experiencing, sensual and empirical subject in the Enlightenment and, at its extreme, the literary genius as *alter deus* in the early Romantic Period. Literature was at that time chiefly associated with its producer. Freudian and Marxist Critical Theory have ventured even further into investigating the personality, psychological disposition, biography and socio-political circumstances of the author, going as far as to ignore the reader and the text altogether.

Third, as a counter-movement to author-centred criticism, literature has been defined in structuralist terms (e.g. Eichenbaum, 1926/1965; Jakobson and Tynyanov, 1928/1971; Jakobson, 1960; Shklovsky, 1988), focusing on language and form. Intending to turn literary studies into a science, structuralists tried to 'amputate' psychological, subjectivist categories such as the author and the reader from the text. Of particular importance here is the notion of literary, or poetic, language as *deviation*, or estrangement (Shklovsky, 1988) from everyday language, which is functionalized by poets to draw the reader's attention to the poetic message as a purpose in its own right (Jakobson, 1960). Despite the teachability and assessability of structuralist literary criticism, which manifests itself in stylistic text analysis, there has been harsh criticism, especially regarding the fact that such analytical methods do not look beyond the (poetic) text. Therefore, stylistics as a discipline has recently reached out into more reader-oriented areas such as cognitive psychology, and also started to look at non-poetic/non-literary texts, using methods of (Critical) Discourse Analysis.

Fourth, literature has been seen in functional and pedagogic terms, particularly by teachers and curriculum makers. The Horatian motto *prodesse et delectare* puts literature's moral and ethical function first, as literature's function is 'to be useful *and* to please'. This concept was particularly predominant in Renaissance humanism and the Enlightenment (see Lessing's moralistic re-evaluation of *catharsis*). Today, the conceptual educational value of literature lies very much in its potential to help readers develop a sense of individual, cultural and – not uncontroversially – national identity. In fact, the underlying conduit metaphor of literature as a vehicle for the transfer of information and values has been and still is exploited for ideological infiltration in various ways, particularly in Imperialist and Totalitarian contexts.

Fifth, and most importantly for this study, literature has been viewed under the pretext of its effect on the reader, in other words, its 'aesthetics'. The term is used here less in its generic sense of *l'art pour l'art* ('art for art's sake') than in terms of the role of the reader as the major element of the reading *process*, in other words the procedurality of literature.

Genealogically, literary aesthetics derives from the Greek *kalokagathon* ideal, epitomized by the Muses, who represent the equation of divinity, goodness and beauty. Since Baumgarten's *Aesthetica* (1750) and particularly Kant's *Kritik der Urteilskraft* (1790), beauty has come to be considered as a subjective matter dependent on sensual perception rather than reasoning. At the same time, the notion of evaluative subjectivity was established as a valid criterion for judging artistry. As a result, 'literature' came to connote appraisal, a notion which it still maintains today (see Lyas, 1969; Davenport, 1978; Lamarque and Olsen, 1994). Critical voices, on the other hand, lament the binding nature of such an understanding and seek a compromise in agnosticism and/or individual judgement (e.g. Beardsley, 1973; Hirsch Jr, 1978).

The procedural aspect of literary reception has been the focus of a variety of critical schools since the late 1970s, and a wide range of phenomenological approaches can be subsumed under this umbrella notion. The emphasis on reading in the sense of experiencing, or exploring, literature was pioneered as early as the 1930s by Louise Rosenblatt (e.g. 1976, 1985), yet did not become the focus of major attention until the Constance School of literary critics was established (e.g. Iser's [1978] reader-response theory, with its emphasis on textual indeterminacy and the semantic gap, and Fish's [1980] assumption that textual meaning develops in the process of textual experience). Drawing on Roman Ingarden's 'schematized views', Iser regards the reader as the decisive element in the process of creating textual meaning. According to him, 'reading causes the literary work to unfold its inherently dynamic character' (Iser, 1974: 275). Similarly, Jauss (1982) argues against traditional historical criticism on the grounds that its methods fail to mediate between history and literature. In his so-called reception theory, he seeks to emphasize the dialogue between reader and text, which creates continuity rather than separation. The literary work is thus re-instantiated and updated with every reading, according to changing historical, social and personal circumstances. Hence, the 'work' as such both depends on and changes readers' 'horizons of expectations' (cf. Gadamer, 1979), i.e. previously known sets of formal, thematic and generic characteristics. Jauss refers to the discrepancy between the first and latest readers' horizons of expectation as 'aesthetic distance', which ultimately determines the work's artistic character.

As will be elaborated below, literary hypertext exceeds the level of indeterminacy displayed by linear media and therefore heightens the procedural, constructive effects of individual reading. Consequently, it categorically defies critical (e.g. Marxist) positions that see literature in contingency with social ideologies as a whole (e.g. Eagleton, 1983). Such collectivist approaches cannot sufficiently account for the subjective nature of the reading process, because they sacrifice the individual for the sake of a culturally or even nationally all-embracing readership, which, of course, can never be homogeneous.

Finally, aspects of mediality have to be considered, not least because recent literary theory (e.g. Ryan, 2004) sees the concept of *narrative* spreading 'across media', i.e. beyond the book. It now includes still pictures, moving pictures, music and, in particular, the digital media, thus including a wide range of different semiotic modes, whose role changes in alignment with the medium in which they appear. Highlighting the harmonizing effects of digitization, particularly in hypermedia, Bolter (2001) refers to the 'remediation of print', i.e. the remapping of largely sequential writing structures into nonsequentially organized, digital textual networks that incorporate other media through the use of a homogeneous underlying code. A working concept of literature in the Digital Age needs to embrace these tendencies, which suggest a departure from the largely monomedial and/or monomodal views associated with paper-based writing.

Having outlined the implications of a medially extended, procedural, reception-oriented concept of literature, I will, in what follows, examine the phenomenon of the literary canon. It may be seen as the ultimate manifestation of underlying ideologies of literature as well as of its functions in society. As the title of this book suggests, my overarching aim is to provide a theoretical and practical backdrop to a 'canonization' of hypertext. In order to do this, however, I will first need to explain and critically evaluate the very notion of 'canon'. As we shall see in the course of the following sections, the canon concept needs to be modified in order to be applicable to the specific intrinsic qualities of literary hypertext.

2   The Literary Canon – Definitions, Processes, Effects

This historical sense, which is a sense of the timeless as well as of the temporal and of the
timeless and of the temporal together, is what makes a writer traditional.
(Eliot, ' Tradition and the Individual Talent': 49)

A major concern of this book is to investigate hypertext's potential for canonization, but also to examine at what stage of a possible canonization process hypertext is at the moment. To do so, a workable concept of 'canon' – a polysemic and semantically malleable term – needs to be identified. Such a concept needs to take into account postmodern social structures, literary practices and the dictates of the digital medium. This section therefore discusses the meaning(s) of the term; the social implications of having either one or indeed multiple, competing canons; and, finally, the relationship between canon and curriculum. Reference is made primarily to relevant chapters in Assmann and Assmann (1987), Arnold and Detering (1997) and John Guillory's seminal study, *Cultural Capital* (1993), which takes a Marxist approach to the relationship between canon and power.

The etymology of the word 'canon' suggests a logical connection between definitions of literature as discussed in the previous section and the canonization of literary works. Derived from the Sumeric word for a straight cane or bar used as a measuring rod, 'canon' (Greek) means 'rule', 'standard', 'list' and 'catalogue'. Applied to literature, the term refers to a compilation of literary works which, during a certain period, are considered 'seminal, normative and timeless' (Schweikle and Schweikle, 1990: 232 – my translation). Knowledge of these works is regarded, institutionally, as a requirement for academic progress and, socially, as a sign for a certain level of education as well as, in meritocratic political systems, membership of a higher class.

Viewed socio-critically, canons comprise texts which are considered culturally valuable by a certain group or society, and therefore 'worthy' of being handed on to posterity (Winko, 1997: 585).[2] They are fixed, self-contained, closed, exemplary and prescriptive in nature. Assmann and Assmann (1987) claim that the term is best defined by ways of institutionalized permanence, presence, propriety and resilience to temporality – 'institutionalized' because canons are *per definitionem* imposed by governmental institutions, with the aim of 'constructing' cultural unity and identity. Guillory explains the driving power of canonization in Marxist terms: 'Judgments with canonical force are institutionally located' (1993: 29), and are most strongly driven by the decisions of educational bodies, which, in turn, are subject to higher organs of power.

Canons are selected by institutional authorities to stabilize a common ground and to highlight certain elements of tradition which, according to an elitist world view, help create and sustain identity within a certain community or peer group. Indeed, canons have a considerable psychological and social(izing) effect in that they enable discourse and a sense of belonging among members of those social groups who are familiar with the works in question. Having said that, imposed, 'top-down' canons can only operate successfully in rather small, totalitarian societies. In large, multi-layered societies, alternative catalogues frequently undermine imposed canons, as was the case with the German 'Klassikersturz' during the 1970s (Grübel, 1997: 618). Alternative canons arise from 'situations of need' (Hahn, 1987: 33), where minority social groups are jeopardized by subjugation, discrimination, marginalization, expulsion or exile. Similarly, the recent empowerment of marginalized social groups across Western societies has subverted mainstream ideological unity, resulting, for instance, in alternative canons of feminist, gay and lesbian, African American and Caribbean writing.

The correlative instrument of the canon is censorship, which is motivated and controlled by the canon. As a matter of fact, canon and censorship stand in dialectic opposition to each other, as their existence and effectiveness are reciprocally conditioned. Underlying both canon and censorship is a catalogue of intra-literary and extra-literary values, pertaining to intrinsic and extrinsic features of a literary text. Not belonging to a canon implies censorship of varying degrees, ranging from being neglected by readers or critics to being banned by law.

From an aesthetic perspective, canons are traditionally considered catalogues of works that are exemplary, admirable, and worth emulating, and thus
create patterns of artistic excellence. Implicitly, a canon follows as well as represents an implicit or explicit set of rules, which may be used as restrictive and
generative principles of production and reception (Hahn, 1987). Ultimately,
therefore, canons are manifestations and concretizations of literary concepts,
which reflect the 'tastes' of dominant social groups. The Western Canon
(Bloom, 1994), or indeed any other 'traditional canon', therefore connotes normativity as imposed by oligarchic elites of literary criticism, such as I. A.
Richards (1929), T. S. Eliot (1932) and F. R. Leavis (1948).

Literary value judgements can occur either implicitly (through tacit acts of
exclusion and inclusion) or explicitly (by means of verbal criticism), and per-
tain to all areas of literary interaction: production, reception, distribution, and
application to pedagogy and criticism (Winko, 1997: 586–9). Needless to say,
selection always implies the exclusion of the majority, which is not only precarious from a scholarly point of view. It has in fact a fundamental educational
disadvantage: students who are given lists of 'must-reads' that are largely unaccounted for are prevented from forming their own, subjective, critical stance in
distinguishing good from not-so-good literature.

Contrary to most definitions, canons are by no means as stable as their 'selec-
tors' would wish them to be. They are indeed highly subject to paradigm shifts
within a particular society. To give an example, the emergence of the vernacu-
lar English primary school curriculum in the eighteenth centuries was closely
connected to a new image of literature, which not only included the ancient
classics but was extended to English writing and thus began to follow the purpose of bourgeois nationalist education. The subsequent inclusion of the realist
and modernist novel in the nineteenth and early twentieth centuries was as
inevitable as that of film since the 1960s, which naturally resulted in a gradual
reduction of the number of works from Greek and Roman Antiquity. In other
words, due to the dynamic nature of human culture and society, the stability of
tradition, which has often been taken for granted by supporters of the traditional canon, is as wrong an assumption as the eternal gospel truth of 'great'
works (Assmann and Assmann, 1987).

Canonization processes are evolutionary in nature. This implies, in Darwinian terms, a permanent process of adaptation to changing environmental
(i.e. social) parameters, or values. According to Assmann and Assmann
(*ibid.*: 16), literary works 'return' to enter a canon after a process of initial
'renunciation', or censorship, which often verges on iconoclasm. Returning to
previously censored works is motivated by an emerging historical interest in
periods gone by and their artistic and literary output, precisely because they
were previously renounced. Günther (1987) elaborates this idea by proposing
five stages that make up the process of canonization. First, a preparatory 'pro-
tocanon' evolves, in which texts of a certain type accumulate. This is followed
by the actual stage of canonization, in which a canon is selected and formulated in opposition to other, existing canons. During the subsequent stage of

implementation, the canon is used, for example for educational and socio-integrational purposes. The last two stages are revertive, in that they reflect the gradual disappearance of a canon. During decanonization, a canon ceases to be binding and, subsequently, becomes obsolete. Finally, the postcanonical stage describes the existence of decanonized texts, which still exist but have vanished from curricula and reading lists.

One of the most controversial aspects of previous canonization processes is their contingency upon the materiality of the written work, i.e. its physical manifestation and preservation in script and print. As Assmann and Assmann (1987) argue, the ideal medium for canonization and thus preserving cultural heritage is the book, as primary means of consolidating script. Books symbolize coherence, density, closure, completeness, unity and physicality, all of which are essential for immortalizing a literary work. Nevertheless, the authors concede that ultimate belief in the preserving power of script is treacherous, as written documents are, under adverse circumstances, nearly as much prone to oblivion as orally transmitted text.

Hypertext oddly inhabits a niche inbetween physical presence and oral evasiveness. It is, by definition, non-printable and thus cannot be turned into a concrete, material object. Whether or not this renders it more prone to evanescence than print literature is an intriguing question. Clearly, the permanence of its existence is far more in the hands of its author-programmer than in the case of print literature. One mouseclick suffices to remove the all-important link which connects a hypertext to the World Wide Web. Publication, therefore, literally hangs by an (electronic) thread. On the other hand, the hypothetical storage potential and economy of digital literature clearly exceeds that of print literature. In other words, the question of whether or not a code can have a stronger preservative power than binding, cardboard and paper is indeed a delicate one.

From a commercialist viewpoint, institutionalized canonization is most efficiently enhanced by means of literary anthologies. By creating different types of anthologies, authoritative editors perform two simultaneous tasks. On the one hand, they re-emphasize the cultural importance of previously canonized texts, in other words 'the historical canon' (Schmidt, 1987: 337). They do so by re-adopting canonical works into new editions of, for instance, *The Norton Anthology of English Literature* or *The Norton Anthology of American Literature*. On the other hand, they have the power to establish and promote 'alternative' (Guillory, 1993: 29) or 'acute' (Schmidt, 1987: 337) canons, which are thus made to compete with the traditional Western Canon without, however, undermining it altogether. Examples of such alternative compilations are *The Norton Anthology of Literature by Women*, *The Norton Anthology of Afro-American Writing* and indeed *The New Media Reader*. The culturally or sub-culturally seminal works contained within those anthologies are chiefly directed at an academic or scholarly audience, some of whom are, *nota bene*, aspiring anthology editors-to-be.

The concept of the canon as a closed, fixed, prescriptive catalogue of set texts has met with a great deal of criticism. The most compelling reason for this is given by Hahn (1987), who, referring to Tenbruck's (1962) tripartite typology of society, comes to the conclusion that an imperative canon becomes only necessary and indeed feasible in 'civilized societies' ('Hochkulturen'), where unity can only be achieved at an abstract level, by imposing an obligatory canon on a stratified, divergent society.[3] Our modern, contemporary Western society is, by contrast, 'complex' in that it organizes itself in terms of functional differentiation. Every individual refers to a variety of peer groups, for each of which he or she fulfils at least one distinct role. Similarly, art and literature form subsystems among other subsystems within a highly diversified society. Cultural coherence no longer derives from a holistic world picture, but rather from an 'interplay of functionally differentiated subsystems' (Hahn, 1987: 36 – my translation). Each of these subsystems propagates its own canon, thus contributing to the contemporary trends of pluralization, partialization and functionalization (Schmidt, 1987). In view of that, it is plausible to assume that each individual follows a variety of rule and text canons, which, in themselves, are flexible and dynamic and are used in an eclectic manner.

The divide between supporters and enemies of a unified, traditional canon, has, since the 1980s, led to the so-called canon debate. Traditionalists (e.g. Kermode [1985, 1990] and Bloom [1994]) follow in the wake of such renowned critics as Palgrave (1861, 1897), Arnold (1880/1988), Eliot (1919/1972) and Leavis (1936, 1948). They argue against the so-called 'School of Resentment' (Bloom, 1994: 4), who are trying to deconstruct the concept of the canon for the sake of a higher degree of social and ethnic egalitarianism (e.g. Gramsci, 1957; O'Donnell, 1984; Blackledge, 1994; Richardson, 1998).

Harold Bloom's monograph *The Western Canon* (1994) seems particularly anachronistic as it obstinately insists on the retention of the traditional canon, with Shakespeare at its centre. It is hardly surprising that Bloom does not include examples of hyperfiction. What is surprising in fact is that Bloom adopts Vico's term 'Chaotic Age', which 'will amalgamate with the Computer Era, already upon us in early versions of "virtual reality" and "the *hypertext*" ' (Bloom, 1994: 310 – emphasis mine). His greatest concern is that technological advances will 'cancel the literary canon once and for all. The novel, the poem, and the play might all be replaced' (*ibid.*: 310). My aim is to annul this concern. As we have seen in Chapter 1, hypertext does not abolish traditional genres like the novel, the poem and the drama: it expands them medially.

It has been argued by many canon theorists that, ever since the advent of the Modern Age, which emphasized individuality rather than collectivism, a singular, prescriptive, normative canon has come under threat. A recent *New York Times* article stipulates the futility of the canon debate *per se* 'in an age where there's no canon, where there are so many other forms of information, and where we're returning to medieval-like oral culture based on television' (California State Librarian emeritus, Kevin Starr, quoted in Weber, 2004). Although Starr's opinion can only partly be accepted, he does have a point in mentioning the crucial impact of television. However, this is not so much because of the orality it reinforces but because of the visuality it has reintroduced into society.

The postmodernist paradigm has subjected the canon to the segregation of diverse cultural value systems, each of which sets out to establish their own rule and text catalogues. The 'atrophy of pan-cultural thinking' (Assmann and Assmann, 1987: 24 – my translation) is indicative of a somewhat post-historical situation, which has resulted in canon apathy, yet has not been able to eliminate canonicity altogether. Evidently, it is becoming increasingly difficult to establish a common foundation for literary scholars and lay readers alike, and it would seem as if egalitarian and equally informed scholarly discourse might become an increasingly utopian ideal.

Contrarily, the past few decades have seen new canons emerge, for example in feminism, postcolonialism, multiculturalism and working class writing. The major argument in favour of them is that they represent pluralist, quasi-egalitarian Western values. As such, the canon functions as an instance of 'imaginary politics' (Guillory, 1993: 7), as 'cultural capital' (Pierre Bourdieu's coinage) mirroring stratified societies. At the same time, however, the promotion of alternative canons paradoxically implies an acceptance of the traditional canon. Ironically, alternative canons epitomize exclusion by calling themselves 'non-canonical', and therefore strengthen policies of discrimination and hegemony. On the other hand, discrimination and hegemony are pervasive symptoms of our so-called multicultural Western societies and cannot be denied or 'canonized away'. Hence, alternative canons carry an enormous symbolical weight and are likely to trigger heated classroom discussion.

The connection of the canon to identity and culture raises the question of whether and how *virtual* culture has hitherto been utilized to reflect social strata. Particularly the younger generations are strongly influenced by the expansion of digital media, such as digital television and film, 'Skype' (digital telecommunication), as well as, of course, the World Wide Web, with all its communicative, entertainment, creative and epistemological facilities. The human body itself is increasingly merging with technology. Human-machine hybrids, such as cyborgs (Haraway, 1991), avatars, and androids, which we encounter in science fiction and cyberpunk film (e.g. *Terminator, Batman, The Matrix Trilogy*), print literature (e.g. by William Gibson, Neal Stephenson, Douglas Coupland, Philip K. Dick), computer games (e.g. *Tomb Raider, Civilization, Age of Empires, Quake*), MUDs and MOOs, is developing in cyberspace as a working alternative to human fleshliness and vulnerability. Virtual communities are arising from internet chatrooms, MUDs, video conferences and other virtual networks. Digital environments offer to many of their users a more flexible, experimental, secure environment than real-life communities, and subjects discover other, potential existences by adopting and exploring various sexual, cultural and historical identities (e.g. Turkle, 1996).

Bloom's (1994) monstrous elegy on the fall of literary studies and the rise of 'Cultural Studies' is in line with Weber's aforementioned pessimistic outlook. I largely disagree with these prognoses, because, although we do indeed listen and watch more than we used to before the age of hypermedia, we also read more than we used to. Reading different media requires different reading techniques and a flexibility in applying them, according to what medium one is dealing with. Hence, what contemporary educational theory and practice needs to do is embrace the affordances of the New Media, including hypertext, and expand their didactic toolkit accordingly.

This brings me to the last point of my discussion. With respect to the educational function of the canon, we have to differentiate between the concepts of 'canon' and 'curriculum' (or, more narrowly, 'syllabus' in the sense of a 'synecdochic list' [Guillory, 1993: 34] used as part of the English curriculum). 'Curriculum' does not simply equate to 'teaching practice'. It is indeed a fallacy to assume that the curriculum is a manifestation of an imaginary construct called the 'canon'. Contrarily, it is the curriculum, or rather curriculum makers, that produces the canon. Along with reading lists and anthologies, these syllabi are the only way of accessing the imaginary list of literary works which represents, materializes, and, not least, commodifies the English canon.

In logical consequence, a revision of the canon is only possible through a revision of the curriculum, particularly when it comes to including New Media phenomena such as literary hypertext. Taking a closer look at the National Curriculum of England and Wales, the question arises whether a potential for integrating hypertext is indeed in place.

Since the arrival of the National Curriculum of England and Wales in 1989/90, questions of canonicity and curricular selectivity have become central: 'To list or not to list became one of the main questions in the politicisation of English teaching' (Benton, 2000: 273). Eventually, the prescriptivist camp, who supported the Saidian notion of 'self' as being English and therefore distinct from the 'other', outnumbered the anti-prescriptivists, who advocated a culturally more diverse and open curriculum. Consequently, the only allowance made in the 1995 version of the English Curriculum was an apologetic invitation of works from 'other cultures and traditions' (Benton, 2000: 275), but the heritage model was institutionalized all the same.

In 2000, Benton postulated a 'less dictatorial structure' (*ibid.*: 276), which focused on the teaching of 'literature in English' rather than 'English literature', and introduced limitations only in terms of genre and literary history, not in the choice of textual material. Similarly, the 2000 and, to a greater degree, the 2003 Curriculum show a much higher demand for ICT (Information and Communication Technology), as well as what is called 'media and moving image texts'. ICT is propagated mostly as a teaching tool and environment for autonomous learning (Clarke *et al.*, 2004: 353). It includes the use of electronic whiteboards, specialized presentation and layout software (PowerPoint, Clicker, Publisher), and the internet as an information resource, as it contains a vast range of canonized paper-under-glass literature, which pupils can engage with as they learn basic IT skills such as cutting, pasting and drag-and-drop, as well as the reflected combination and presentation of various digitized media (image, text and sound). 'Media and moving image texts', on the other hand, covers mostly film and prevailingly expository texts found in newspapers, magazines, on television, and in advertising.

The emphasis of media and ICT education appears to be focused on the development of critical skills in terms of using *informative* multi- and hypermedia sensibly and reflexively. It therefore does not come as a major surprise that *literary* hypertext is not mentioned anywhere in the National Curriculum. That said, the inclusion of other media, which are not perceived as literary media in the conventional sense, in the literary classroom suggests that, in all likelihood, it is only a matter of time until other 'narrative' media such as computer games and hypertext will be integrated. Meanwhile, however, even the leading teacher training manuals fail to interpret the National Curriculum in such a way as to include literary hypertext in their interpretations. Pike (2004) carefully hints that 'writing a poem is different on a computer but one of its advantages is that text can be so easily manipulated' (125), without, however, making any specifications as to what kind of electronic poetry he is referring. Clarke *et al.* (2004: 353) venture a considerable step further by claiming that:

> our concept of literacy has altered through the challenge of invisible, unreliable authors and multi-authoring, non-linear text and hotlinks that the computer screen, and especially the web, offer us. Even the way we think may have changed to thinking in whole chunks of movable text rather than discrete words or sentences. The public, collaborative nature of these new texts on the Web, and the centrality of the visual image, graph or icon, has also transformed the way we read, view and write texts.

Evidently, the authors do use expressions that evoke associations with hypertext terminology without, however, spelling out the word itself. One is thus tempted to suspect that hypertext is mentioned neither in commendation nor derogatorily because it simply has not yet been popularized among English teachers and curriculum planners.

In sum, it may be argued that the major steps towards facilitating an inclusion of hypertext have been taken. Despite the facts that hypertext is not explicated in the Curriculum and, as a result, only a marginal number of English teachers are familiar with it, the increasing importance of hypermedia in the Curriculum may reflect the need for alternatives to literature in print.

To conclude this section, a literary, script-based culture, which manifests itself *idealiter* by a shared passion for reading among its members, can only be maintained if the New Media and their specific poetic manifestations are taken on board. After all, learners have to be picked up from where they are, and the technological evolution can be denied by neither literary traditionalists nor teachers of literature, as it is so willingly received by the younger generations. If the contrastive literary use of New Media in the classroom is supported by teaching staff, educational authorities, and students alike, I am convinced that the end of the book as foreseen by Marshall McLuhan (1962) and Jacques Derrida (1976) is not impending after all. However, we are indeed witnessing the end of a unified, exclusive, print-based canon as the gospel truth of literary value.

Under the pretext of the preceding discussion, the title of this book may seem like a contradiction in terms. In fact, we can only use the term 'canonizing' for hypertext given that we abandon the rigidity and normativity it implies. Instead, 'canon' is used in this study in a creative rather than restrictive sense. The catalogue of selection criteria listed at the end of this chapter forms a deliberately flexible and dynamic 'rule canon', which produces a canon of hypertexts which is neither compulsory nor rigid in nature. Rather, it outlines a number of what I consider outstanding works of the genre, which, for educational, academic and aesthetic purposes, are 'worthy' of entering an educational paradigm.

3   Canonizing Hypertext – An 'Apologetic Crusade'?

Literary systems are comprised of canons, and 'novelization' is fundamentally anticanonical. It will not permit generic monologue. Always it will insist on the dialogue between what a given system will admit as literature and those texts that are otherwise excluded from such a definition of literature.
(Holquist in Bakhtin, 1981: xxxi)

Literary hypertexts have been written for over 20 years, yet still cannot be considered 'canonized', either in the sense of representation through individual specimens in anthologies or university readers, or in a generic sense, as an abstract phenomenon in the minds and discourse of the reading public, as Shakespeare, Milton and James Joyce are. In fact, as Gates (1997) cogently argues, whereas the 'traditional English and American canon' has quite readily adapted to the new (digital) medium, works written *in* and specifically *for* the new medium are by no means as easily adopted by the canon. This is hardly surprising, as we are dealing with a form of writing that became materially possible only a few decades ago, through the evolution of personal computing, software applications and, not least, the internet as the primary medium of communication and research in the First World. Stressing the chiefly sociological implications of this development, Becker argues that, before the mid-1980s:

> there were no programs to make hypertext fictions, there were no authors, no body of works to constitute the beginning of a 'canon', no publishing companies to manufacture and distribute those works, no readers who had acquired the skills necessary to read them and who had read a number of them and therefore were prepared to be a 'public' for them, no critical writing about that body of work to inform the public about their existence and virtues – in short, no *world* of hypertext fiction. (1995 – emphasis in original)

Nevertheless, unlike many other web-based text types such as portals, discussion and chatrooms, online magazines, wikis and blogs, internet-based creative writing of any kind has not entered media-reported public discourse in the UK. A database search of *LexisNexis*, a leading international digital newspaper archive, proves the virtual non-existence of the term 'literary hypertext' and other related expressions across the British press media landscape, both broadsheet and tabloid. As a matter of fact, over the period of the past fifteen years (1990–2005), a timespan which approximately corresponds to the existence of internet-based literary hypertext, no instances of 'literary hypertext' and only eight occurrences of 'hyperfiction', two occurrences of 'hyperdrama', and two occurrences of 'hyperpoem' are retrievable.[4] The distribution of those instances across various British newspapers is demonstrated in Table 1. Perhaps not surprisingly, only 'serious' newspapers are represented, as the database search did not yield any tabloid occurrences. This observation may support the fact that literary hypertext has, from the outset, been associated with academic and scholarly rather than popular interest. A certain 'peak' of discursive engagement – if, in the face of the generally low number of occurrences, one may use such an expression – happened around the mid-1990s, which was the time when the internet was experiencing its first surge in popularity among a wide public sphere.

Thematically, the eight tokens of 'hyperfiction' are used in either marginalizing or even pejorative contexts. They occur in book reviews, for instance in a discussion of the labyrinthine *Shadow of the Wind* by Carlos Ruiz Zafon, where 'the same old self-deconstructionist hyperfiction shuffle' (Jones, 2004: 8) is assigned a derogatory connotation, to highlight that Zafon has managed to avoid the confusion typically associated with reading hypertext structures. Another instance appears in a review of Noah Wardrip Fruin's *Hypermedia Reader* (Mackintosh, 2003: 25), yet only marginally, as part of Fruin's homepage URL. Other occurrences appear in letters or questions to the editor, e.g. in the *Daily Telegraph* section 'over2you' (25 January 2001), without, however, being elaborated or discussed in greater detail. Only three out of the eight instances of 'hyperfiction' present the genre in a more informative, less partial way. Interestingly, it is an article in the *Financial Times* (Griffith, 1996) which gives the most exhaustive detail about 'hyperfiction', characterizing it as a 'slowly expanding volume of narratives' (15). Griffith mentions Nelson's (1984) widely acknowledged definition, provides a short historical overview of

Table 1   Distribution of 'literary hypertext', 'hyperfiction', 'hyperdrama' and 'hyperpoem' across British newspapers between January 1990 and September 2005

	'literary hypertext'	*'hyperfiction'*	*'hyperdrama'*	*'hyperpoem'*[5]
Guardian	none	1 (2003)	1 (1992)	1 (1992)
Daily Telegraph	none	2 (2001; 2004)	none	none
Independent	none	1 (1999)	none	none
Observer	none	1 (1997)	1 (2001)	none
THES[6]	none	1 (1996)	none	none
Financial Times	none	2 (1994; 1996)	none	none

hypertextual phenomena, outlines the major structural and thematic principles of Shelley Jackson's *Patchwork Girl*, and does not fail to draw attention to the perceptive challenges evoked by hypertext structures without, however, condemning the genre for precisely this propensity.

As Table 1 shows, 'hyperdrama' occurs only twice: once in the *Observer*, where it is used in the sense of 'overdimensional American television soap opera', exemplified by *Dallas* and *Dynasty* (Anthony, 2001: 20). Even more deviant from the concepts propagated by Ayckbourn and Deemer is the use of 'hyperdrama' in the second article from the *Guardian*, in which the term refers to 'the hyperdrama of our futures' (Waters, 1992: 23), thus expressing a realistic, socio-political meaning. The sole instance of 'hyperpoem' also comes from the *Guardian*, where it features in an article which is, exceptional though it may appear, dedicated to the Apple-based hypermedia poetry written and displayed by artist and poet John Cayley at the Poetry Library in the London Royal Festival Hall (1992/93). However, the author of the article implicitly denigrates the poetic potential of Caley's art by quoting the poet's reply to the question of whether he would refer to his poetry as 'art': Caley refuses to 'make any aesthetic judgments about the value of the work', leaving this 'up to other people' (Moody, 1992: 33). The fact that the statement stands uncommented at the end of the article is indicative of Moody's personal opinion, which is made to remain in his readers' memory beyond the reading event.

To give further evidence of whether and to what extent hypertext – despite or, in fact, in addition to the bleak picture presented by the press – has entered teaching practice in England, I conducted a telephone-based survey among secondary English departments in May and June 2005. The results unambiguously reflect the impression given by the newspaper search. Out of 85 English teachers from secondary schools in and around two representative northern England industrial cities (Leeds and Newcastle upon Tyne),[7] 70 (82 per cent) had never come across the terms 'hypertext' or 'literary hypertext'. Fifteen (18 per cent) were familiar with the term 'hypertext' as used in 'Hypertext Mark-Up Language'. None had ever heard of Eastgate Systems or any of their products. Forty-two (49 per cent) said they were using the computer and internet to a great extent for student projects, e.g. SmartBoard, interactive whiteboard, and game-type software for analysing set texts such as *Of Mice and Men*, *Macbeth* and *Romeo and Juliet*. Twenty-one (25 per cent) maintained they were using the computer solely for teaching basic word processing and graphic design, which was, according to the respondents, partly due to limited access to computers in some schools. Thirty-four (40 per cent) explained they were using the internet for literary research, e.g. to investigate First World War poetry at A-level, finding materials on Shakespeare for the SAT exams,[8] or downloading electronic versions of set texts. Eight (9 per cent) replied they were using the internet only for weblogs. Another 15 (18 per cent) stated that they taught computer-based, yet traditionally linear creative writing. Finally, as few as eight respondents (9 per cent) had also experimented with creative writing in hypertext format, using, for instance, the free internet service *think.com*.

The empirical data suggests that hypertext is, to use Günther's (1987) terminology, still in a 'protocanonical' stage. Simanowski (1999b) specifies this stage, which has not moved on considerably since the publication of his article, in terms of a developing 'literary field' (a Bourdieuan term). This development is characterized by competitions, commercialization, as well as the emergence of reviewing platforms and scholarly expertise manifested by specialized academic seminars, research talks, publications and dissertations. The main dilemma of hypertext criticism, however, surfaces particularly in competitions: the lack of evaluative criteria, which would, if they did exist, do justice to the vast range of different aesthetic phenomena and would help scholars, critics and editors to 'sift the wheat from the chaff'.

Conversely, Coover (1999) claims that the Golden Age of hypertext is already over and will by replaced by a 'Silver Age', 'a miniboom', which is determined by the chaotic, unstructured, largely pictorial and reductionist character of the web. To a certain extent, this ties in with Moulthrop's observation (1993: 73) that hypertext:

> has been bumped from the limelight by hazier and more glamorous obsessions: cyberspace, virtual reality, and the Information Highway. Such changes of fashion seem a regular hazard of the postmodern territory – taking *post modo* at its most literal, to mean 'after the now' or *the next thing*.

Rather than bidding hypertext farewell, however, Moulthrop concedes that 'a certain circularity seems to be in play' (*ibid.*: 73), in that hypertext appears to be coming in and going out of fashion quasi-cyclically. Coover (1999) adds to this observation that, as a result of such an evolution, literature *per se* will look entirely different from what it used to, and so will the readers of the future.

Coming back to Assmann and Assmann's (1987) concept of renunciation and return (see Chapter 2.2), I would argue that hypertext has by no means passed the first stage of the two, at least not in the UK, where, as previously evidenced, hypertext scepticism and ignorance are only gradually being replaced by curiosity and open-mindedness, at least among literary and linguistic academics.[9] On the other hand, with respect to hypertext-friendlier nations such as the USA, Germany, Austria and Switzerland, one may tentatively speak of a gradual transition to a 'return', which manifests itself in a considerable number of university syllabi geared towards including hypertextual phenomena and their theoretical underpinnings.

Hypertext *censorship* is of an essentially cathectic kind (see Hahn, 1987), i.e. hypertext is most frequently denounced for its incapability of arousing aesthetic pleasure in the reader. In fact, readers' responses to first hypertext exposures tend to be radically divided and polarized. They are 'either delighted or annoyed' (Schnierer, 2003: 96). At the same time, critiques by first-time readers show a tendency towards premature, overgeneralizing conclusions about hypertext as a genre, rather than towards analysing individual works.

Reader bewilderment and resentment are due to a number of factors. On the one hand, most of them lack theoretical and practical media knowledge, i.e. the ability and confidence to use particular kinds of media text, as well as an awareness of typical macro- and microstructural features (Flender and Christmann, 2002). Media knowledge normally comes with regular exposure and experience, and these are prerequisites to processing hypertext.

Clearly, hypertext's anti-monolinearity has an alarming effect on many readers, insofar as there seems to be a lack of perceivable author intentionality, and, as Ryan (2000) controversially argues, a 'deficiency, compared to traditional narrative in the area of immersivity ...' I do not subscribe to her point of view, as many hypertexts do enable reader immersion, albeit by different means than traditional narrative. In a nutshell, the most common complaints revolve around structural complexity, semantic opaqueness and logistic impediments. Furthermore, a lack of navigational guidance and macrostructural standards aggravates readers' impression of having lost or being incapable of gaining control of 'their' text.

As a matter of course, hypertext does not set out to encourage culinary hammock-reading.[10] On the contrary, one of the major intricacies, if not pitfalls, of hypertext is its inherent expectation of an 'ideal' hypertext reader, who will readily adapt to an unfamiliar reading situation, which introduces not only a new, bi-dimensional, in most cases even bulky medium, but a level of complexity and arbitrariness in textual organization that defies the conventional *delectare* effect. As a result, readers may be tempted to develop a hypertextual 'zap mentality' (Auer, 2004: 281), which is caused by a shift in attention from the text to the link and its target. Wingert calls this the 'centrifugal powers' (1996: 202) of hypertext reception.

A further reservation relates to the incompatibility of operating systems and the resulting difficulty in accessing a great number of hypertexts. As Glazier (2002: 156) points out, '[t]he most notable controversy here is the PC versus Mac conflict'. In fact, '[e]ven academically mainstream texts, such as *Uncle Buddy's Phantom Fun House* and Michael Joyce's *Twilight, a Symphony*, cannot at this writing be run on Windows' (156). Nor, indeed, can they in summer 2006. It is mostly for this reason that only a comparably low number of Mac-based hypertexts could reasonably be adopted in the hypertext canon featured in Chapter 3.

Further issues of concern are the so-called 'anarchy' of the web and the issues of authenticity and copyright it brings along. Walter Benjamin's (1977) famous tenet of the lost 'aura' of the original artwork in the face of infinite reproducibility, reinstated through digital encoding, almost inevitably springs to mind. As a matter of fact, copy and paste, as well as 'Surf – Sample – Manipulate' (Amerika, quoted in Beiguelman, 2004: 173), are web-inherent activities that categorically undermine authorship in the traditional sense and turn online documents into fair game, into 'second-hand originals' (*ibid.*), which are exposed to any hacker's or internet surfer's free will.

Another inherent problem of hypertext is its resistance to anthologization, especially when it does not come in the format of a handy-sized data carrier such as a CD-ROM or a floppy disk. Hypertexts most frequently appear on the internet, the anarchic, dynamic nature of which subjects them to ephemerality and evasiveness. Similarly, some attempts have been made to capture the swiftly expanding body of hypertextual writings by means of exhaustive listings online. Nevertheless, an explicit canon, operating on the basis of distinct selection criteria, has never been formulated. Admittedly, Glazier (2002) draws up a catalogue of the most prominent hypertext practitioners, induced from three quasi-anthological web-based lists. However, his results are no longer verifiable, as none of those lists exists any longer. Furthermore, neither Glazier nor the authors of those lists base their selections on any evaluative criteria, but proceed in an uncritically statistical fashion, by giving the names most frequently found on the internet, which are: Ted Nelson, Michael Joyce, Jakob Nielsen, Laurence Sterne, Paul Delany, George Landow, Jay David Bolter, Jane Yellowlees Douglas, Gregory L. Ulmer, Jerome McGann, John Tolva and John Unsworth. This approach, objective as it may appear, implies the inherent fallacy that the mentioned authors venture to publicize their own names as frequently as they can and therefore skew the data found in web searches.

By the same token, the past few years have seen the launch of a number of print compilations focusing on cyber-theory, hypertext criticism and hyperfiction. The process was initiated by the 1997 edition of *The Norton Anthology of Postmodern American Fiction*, which features referenced excerpts from Michael Joyce's *afternoon* and Jane Yellowlees Douglas's *I Have Said Nothing*. Further progress with regard to anthologizing hypertext theory can be seen in the launching of Victor J. Vitanza's *CyberReader* (1996) and Neill Spiller's *Cyber_Reader: Critical Writings for the Digital Era* (2002), the first compilations of theoretical essays about computer aesthetics, cyberculture and digital literature. They do not, however, contain any digital literature. On the other hand, Vitanza supplies a multitude of web addresses at which the keen reader may find related and supporting materials. The essential step towards including creative digital media was accomplished by Wardrip-Fruin and Montfort in their *New Media Reader* (2003), which encloses a CD-ROM with selected hypertexts, most of which are, however, only readable on a Macintosh computer.

As previously discussed, postmodern Western society is characterized by plurality, globality and, perhaps most importantly, rapid change. It is also increasingly dominated by hypermedia, which are currently taking over the world of television, telephone communication, and epistolary writing. Arguably, therefore, the future literary mainstream will at least partly be situated in virtual space, which will retain its fluidity and thus create ever-changing forms of literary art. It will also, in all likelihood, integrate the visual to an increasing extent. For this reason, educationalists have to find ways of meeting the needs and interests of the new generation without, however, allowing the vanishing of the written word to proceed any further.

Therefore, to conflate the ostensibly conflicting concepts of hypertext and 'canon', I contend that the very concept of canon can no longer be understood as it was in the nineteenth and until well into the twentieth centuries. As a matter of fact, the situation experienced by Western society in the Digital

Age curiously resembles that of late eighteenth-century Europe, particularly France, when the Ancient Régime was struggling to regulate an oozing, anarchic mass of Enlightenment writings. Such writings were naturally frowned at, however, not censurable as a whole – which correlates with the usual attitude towards online publishing. Although the political situation is, of course, entirely different now, the dilemma of facing a virtually uncontrollable host of anarchically distributed documents is indeed comparable to that experienced by Louis XVI and his Conseil du Roi.

While departing from the traditional canon, a hypertext canon must inevitably adopt components of radically subversive *avantgarde* canons, which have influenced poetry and art since the 1920s. Among their components are the claim for innovation (a derivate of technological progressivity and the concept of evolution); the concept of style as manifested subjectivity; and the use of (meta-)theory as an instrument of transforming art and literature (Schmidt, 1987). Rather than eliminating the canon idea entirely, we thus have to part with its traditional self-contained, closed, and rigidly exclusive connotations. Instead, an inclusive, open concept has to be adopted, which works in terms of a continuous process of integration, modification and discharge.

Hypertext writers generally adhere to the aforementioned *avantgarde* criteria, which will be recorded in the 'rule canon' listed at the end of this section. Furthermore, translating the dynamic character of hypertext production and reception into a hypertext canon reconfirms the validity of hypertext's inherent properties. Finally, a hypertext canon can be considered a useful instrument for members of distinctly hypermedia-friendly communities to establish a common ground for shared reading experiences.

The crucial problem with 'canonizing' hypertext in the sense of creating a catalogue of outstanding works is the question of how to 'judge, analyze, write about a work that never reads the same way twice' (Coover, 1992: 25). Clearly, the Aristotelian absolutism of beginning, middle and end does not hold true for hypertext, as there are a number of possible middles and ends (even if all readers start from the same lexia). In fact, a hypertextual canon can only work if we replace the idea of a unifying experience through reading 'identical' texts by the idea of unity through individual readings (see Bolter, 2001: 11). Paradoxically, as didactic implementation has shown, critical meta-discourse is not only possible but indeed lively and enriching, despite or precisely because readers are made to debate their personal versions of the same hypertext.

Setting up a canon of aesthetically, cognitively, spiritually and morally appealing hypertexts is in fact not an 'apologetic crusade', as Aarseth (1997: 22) calls any such theoretical or practical attempt. I also disagree with Aarseth in that, rather than not searching 'for traditional literary values in texts that are neither intended nor structured as literature' (*ibid.*: 22), I concentrate on texts that are maximally close to 'traditional' print literature and therefore do not require a complete redefinition of 'literature'. 'Good' hypertexts do not require an *apologia* but rather emphatic vindication, which may ultimately direct them towards curricular integration. For this purpose, this chapter is dedicated to drawing up a concise catalogue of aesthetic, paedagogic and conceptual criteria. This 'rule canon', or 'set of values', forms the basis of my evaluation and selection of hypertexts. In order to do so, however, we must not forget that reading hypertexts has to be learned and practised in order to appreciate their distinctive aesthetic potential. As I pointed out previously, some hypertexts exhibit deliberately intricate navigational systems, which form a constitutive part of their aesthetic programme.

Aesthetic value judgements of any kind are problematic in that they are not only highly subjective, but essentially dependent on the qualitative conceptions of different groups in society. Hence, venturing to suggest a hypertext canon single-handedly may seem hubristic if not downright impossible. Having said that, the digital medium facilitates two aspects of reception which, in print media, are, for pragmatic reasons, less feasible: direct, often even textually interventionist interaction with the product on the one hand, and direct communication with the author on the other. To put it differently, the reading subject is autonomous in terms of being able to respond immediately to the individual reading experience – without even changing the medium of interaction. The author's email address is normally given on the website in question or, if not, it can be 'Googled'. In my experience, hypertext authors tend to be interested in and swift to reply to readers' questions. Notably, this sense of reader autonomy does not imply an approval of the convergence theory as discussed in Chaper 1. Rather, it supports the notion of personalized hypertext and, along with it, the plausibility of a single-handed canon.

Strictly speaking, my hypertext canon is only single-handed with regard to its selector anyhow. The actual selection process operates by means of (electronically) networked reading and scholarly discourse. In other words, the text catalogue reflects an individual opinion derived critically from many other opinions. This renders the selector a subjective reflector and catalyst of scholarly opinion. To emphasize this aspect, Chapter 3 provides not only an alternative canon, but discusses existing reviews and critical essays focusing on the selected hypertexts.

Another pervasive argument in support of (alternative) canons is the mundane fact that reading time is short for the average member of the First World, and selections have to be made, considering the sheer host of reading matter on offer. Therefore, I agree with Winko, who argues in favour of retaining canons, mainly because they facilitate selection. Her only reservation is that, in order to compensate for subjectivity, relativity and changeability, any underlying 'axiological' value judgements have to be well-founded and explicated (Winko, 2002: 2).

With this in mind, I suggest a hypertext canon (see Chapter 3) that is based on a set of such 'axiological values'. These values have to be exclusive enough to bring forth a 'manageable' choice of hypertexts. Simultaneously, they need to be sufficiently open to allow future additions, modifications and reductions. I propose four overarching categories, which are in alignment with the classical semiotic triangle as suggested by Bühler and echoed in a range of approaches to literary value judgements (e.g. Grübel, 1997; Winko, 1997). The categories are: (1) production (relating to circumstances of authorship); (2) object (relating to the subject matter); (3) form (linguistic and other structural devices, including navigational strategies); and (4) reception (relating to the reader in the widest sense, which includes lay readers, critics, editors and pedagogues alike).

Considering the productive element, innovation and originality, which Winko categorizes as 'relational' values (Winko, 1997: 594), play an important part. An aesthetics of innovation implies, according to Fricke (1981: 209), a deviation from quasi-norms dictated by literary history and generic conventions. The innovation claim is, as mentioned previously, a central constituent of *avantgarde* canons and adhered to by most hypertext authors.

Another feature to consider with regard to production is the extent to which technology is used to reflect the subject matter. Clearly, technological expertise is perceived to be of less significance than poetic and narrative skill when it comes to assessing an author's potential for (literary) canonization. Evidently, the mere ability to use sophisticated hypermedia software and mark-up languages does not necessarily result in a literary or multimodal masterpiece. Instead, a central formal concern will be transmedialization, i.e. the meaningful combination of hypermedia (in the case of second- and third-generation hypertext mainly), and, more generally, the implementation of intertextuality in the sense of textual and semiotic interplay.

Thematically, the focus will be on the text's 'ability' to make readers reflect, to influence their world picture, or expand their horizon of expectation. This includes not only topicality of subject matter and reference to theories of philosophy, sociology, politics, psychology, ethics and religion (Winko, 1997: 549): hypertext's characteristic self-referentiality necessitates that meta-fictional, meta-hypertextual, meta-medial and meta-critical issues are intelligible as well (Löser, 1999: 1; see also Block *et al.*, 2004). Such self-reflexive aspects entail a high degree of implicit and explicit intertextuality, thus signalling the thematic, inter- and transcanonical network a hypertext may allude to and evoke in the reader's memory.[11]

Formally (pertaining to the sign-element of the semiotic triangle), I will look at microstructural and macrostructural features as discussed in Chapter 1.5. Formal-aesthetic values are traditionally associated with the beauty of sound, connotational density and ambiguity, completeness, coherence and 'magnitude', as Aristotle puts it in his theory of tragedy. That said, formal excellence depends largely on the theory of literature applied to a text and the degree to which the text meets the requirements of such a theory. Hypertext theory specifically believes in the effects of narrative antilinearity and the resulting increase in reader responsibility; the lexia as the smallest and decisive textual unit; the absence of closure; and rhizomatic infinity, as well as the tripartite structural interplay between link, node and network. As linking patterns and navigational strategies are among hypertext's most characteristic and unique formal features, particular attention will be paid to how authors use them to achieve distinct aesthetic effects.

In terms of reception, I will examine cognitive, emotive and existentialist effects on the reader in general, insofar as they can be examined from published documents. These include, on the one hand, responses written by professional critics by means of reviews and critical articles, which have been published in (online) journals, books, and other electronic or print media resources. Of further interest are awards won in hypertext competitions, as well as the publishing situation in general. In terms of distribution, we need to ask, for instance, whether the copyright of a particular hypertext is owned by a registered publisher, such as Eastgate Systems, as this implies peer review and professional editing. Contrarily, a text may have simply been put on the internet, without there being any instance of peer review. The role of the reviewer is particularly important in the case of collaborative writing projects, as here the act of reviewing often completes the otherwise never-ending hypertext (see Wirth, 2001: 60). In other words, editorial power often surfaces in the 'right' of the reviewer to finalize an open-ended hypertext sometimes to the relief of the co-authors.

Another question with regard to hypertext dissemination is the degree to which it has been anthologized, i.e. integrated into readers (books or CD-ROMs). Such compilations are among the most suitable pedagogic tools as they may be set as prescribed reading for courses in Media Studies or contemporary literature.

Perhaps most importantly, but also most subjectively, the rule canon highlights aesthetic qualities that are likely to have a motivating effect on readers. Ways of making readers 'read on' are manifold, even though they are reading from a screen and cannot expect any sense of closure or completeness from the text in question. Aesthetic effects include suspense, surprise, playfulness and 'intellectual exercise' (Schnierer, 2000: 544), i.e. the challenge of exploring and making sense – or well-grounded non-sense – of a text that may defy cognitive comprehensibility, both structurally and thematically. Aesthetic features are necessarily dependent on other, mostly formal, properties of a literary work, and will thus be discussed in relation to these properties. Table 2 summarizes the axiological criteria explained in this section, which will serve as a catalogue of criteria, i.e. a 'rule canon' in note form, for the hypertext canon compiled in Chapter 3.

It is important to note that such a norm catalogue is creative rather than restrictive in nature. It legitimizes and produces a canon which, on the one hand, excludes works that do not sufficiently fulfil the criteria in question. In other words, it adds an element of 'scholarly control' to the anarchy of the web, as well as to commercially biased reviewers and editors as represented by Eastgate Systems. Moreover, the norm catalogue allows for dynamics in the sense of facilitating the adoption of new works. The criteria are formulated so as to yield to value-related paradigm shifts. Hence, rather than mapping out a limited number of 'exemplary' role models, the catalogue invites modifications of the works it brings forth, depending on individual opinion.

In a field as fluid as digital literature, new, groundbreaking technology as well as writerly creativity proliferate new works, most of which, sadly, do not

Table 2 'Rule canon'

Production	Innovativeness	• deviation from literary/hypertextual traditions • interrelation between technology and subject matter
Object	Thematic depth	• topicality • thematic message • self-reflexivity • metatheoretical concept • intertextuality
Form	Aesthetic overstructuring (microstructurally/macrostructurally)	• rhetorical devices • linking patterns • navigation • hypertext structure
	Semiotic interplay	• transmedialization • implemented intertextuality
Reception	Criticism	• critical acclaim • awards
	Anthologization/degree of canonization	• readers (print/CD-ROM) • university reading lists • curricular presence
	Motivation/effect on reader	• suspense • surprise • playfulness • 'intellectual exercise'

meet the standards of a literary scholar. Some exceptions, however, give evidence not only of technological expertise, but, more significantly, of an overwhelming combination of poetic and artistic aestheticism. Such works should be invited into a hypermedia canon, which, as its underlying medium, is inherently open-ended, yet, at the same time, internally well-structured and thought-out.

Chapter 3

A Hypertext Canon

Epiphany subsides once experience sets in.
(Schnierer, 2003: 97)

Thus, I would argue that the task ahead is one of placing hypertext in the correct context,
of working toward a more useful definition of e-writing, and of establishing a newly
envisioned canon of e-literature.
(Glazier, 2002: 95)

This chapter proposes a selection of 23 hypertexts from three generations that meet the criteria outlined in Chapter 1 and may thus be considered suitable for inclusion in a hypertext canon. The selection was made out of a total of more than 200 hypertexts. As a preliminary note, the selection was made from a clearly subjective point of view – as any selections are. Hence, any evaluative statements expressed in the following textual analyses have to be taken as such – as value judgements based on subjective aesthetic impressions, which other readers may entirely disagree with although, as pointed out before, they are grounded in a matrix of quasi-objective evaluative criteria (Table 2).

A tendency that can be observed when traversing the list chronologically, particularly between first- and second-generation hypertext, is the increasing endeavour, performed successfully in the selected works, to abide by Ryan's (2000) dictum that

> [t]he next generation of hypertexts will have to be visually pleasurable, and hypertext will be a work of design and orchestration as much as a work of writing ... To remain readable, these conceptual hypertexts will have to be shorter than the hypertext novels of the first generation. And it will be necessary to give a strong allegorical meaning to the action of moving through a textual network – not an invariant generic message inherent to the medium, but a meaning unique to each particular text, and ideally recreated with every use of the device.

What Ryan suggests is that hypertext writers need to take into account the material circumstances under which their works will be received as well as the idiosyncratic mediality of digital writing, which encompasses macrostructural nonlinearity and microstructural intersemioticity. 'Visual pleasurability' is, of course, not only a value-ridden concept, but also somewhat naïve in its outlook. In fact, it conjures up Edmund Burke's distinction between 'the sublime' and 'the beautiful', which renders the two binary concepts mutually exclusive and thus inapplicable to a great number of works. Deliberately provocative and aesthetically disturbing visualizations, such as the wired head depicted in the introduction to Urs Schreiber's *Das Epos der Maschine*, would be doomed to fail under the auspices of pleasurability, which, in many cases, would be highly inappropriate. In fact, the major aesthetic effect of *Das Epos der Maschine* relies on precisely that mixture of aural and visual displeasure and verbal, i.e. poetic, *belcanto*. Consequently, as far as the interplay between verbal, aural and pictorial elements is concerned, 'pleasurability' ought to be supplanted by 'meaningfulness', which would pay tribute to the author-programmer's specific textual conception and the semantic significance attributed to every single textual component.

Ryan's brevity postulate, however, seems plausible indeed, as relatively short texts minimize the physical effort of reading from a CRT (cathode ray tube) screen, which has medically been proven to be slower and more strenuous – although not of lesser cognitive-mnemotic quality – than reading from paper (e.g. Ziefle, 1998). Similarly, the meta-level of allegorizing virtual, hypertextual space is a popular concept among hypertext authors and forms part of hypertext's self-referentiality. Making it a *sine qua non*, however, would significantly reduce the author-programmer's creativity, particularly when it comes to technologically more sophisticated manifestations. Therefore, Ryan's claim needs to be qualified and replaced by a more descriptive approach that takes into account hypertext's innovative potential.

Various attempts at providing lists of hypertexts and other projects of New Media Writing have been made offline (e.g. by Suter and Böhler, 1999; Heibach, 2003), and via online databases (e.g. by Suter, 2001), without, however, explicating any systematic selection criteria. To compensate for this absence, the preceding section of this study proposed a 'value canon', which indicates clearly why certain hypertexts fall within the range of a possible canon, while others do not. For each hypertext in my list, I will provide an approximate synopsis,[1] representative examples of previous research and reviewing activities, a formal analysis (macrostructural, microstructural, narrative and [trans-]semiotic features: see Table 2), and an interpretation of the effects the text has on me as a reader. While it is not necessary, or in fact possible, for any hypertext to meet all the criteria listed in Table 2, the selected examples follow the majority of them in various weightings.

To be shortlisted for a canon in the first place, a hypertext needs to exhibit a range of essential, rather obvious properties, which are again production-oriented, thematic, formal and aesthetic in nature. Perhaps the most salient quality is functionality. Some hypertexts, particularly hypermedia, contain huge files which take so much time to load even high performance computers that the reader loses patience and is likely to close the application before it has even opened (e.g. *Tyrell.Hungary* by EastEdge, 1998, or *Zwei Tote?* by Romana

Brunnauer). Similarly, hypertexts containing links to external pages that are not updated on a regular basis are prone to become obsolete in the course of time. Links leading to pages that no longer exist cause frustration in the reader and undermine the integrity of the text.

Another important exclusion criterion is lack of originality. There have been various attempts at recycling pre-existing literary print material by re-arranging it into a hypertext structure. In fact, they give the impression of an unauthorized postmodern pastiche, assembled by experimentally minded, artistically inclined 'tekkies'. The originality of any work of art is an essential component of its productive process. In other words, the crucial function of an author – or, in the case of hypertext, author-programmer – cannot be replaced by that of an editor, whose function lies in (re-)assembling previously written material (see Wirth, 2001).

One example of hypertextual recycling is Edward Falco's *A Dream with Demons* (1997), which is largely based on a novel by Preston Morris. Apart from the fact that hyperlinks are available for navigation, the hypertext reads like a linear novel. Its lexias are chapter-long, so the reader has to go to the trouble of using the scroll-bar extensively, which complicates and aggravates the reading process.

Of particular significance in the evaluation of hyper*fiction* are considerations regarding character and narrative. As in traditional print literature, characters are most compellingly rendered if they are psychologically complex (rounded) and undergo a certain degree of development, which depends to a large extent on the spatio-temporal dimensions of a text. Similarly, narrative structures are used either, traditionally, to achieve the reader's 'willing suspension of disbelief' or, in a poststructuralist paradigm, to deconstruct it. If hypertexts lack elements of either or both of those two major features, they cannot reasonably be placed in a diachronic canon of similarly structured works. Sarah Smith's science fiction hypertext *King of Space* (1991), for instance, displays a lot of attributes listed in the rule canon. Nevertheless, Tam Ross, the protagonist, does not come across as a profound, intricately structured character, as he seems to be largely driven by sexual and other basic physical instincts as well as the melodramatic, heroic desire for achievement, conquest and mundane fame. His actions are mostly listed rather than attributed to any psychological motivations. Although the story is narrated from Tam's point of view, it does not reveal many of his thoughts and emotions. A few neutrally reported dreams are the only psychoanalytical insight granted to the reader, who is bound to feel excluded from the narrative essence of the text.

The receptive side of the value canon is one of the most controversial aspects, as critical voices on hypertexts and their authors are hardly as unanimous in terms of praise and condemnation as they are on traditionally canonized writers such as Shakespeare, Milton, Joyce or even Pynchon. The research situation with most hypertexts is such that reviews and academic papers are written by hypertext supporters. Therefore, criticism tends to be rather opinionated and to emphasize the academically interesting sides of a hypertext rather than its cumbersome attributes. Evaluations on aesthetic quality from my own point of view are therefore added to reinforce, supplement or indeed oppose other critics' appraisals. Reviews are taken from established literary and critical websites such as Robert Kendall's *Word Circuits*, Roberto Simanowski's online journal *literatur.digital*, Beat Suter's commented hypertext collection at *www.cyberfiction.ch*, and Johannes Auer's (2005) exhaustive :: *Projekte* :: *Netzliteratur//Hyperfiktion*. These sites are constantly updated and outline a variety of critical responses.

The hypertext canon contains hypertexts written in German and English. This is due to a number of factors. First, English and German are, at the time of writing, the two leading languages of the internet.[2] Second, due to its contingency on the computer and, in particular, the internet, hypertext literature is a generically global phenomenon. Owing to the 'anarchy', or 'liberty', of the web, hypertext writers are more inclined to write in and experiment with languages other than their own mother tongues than they are in print literature, where getting established as a creative writer in a foreign language culture tends to be met with a greater degree of scepticism and colonialist prejudice. As a matter of fact, Glazier regards digital writing, for its nomadic tendencies, as a side-effect of globalization, placing it in the international tradition of Concrete Poetry (2002: 151–2). Finally, the Anglophone and German-speaking hypertext communities are probably *the* most prolific resources of 'canonizable' hypertext, from both a creative and a critical perspective, as the majority of publications as well as publishing bodies at the time of writing happen to be based in the USA, Germany and Switzerland.

1   First-Generation Hypertext

1.1   Michael Joyce, *afternoon, a story* (1987/1990)

Michael Joyce is widely acknowledged as the first ever significant hyperfiction author. His hyperfiction *afternoon, a story*, created in Storyspace and published by Eastgate Systems, predates the antilinear possibilities of the internet. It is predominantly script-based, and self-contained in that it does not offer any hyperlinks to external systems or web pages. Excerpts of it were included in the 1998 edition of the *Norton Anthology of Postmodern Literature*.

The text follows essentially in the tradition of the psychological novel, as the story is told from the point of view of a first-person narrator, who is deeply disturbed by his personal bereavement, his feelings of guilt and failed responsibility and his general inability to come to terms with his existential situation as well as his social environment. Other than comparable narrative and dramatic male, essentialist psychograms like Franz Kafka's *The Trial* (1925), J. D. Salinger's *The Catcher in the Rye* (1951), Samuel Beckett's *Krapp's Last Tape* (1958) and Raymond Carver's 'The Bath' (1981), however, Joyce's pioneering work is primarily concerned with its own macro- and microstructural intricacies, which, after all, make it *the* prototypical first-generation hypertext. After all, the resolving 'afternoon' events alluded to in the title and in the first, inevitable lexia [*begin*] are not revealed in every possible reading experience of Joyce's hypertext.

Afternoon has had a trendsetting impact in that it features the complexities of digital, nonlinear text organization in an unprecedented way. As a matter of fact, the sheer infinity of possible readings makes it virtually impossible to summarize the 'story' in a comprehensive, all-encompassing way. Nor does Joyce intend his readership to discuss and analyse the hypertext with conventional 'ease' and relative unanimity. In fact, the story exists on various levels and changes according to chosen paths, such that even previously visited pages change in terms of designated and hidden links. Every reading results in a different story, and it is this particular quality which elucidates the hypertext's affinity to poststructuralist concepts, such as the rhizome, and the deconstruction of centrality and of unified meaning. The text presents itself as a cycle, which becomes more adamant as the reading process advances. Readers reach a point at which they seem to have read everything, without, however, being able to come to a conclusion as to the actual contents of the novel.

Peter, the first-person narrator, is a technical writer, who has recently been divorced from his wife Lisa. One morning he witnesses the aftermath of a car accident, which becomes the focus of nightmarish musings pervading the whole novel. He believes he has seen his ex-wife and son Andy killed in the accident, and cannot stop reproaching himself for passing by without helping the injured. This neurotic state is borne out by the ever-recurring sentence 'I want to say I may have seen my son die this morning' [*I want to say*], which is built into a loop, causing readers to revisit the same lexia repeatedly as they go along. Paradoxically, Peter finds himself incapable of fantasizing: 'I sit here, unable to dream' [*yesterday*]. This lexia also keeps recurring, thus assuming an equally central position within the hyperfiction. Peter is stuck in a mental cul-de-sac. He is numbed by feelings of guilt, jealousy and inertia. Dream and reality merge, a phenomenon which may be indicative of cyberspatial psychology. His musings revolve around the two other main characters, Wert, his wife's new boyfriend, and Lolly, a secretary and prostitute. The hypertext centres around the accident, yet also reveals the multifarious ways of the characters' mutual promiscuity. These two 'poles' determine the protagonist's and narrator's paralysed mental state, which renders him unable to take rational action.

As a matter of fact, the fragmentary character of *afternoon* is augmented by the unreliable narrator, who never appears capable of forming any conclusive thought. His stream of consciousness reveals a high degree of uncertainty, speculation and disorientation. This impression is reflected by the absence of clear navigation aids. Rather cynically, the implied author remarks: 'The lack of clear signals isn't an attempt to vex you, rather an invitation to read either inquisitively or playfully and also at depth' [*read at depth*].

Joyce's central intention is to illustrate how hypertext embodies postmodernist writing and poststructuralist theory. In the first place, Joyce is, as Landow puts it, 'suspicious of closure' (1992/1997: 192). And indeed, in one lexia the implied author proposes his paradoxical programme, which may well serve as a guideline to hypertext readers in general:

> Closure is, as in any fiction, a suspect quality, although here it is made manifest. When the story no longer progresses, or when it cycles, or when you tire of the paths, the experience of reading it ends. [*work in progress*]

Setting, narrator, characters and plot keep changing throughout the reading experience. Even so, the reader is able to connect fragments of information into a somewhat coherent, yet subjective picture, and having achieved this element of 'closure', is likely to leave the text.

Furthermore, *afternoon* lays open its intertextuality. It not only draws on, but overtly mentions sources like the *Odyssey*, Grimms' *Kinder- und Hausmärchen*, Goethe's *Werther*, Tolstoy's dramatic theory and Pynchon's novels. Joyce self-critically questions the act of writing itself by confronting the reader with cynical metafictional remarks such as 'I am not sure that I have a story. And, if I do, I am not sure that everything isn't my story or that, whatever is my story, is anything more than pieces of others' stories' [*me**] and 'And, as a poet, you know more about the world than anybody?' [*Mefisto*] – 'Some poets like to think so' [*there you are*].

The language of *afternoon* exhibits distinctly lyrical qualities. It is highly expressive and captures the reader's attention by its aesthetic impact alone. The winter landscape seems animate with powerful personifications, animal and botanic metaphors: 'the afternoon melt freezes again across the blacktop into crystal octopi and palms of ice ... the snow moaning beneath our boots' [*begin*]. Similarly, Peter's internal monologue renders a realistic psychogram of his intricate, disorderly feelings. His stream of consciousness is reminiscent of similar passages in *Finnegans Wake* and *Ulysses*, e.g.

> No wonder. Says it exactly. And I am taken by the medievalism of Hours, to think of the day so. In this season the day has only long hours. Mornings, when I walk, I pass through zones of odors: chemical fertilizer, cigar, smoke, lingering exhaust fumes, an occasional talcum scent when an infant has been ferried from the car to home or vice-versa. [*no*]

The narrator's mental hopscotch is believable in that it evokes the image of authentically disconnected yet curiously coherent, associative pondering.

Joyce's *afternoon* is widely used by teachers of hypertext from all over the (electronically networked) world as the first significant example of its kind ever written – referenced too widely to mention every single module that focuses on it. Nearly every hypertext seminar in the Western hemisphere features it on its schedule. Furthermore, critical acclaim for *afternoon* has been plentiful. The hypertext appears in virtually every scholarly publication on literary hypertext (e.g. Landow, 1992/1997; Aarseth, 1997; Murray, 1997;

Bolter, 2001; Hayles, 2002; Simanowski, 2002b) as the prime example of digitized, nonlinear structures and multilinear reading.

1.2 Stuart Moulthrop, *Victory Garden* (1991)

Like *afternoon, a story*, Stuart Moulthrop's *Victory Garden* is one of the first as well as most widely read and taught hypertexts. It was written in Storyspace and published by Eastgate, and a sampler is available on the internet. Due to its enormous scope (approximately 1,000 lexias and 2,800 hyperlinks), it is barely readable in a single go. Thematically, it represents a mixture between American campus novel and anti-war novel and may thus be contextualized within the traditions of books like *The Groves of Academe* (Mary McCarthy, 1952), *Pictures from an Institution* (Randall Jarrell, 1954) and *Pnin* (Vladimir Nabokov, 1955), as well as *All Quiet on the Western Front* (Erich Maria Remarque, 1929) and *Tin Soldiers: A Novel of the Next Gulf War* (Michael Farmer, 2003). Like Michael Joyce, Moulthrop lays open his intertextual references. He draws mainly on Jorge Luis Borges's *Labyrinths* (1964), as well as song lyrics written by John McDaid, Mojo Nixon and Two Nice Girls. *Labyrinths* is the primary resource and analogy for the title-giving garden metaphor, which again is derived from Borges's short story *The Garden of the Forking Paths*.

Victory Garden is set primarily in Tara, an imaginary North American sunbelt state, during the Persian Gulf War of 1990–91. It centres around the influence of the media in war correspondence and strategy. Moulthrop explains: 'Hypertext seemed the right choice – indeed the only choice – to capture the bewildering complexity of such a massively convoluted, hyper-mediated experience' (quoted in Simanowski, 2000b). The vast array of characters employed by Moulthrop is almost Dickensian in nature, and the reader finds it difficult to identify a protagonist. One may speak of a set of recurring characters, none of whom is textually explored in psychological depth. Going by the surface text as displayed by the lexias, the impression is rather that of a cross-section of media-oriented American society against the backdrop of postmodern warfare. Only upon repeated reading and venturing deep into the hypertext does the reader recognize an underlying 'intrigues and love' story. By the same token, the reader's existing schemas relating to the complexities of human relationships and psychological dispositions are activated and added to the reading experience as such. These cognitive processes cause textually flat characters to become rounded, and opaque relationships to turn into an intricate and conflicting, yet subjectively transparent, social network.

The love story unfolds between Jude Bush, a misanthropist undergraduate, and Victor Gardner (from whose first name the first part of the title is derived),[3] a graduate student, who is unhappily in love with Emily Runbird, a young soldier in the American Forces, who, in turn, has fallen in love with Boris Urquhart, a professor at her university. Jude, pretending to be Emily, perversely seduces a spiritually disembodied Victor before telling him about her own, homoerotic, passion for the girl.

What Jude is trying to do (she recognizes her desire as both 'deeply symbolic' and 'radically perverse') is 'to create a link that would unite all three of them, a symbolic link outside of bodies and time,' a desire shared in some respects by Mr. Moulthrop and exhibited in his multidirectional, atemporally linked hypertext structure. (Coover, 1999)

In another strand of the story, Emily is killed in a bomb attack. In yet another one, the reader is taken back to pre-war times, finding Emily and Victor making love. Other central characters who (potentially) appear during the reading process are Dorothea Agnew ('Thea'), a professor, who is waiting for a visit from her rebellious son, Harley; Veronica Runbird (Emily's sister); John Law; Leroy; and Miles Macarthur, a university lecturer, whose aim − in alignment with the principles of hypertext perception − is to dissuade his students from the principles of necessity and determinism.

One of Moulthrop's major novelties is a topographical map representing the narrative 'Garden', offering the reader a variety of entries into the hypertext. While the map does not give an exhaustive view of all lexias and thus refrains from giving insight into the text's overall scope, it serves as a superficial navigation aid, which foreshadows hypermedia synaestheticism (see also Deena Larsen's *Marble Springs*). It represents a paradox, in that beyond it lies a host of intricately interlinked lexias, which seem to come to life under the surface of a treacherously simple, visual navigation device.

One of the crucial differences between Joyce's and Moulthrop's hyperfictions is the use of language. Whereas Joyce entangles the reader in an almost psychedelic lyrical monologue, Moulthrop's style is highly prosaic, almost colloquial at times. He captures the speech of young American adults, without, however, distorting the narrative by a surplus of slang expressions. This down-to-earth quality has a powerful effect, particularly in violent, emotional scenes such as Emily's thoughts preceding her death. The author chooses free indirect speech and dialogue for most of his lexias. He focuses on a range of characters without having to provide any smooth transitions, a technique which is facilitated by the modularity of lexias. Sentence fragments and scattered, single words intensify the evocation of media communication and information distribution.

In his extensive analysis of *Victory Garden*, Coover (1999) calls Moulthrop one of the 'creators of the early classics' of hypertext. His sobering, generic judgement runs as follows:

And yet *Victory Garden* is, essentially, a very conventional academic novel, easy to follow, easy to read, about a group of professors and students at a Southern university at the time of the gulf war in 1991. There are the usual intellectual affairs and passionate disputes, the parties, the politics, the familiar bedroom and campus tavern scenes, along with protests and counterprotests about the war, curriculum reform and other hot topics. It is all stitched together with the customary epigraphic gathering of the author's favorite quotations, a kind of 'interanthology'.

It is indeed subject to individual opinion whether or not *Victory Garden* is an 'easy' read in the conventional, culinary sense of the word. Having said that, there is no doubt that, due to its explosive thematic content, its suspenseful way of narrating (although – or even because – it is fragmented), its rounded characters and sociocritical message, on top of its structural idiosyncracies, the text is rightly mentioned and commended by most hypertext critics and theorists (e.g. Landow, 1992/1997; Suter, 1999; Bolter, 2001; Joyce, 2002; Simanowski, 2002a, 2002b) alongside Joyce's *afternoon*, as one of the leading pioneers of the genre.

1.3   Carolyn Guyer, *Quibbling* (1993)

'Carolyn Guyer's *Quibbling* is one of the mothers of feminist hypertext and it is still one of the best,' maintains Carolyn Guertin (1998), another eminent hypertext writer and critic publishing with Eastgate. *Quibbling* is one of Eastgate's early products, being purely script-based and created in Storyspace for Windows or Macintosh.

Like Matthias Goldmann (2002) in his German hyperpoetry cycle *Schreiben auf Wasser*, Guyer chooses water as a metaphor for writing in e-space. Other than Goldmann, however, Guyer's concept of water symbolizes more than just the fluidity and changeability of text. It is used as a metaphor for womanhood and, exceeding it, for 'life itself' (Guyer, 1992: 258):

> in that rhythmic sense of ebb and flow, of multi-directional change, of events that disappear before they are quite intelligible but somehow come to mean something, that *Quibbling* was made . . . A lake with many coves is how I saw it. The coves being where we focus, where individuals exist, where things are at least partly comprehensible; the lake being none of that, but, naturally, more than the sum of the coves, or more than what connects them.

The text's emphasis on water as a gendered natural element places it in the context of other, similarly inclined feminist narratives, such as Virginia Woolf's *To the Lighthouse* (1927) and Jean Rhys's *Wide Sargasso Sea* (1966).

The 'quibbling' of the title refers to the conversations between at least five couples – Agnes and Will, Margaret and Henry, Angela and Jacob, Hilda and Cy, and Heta and Priam – viewed from the perspective of the women. Each of the couples' 'plots' can be read in a linear fashion, by navigating with the enter key. For example, Heta and Priam's story largely centres around Heta's musings on making her partner understand her needs and feelings. She mentions aquatic elements like Lake Michigan and the ways in which it reflects the endless sky, the colour of her lover's eyes and clothes: 'is there anything as alive and full of light as a body of water?' [*bottle glass*]. She tries to envelop her feelings in a cigar box meant for Priam, yet refrains from giving it to him because she doubts his willingness to comprehend what it means to her. Agnes and Will, both artists, represent the carnivalesque, physical, erotic, almost perverse element of love. They maintain a playful relationship. Once again, bright colours, specifically turquoise, play a dominant part in the life of the female narrator, who, through her art, connects air and water. Margaret and Henry seem to be taken from a novel set in the previous century, as the couple ride along on horseback. In integrating their story, Guyer adds a meta-fictional aspect, a novel written by one of the characters. Each storyline breaks off at a certain point and merges into that of another couple. This macrostructural technique has an integrative, unifying, but also fantastic effect, as the reader seems to jump from person to person in a randomly associative way.

The highly intertextual character of Guyer's hypertext is supported by the extensive list of references she draws on, both fictional and critical, including books by John Fowles, Jorge Luis Borges, Michael Joyce and, most importantly, Deleuze and Guattari's (1987) *A Thousand Plateaus*. The last figures most prominently, as the author found in it ideas she had long been seeking. She prefers nomadic thought to Aristotelian linearity. Her image of narrative is one of flux, and thus matches her cyberfeminist programme of dissolving polarities. In Guyer's view, hypertext comes close to embodying *l'écriture feminine* (cf. Landow, 1992/1997: 206), with its 'decentered contexts', 'the woven practice of women's intuitive attention and reasoned care' (Guyer, quoted in Joyce, 1988/ 2002b: 89), its 'ostensibly female (or perhaps, feminine) characteristics of intuition, attentiveness, and care, all of which are transmitted from one woman to another via the universal experience of having a (certain kind of) mother' (Greco, 1996), and its similarity to 'gossip, family discussions, letters, passing fancies and daydreams' (Guyer, 1992: 258). The female characters in *Quibbling* reflect on the various roles a woman has to play to please everybody around her in the same way: 'A wife can be what her husband needs, but a mother must be everything' [*the impossible*].

Like Michael Joyce's *afternoon*, Guyer's *Quibbling* has appeared on many a reading list of US and Canadian hypertext modules. Her poetic, expressive style arises from an intensely descriptive, colourful vocabulary, which makes for a synaesthetic, realistic reading experience. Colours carry the main symbolical weight, and metonymies of water and liquid permeate the free indirect speech narrative like a *leitmotif*: 'she picked up a piece of cobalt glass from the beach. She had been picking up bits of glass and dropping them again all day . . . a sliver of watery turquoise etched by sand to frothy opacity' [*broken cobalt*]. By applying a mixture of rich symbolism, emotional intensity, contemplative tone, and water imagery, Guyer achieves the intended effect of reading experienced as cradling, lulling and flow, without, however, losing the reader's attention, which is retained by a subject matter to which everybody (especially women) can relate.

1.4   Jane Yellowlees Douglas, *I Have Said Nothing* (1994)

Jane Yellowlees Douglas's hyperfiction *I Have Said Nothing* (*IHSN*) is exceptional in that it has managed to take a first step towards canonization via anthologization. Along with Joyce's *afternoon*, it is the first and so far the only hypertext to have been included, via referenced excerpts, in a major anthology, the 1998 edition of *The Norton Anthology of Postmodern American Fiction*. Initially written in Storyspace and published by Eastgate, Douglas has also created a short version for the World Wide Web (1994). Like Joyce, Moulthrop and Guyer, Douglas has appeared on many (US-based) hypertext literature modules (e.g. Rita Raley's 'Hypertext and Hyperfiction' module, Minnesota).

Douglas created her title from an aphorism by St Augustine: 'I have done nothing but wish to speak; if I have spoken, I have not said what I wished to say' [*But I've said nothing*]. The incapability of speaking after a tragic, avoidable accident, for which one is not responsible, yet the repercussions of which one has to bear, is one of the major themes of the hypertext, and is developed on two levels. The author focuses on the parallels between psychological and textual fragmentation as represented in hypertext. This theme is embedded in a general criticism of contemporary society, emphasizing in particular drink and drug-addicted US youth culture. Unable to vocalize her feelings, the young narrator writes about her experiences in a fragmented, distorted manner. She lets all possible storylines end in the programmatic cul-de-sac sentence: 'That's all she wrote' [*The End*].

Set in Detroit, Douglas's hyper-short-story revolves around two alcohol-related, fatal accidents, the effects and aftermath of which are reflected throughout the story. The order of events is significantly distorted by the lack of a sequential plot. In so doing, Douglas compellingly conveys the confusion of the characters, whose feelings and logical thinking are numbed by the sheer tragedy of events. Following the tradition of the psychological teenage novel and short story (like, for instance, Alex Garland's *The Beach* [1997], Ann Marlowe's *How to Stop Time: The Memoir of a Heroin Addict* [2002] and Melvin Burgess's *Smack* [2003]), the main focus of the story is on the characters' mental struggle to come to terms with their own, corrupted lifestyles, drug addictions and the inability to learn from past mistakes.

From the first-person narrator we learn that Sherry, her brother Luke's 18-year-old girlfriend, was killed in a car accident. One part of the story centres around Luke's autistic withdrawal as he struggles to come to terms with his loss: 'I wish to Christ it'd been you. Why the fuck wasn't it you instead?' [*You sit, you think*]. The narrator reflects upon contemporary media and pop culture, which causes indifference to simulacra yet makes it impossible for human beings to accept real life tragedy: 'She was gone like one of those women in monster films, the ones who inevitably trip a half dozen times before the camera – twitching violently to simulate the ferocity of the oncoming beast . . . How is it, we, who have witnessed eighteen thousand deaths, cannot accept one?' [*Can we accept one?*] The narrator describes Sherry's clothes (polyester, 'come-fuck-me' spiked shoes, six-inch heels), which Luke keeps on his bed day and night, as he fails to let go of his memories and feelings of guilt. Through the narrator the reader learns about Sherry's poor and antisocial family background. Her father wanted her to be buried anywhere, next to a telegraph pole. The narrator recalls Sherry saying: 'I hug my daddy loads of times, but he never hugs me back.' [*He had forgotten*].

Surprisingly or not, Luke soon finds himself a new girlfriend, Juliet. The narrator blames him for 'replacing one living thing with another'. She concludes that 'it's all just a story, something you can spin into a plot with memorable characters and a few good lines that stick in the craw and maybe even something approximating real closure, if you play your cards right ... It's all just fiction' [*A story*], in the sense of distraction from reality. Ironically and rather cynically, Luke's morbid wish comes true as the first drink-related accident is repeated, this time involving the narrator herself, caused by Luke's new girlfriend, who dies in the same accident. The lexias following the event – if read in a linear fashion – are told from the first-person point of view of the seriously injured narrator, who describes her way to the hospital, her medical treatment, the beginning of her anaesthetics: 'That's when I realize I'm bleeding to death' [*You start not making*]. Nevertheless, she survives, just to be faced with the tantalizing memory of a brother twice having been partly responsible for his girlfriend's death.

To match form with content, Douglas interweaves her narrative with passages written in the slang of North American youth culture. The effect this has on the reader is powerful in that it authentically conveys the realism of adolescent alcoholism, the lack of future prospects, and the emotional apathy resulting from the excessive infiltration of television horror and violence: 'All the unfinished business, the pure messiness of life, always sticks around and haunts us' [*Tom Buchanan*]. Effectively, the narrator switches to and fro, from youth slang into contemplative mode, transforming her language into a highly poetic diction: 'The octagon of skin she'd left against one curb, as opaque and delicate as a fragment of ice skimmed from the surface of a pond not yet frozen over' [*Later*]. The speechlessness is further heightened by the author's deliberately abrupt way of intersecting her lexias. Some of them begin, and others end, in the middle of a sentence, with the other half not provided in any preceding or succeeding lexia. In so doing, Douglas reinforces the effect of mental paralysis as experienced by the narrator and the characters in the story. The traumatic memory of both accidents is implemented in the hypertext by looping back to the lexia [*Run over*], which conveys the narrator's despair about the situation: 'It runs over and over in your head, like the loop of film in the Volvo commercial, with the crash test dummies bouncing forward in unison, choreographed in slomo like an overcranked version of *Swan Lake* or an Esther Williams number.' In terms of stylistic design, this passage may be seen as a prime example of Douglas's successful attempt to poetically functionalize the sociolect of North American youngsters. Lexically, the second-person narrative abounds with intertextual and intermedial cross-references, wrapped in densely organized and hence almost hyperbolic similes and metaphors. In fact, the reference to *Swan Lake* may strike the critical reader as somewhat alienated from actual youth slang. By means of foregrounding density of imagery and explicit intertextuality and intermediality, Douglas paints a vivid picture of the traumatized narrator's psychological condition. At the same time, by choosing the uncommon second-person narrative, she exhibits the girl's internal estrangement and narrational unreliability.

1.5 Shelley Jackson, *Patchwork Girl, Or a Modern Monster* (1995)

Shelley Jackson's *Patchwork Girl, Or a Modern Monster* (*PG*) may be regarded as the hypertextual epitome of cyberfeminism, and is, furthermore, one of the most exhaustive and novelistic hyperfictions ever produced. It was created in Storyspace, is distributed by Eastgate, and ranges among the most widely read, discussed and taught hyperfictions of the first generation. Its interactive illustrations bring *Patchwork Girl* close to hypermedia, although the overall emphasis lies on script.

Patchwork Girl is one of the most 'canonical' hypertexts, as it openly declares its affinity to Mary Shelley's *Frankenstein, or, The Modern Prometheus*. In fact, Jackson makes it clear from the outset that her hyperfiction is an outspoken feminist response to Shelley's 1818 gothic masterpiece. The analogy does not only permeate the entire story, it is also evoked by the title and the author's very own pseudonym. Jackson quotes lengthy passages from *Frankenstein*, Derrida's *Disseminations*, Evelyn Shaw and Joan Darling's *Female Strategies*, Carolyn Walker Bynum's *Fragmentation and Redemption: Essays on Gender and the Human Body in Medieval Religion*, Nancy K. Miller's *Poetics of Gender* and Barbara Maria Stafford's *Body Criticism: Imaging the Unseen in Enlightenment Art and Medicine*. *Patchwork Girl* could thus be viewed as a fictional assimilation of the author's research into theories of deconstruction and gender. In fact, the notion of a patchwork quilt runs through the text, piecing together quotations from a plenitude of sources 'in an intuitive, crazy-quilt style' [*sources*]. In the same lexia, the author lists further seminal works of postmodernist and feminist criticism (e.g. Cixous, Deleuze and Guattari, Haraway, Lyotard, Theweleit), which further increases the hypertext's academic, scholarly flavour.

The novel shows a high degree of writerly and artistic self-reflexivity in terms of meta-hyperfictionality, meta-theory, meta-mediality and meta-art (focusing on pastiche). One of the author's central concerns is the corporeality of hypertext, which equals that of a 'monster' patched together. 'Each patch in Jackson's quilt is composed of various other patches, various other texts, from theoretical to fictional, from pop cultural to hearsay, sewn together to form either a sentence or paragraph' (Karyn Raz, quoted in Landow, 1992/ 1997: 199). Hypertext, according to Jackson, represents

> the banished body. Its compositional principle is desire. It gives a loud-speaker to the knee, a hearing trumpet to the elbow ... Hypertext is the body languorously extending itself to its own limits, hemmed in only by its own lack of extent ... You could say that all bodies are written bodies ... all lives pieces of writing. (n.d.)

Similarly, the narrator, Mary Shelley 'herself', compares book and hypertext production processes thus:

> Assembling these patched words in an electronic space, I feel half-blind, as if the entire text is within reach, but because of some myopic condition I am only familiar with in dreams, I can see only that part most immediately before me, and have no sense of how that part relates to all the rest. When I open a book I know where I am, which is restful. My reading is spatial and even volumetric. I tell myself, I am a third of the way down through a rectangular solid, I am a quarter of the way down the page, I am here on the page, here on this line, here, here, here. But where am I now? I am in a here and a present moment that has no history and no expectations for the future. [*this writing*]

The elusiveness, bi-dimensionality, and a-historicity of the digital medium form a strong undercurrent to a story which features a female monster on her quest for a new, a-gendered space for creative self-expression.

Where the story starts is left to the reader. Jackson provides five possible starting points – analogous to the five human senses – and adds a source page. 'A graveyard' 'resurrects' the creature from buried body parts of other people, mostly women. The owners are characterized so as to form a patchwork identity in the female monster originally created, yet 'forsaken' by Mary Shelley in the original novel. 'A journal' contains fictional diary entries by Mary Shelley, recording her feelings towards the female monster. The shock upon first beholding her own creature is reminiscent of Victor Frankenstein's in the original novel. Different to him, however, Shelley manages to overcome her sublime fear, giving way to motherly affection, which, at times, assumes even homoerotic traits:

> It was my monster, stark naked, standing as still as if I had not yet breathed life into her massive frame ... I could not help but quail before the strangeness of this figure from which, I fancifully imagined, the very blades of grass seemed to shrink, but curiosity, compassion, and a kind of fellow feeling was the stronger impulse. [*sight*]

'A quilt' contains only two lexias [*scrap*, *bag*], both displaying the same quote from *Frankenstein*, as Victor embarks on creating a female companion for his monster. By literally 'sewing' her own words into the passage, Jackson demonstrates the actual making of a written patchwork quilt. She uses different fonts and formats to underline her intention. 'A story' is by far the most exhaustive section of *Patchwork Girl*. Surprisingly, it tells a linear story, the 'biography' of the monster, who – following Victor Frankenstein's order – does in fact leave Europe, bound for North America. Like a postmodern frontier woman, she ventures her way through American suburbia and the metropolis, until she finds in Death Valley her ultimate destination. As her physical components gradually dissemble, her legacy is to continue the work of her mother Mary Shelley. She observes that hyperspace is the ideal environment for contemporary women writers, which may be considered one of Jackson's key messages. As Williams (1999) points out, 'because this section ['A story'] emphasizes temporal dynamics, its link structure correspondingly parallels our normal linear perception of time, regularly progressing from past lexias forward'. In the path entitled '& broken accents', the narrator pays tribute to her physical mothers, the women from whom she received her organs. This section forms the most thought-provoking, contemplative part of the hypertext, in that the author raises and discusses the question of postmodern identity.

Jackson's style of writing overflows with allusions to her intertextual resources, which are arranged and formulated in such a diligent, elucidating and emotive manner as to provide the reader with a series of sudden insights and powerful emotions. In parts, *Patchwork Girl* resembles a philosophical treatise, with its many aphorisms, ontological contemplations and meta-poetic, apocalyptic prophecies: 'Metaphors will be called home for good. There will be no more likeness, only identity' [*hidden figure*]; 'If all things are called back to their authors, that is. Mary, Mary, I know you want me back, but I shall be no more than a heap of letters, sender unknown, when I return' [*mementos*]. Jackson refers to Plato, whose tenets she applies to poststructuralist discourse as she discusses them from the point of view of the monster: 'There is thus for Plato no such thing as a written thing . . . – that is, I don't exist. I am a passel of parts and should be returned to their original owners' [*interrupting D*].

Critics have almost unanimously praised Jackson's masterpiece, describing it, for instance, as 'what is perhaps the true paradigmatic work of the era, Shelley Jackson's elegantly designed, beautifully composed *Patchwork Girl*' (Coover, 1999). And although, due to its cumbersome representation – small windows and tiny typescript – it requires a patient reader, it is easy to lose oneself in the 'story':

> for as one plunges deeper and deeper into one's own personal exploration of the relations here of creator to created and of body to text, one never fails to be rewarded and so is drawn ever deeper, until clicking the mouse is as unconscious an act as turning a page, and much less constraining, more compelling.

Reviews and analyses have appeared in great numbers. Seidel (1996) calls Jackson's aesthetics a 'hypertextuality of scars', as:

> scars are analogous to hypertextual links. The monster's scars are intimate, integral, the essence of her identity. Similarly, the essence of hypertext is the linking, the private ways that the author chooses to arrange her piece, and the reader uses to meander through it.

Although scars denote adhesion, they also imply separation and disjunction, and in the Patchwork Girl's case even dissemblance. In other words, Jackson prognosticates ultimate material disintegration, and the enduring existence of cyberspace and its component elements.

Landow (1992/1997) devotes a whole chapter to Jackson's bestselling hypertext, describing it in terms of 'Bakhtinian multivocality' (200) and emphasizing the handing over of 'Frankensteinian' power to the reader, 'stitching together narrative, gender, and identity' (*ibid.*). According to Goldberg, Jackson, as much as Shelley (unwittingly), draws on Baudrillard in that 'Frankenstein and his real-life predecessors ... sought ... to create new life, a copy without an original – Baudrillard's simulacrum' (Goldberg, 1998). In a cyberfeminist reading, Ensslin (2005b) compares *Patchwork Girl* to T. S. Eliot's *The Waste Land*, investigating the implications of liminal spaces like the gendered desert – the ultimate postmodern frontier – for the feminist writer.

1.6   Charles Deemer, *The Last Song of Violeta Parra* (1996a)

As mentioned in Chapter 1, the American playwright Charles Deemer was one of the first writers of offline and online hyperdrama. In his writerly programme, set out in 'The New Hyperdrama', he speaks out against the 'traditional playwright's Single Vision', referring to the conventional passivity of the individual in an audience, who is shown the same drama throughout. To oppose this stance, Deemer created a dramatic form that would give the individual viewer the choice of following particular characters through the drama, through all their 'exits' and 'entries'. For obvious reasons, such a dramatic form would do away with the classical, monolithic centre stage:

> In hyperdrama, the traditional linear narrative line explodes into branches, multiplying the action on a 'stage' into simultaneous scenes occurring throughout a performance space. The bolted chairs of the audience are uprooted to give the audience mobility, an opportunity to follow different branches of the narrative line as they unfold into different, often distant, areas of this expanded new 'stage.' (Deemer, n.d.)

One major dramaturgic effect of this is an increase in dramatic democracy, as minor characters potentially gain as much attention as major characters: they might still not have as many lines, but would be permanently accessible to the interested spectator. Similarly, one may no longer speak of a main plot and a subplot, as every character's story would seem of equal importance. The author creates narratives for all dramatis personae alike, thus avoiding a 'skewing of material' (*ibid.*). The main hyper-dramatic effect is the transfer of choice to the viewer. Naturally, on stage there are no links as there are on an interactive screen. Nevertheless, every decision as to which character to follow may be likened to activating a hyperlink, even if the physical experience of virtually walking after a character on stage may be more memorable than operating an electronic connection. According to Deemer, traditional Single Vision theatre, i.e. deciding to stay focused on one stage only, is a subtype of hyperdrama.

Deemer first started experimenting with offline hyperdrama in the 1960s, a tradition which was also taken up in the 1970s by the English playwright Alan Ayckbourn with *The Norman Conquests, a Trilogy* (1974), and continued with his *House and Garden* (2000). Deemer's unique achievement, however, was to put hyperdrama on the internet. His first original work of this kind was *Chateau de mort*, which he wrote for an MS-DOS system called Iris. Only a hypertext sampler of it is available on the internet, which makes it impossible to fully appreciate the text or write comprehensively about it. *The Bride of Edgefield*, a sequel of *Chateau de mort*, is fully based on HTML.

Deemer's own favourite hyperdrama is *The Last Song of Violeta Parra: A Hyperdrama in One Act*, the first hyperdrama he developed in cyberspace. It was written in collaboration with Andres Espejo, a director in Santiago, Chile. The play offers two parallel online versions in English and Spanish. As *Violeta Parra* was intended to be performed on stage after being displayed for feedback on the internet, Deemer limited it to a one-act drama, for pragmatic reasons. For one thing, a hyperdrama script tends to be three to five times longer than a 'Single Vision' drama, as all parallel plots have to be written out in full. For another, the producers wanted to give the audience an opportunity to view the same play three times on one evening, so they could follow several characters and thus get an impression of the full scope of the drama.

With regard to its overall 'plot' – or rather 'hyper-plot' – the drama follows the tradition of the Wildean comedy of manners. It features a series of highly amusing confusions and intrigues, partly intended, partly accidental, which usually revolve around single objects (such as in *Lady Windermere's Fan* or the cigarette box in *The Importance of Being Earnest*), and ends in a morally instructive dénouement which makes the preceding appear ridiculously and relievingly insignificant. The morbidly contorted, sociocritically loaded storyline further places *Violeta Parra* in a magico-realistic framework reminiscent of Gabriel García Márquez's *One Hundred Years of Solitude* (1970) and Isabel Allende's *The House of the Spirits* (1985).

Set in a Chilean art gallery, which is doomed to close down because the house has been inherited by a recently married couple (Luisa and Alberto), *Violeta Parra* centres around a conspiracy between Juan, the gallery owner, his assistant, Guillermina, and Francisco, an art critic. Intending to sell as many paintings as possible before the gallery is closed down, Juan orders Guillermina to tell the artist, Eduardo, who is madly in love with her, that she and Francisco are having an affair. Burning to take revenge, for both the emotional betrayal and Francisco's slating reviews, Eduardo attempts to kill Francisco, who fakes deadly injury for the police and the potential purchasers. In another strand of the drama, the audience learns that the attack was actually faked by Francisco and Eduardo to impress Guillermina. Juan does achieve his aim. Carmen, a prominent art collector, who initially loathed all of Eduardo's paintings but seems impressed by the artist's sudden outbreak of passion, buys the lot of them in one swoop much to the pleasure of Juan. However, as Carmen indicates that she knows about the charade, Francisco gives himself away. The dénouement brings every character back on one 'stage' to tell the audience in subsequent monologues what happened after the plot. Guillermina tells Eduardo that she made up the love affair between herself and Francisco to discourage Eduardo. Carmen reveals that she has recently purchased the art journal for which Francisco works, and fires him on the spot. In his final monologue, Eduardo discloses that Guillermina works for the police, who, luckily, could not prove Juan to be guilty of any crime. Francisco tells the audience that he was rehired by Carmen and given a solid increment. Eduardo talks about his sudden fame, lamenting the fact that his art is seen less as art than as an investment by most patrons. Juan turns out to have been collaborating with Ana in the socialist Chilean underground. After Ana is found out, both have to leave the country to plan their next move in attempting to reveal to the world the truth about the death of Violeta Parra, a political Chilean songwriter.

One of the comic highlights of the hyperdrama, which in fact shows the very potential of the genre, is the fact that Luisa and Alberto do not learn what is going on in their house throughout the play. Nor does the viewer, who follows their story all the time. Similarly, those members of the audience who do not follow the conversation between Ana and Eduardo in the second bedroom do not learn about the political significance of the title, which adds a second level of meaning to the otherwise rather superficial, light comedy. According to Eduardo, Violeta Parra was murdered by the CIA in 1967 over allegations of socialist activities in support of Allende. Ana, who owns some of Parra's tapes, suddenly appears to be in great danger, especially because she works for the police.

At a third level of meaning, *Violeta Parra* follows many of its hypertextual forerunners in that it raises a variety of points in meta-fictional, meta-critical, meta-hypertextual and meta-dramatic self-mockery. Criticism of the critic is uttered by Carmen, the art collector, upon observing the apparently dying Francisco: 'I wish all his readers could see him now. All the misguided people who take his word as gospel, who don't go to an opening because he writes that there's nothing there worth seeing. It's appalling how much power art critics have' [*Livingroom II script*]. Another meta-fictional remark by her runs as follows: 'God save us from poets and prose writers. They only look for personal freedom' [*Livingroom II script*].

Despite the possibility of performing hyperdrama on a multiple stage, Deemer is still intrigued by the 'natural marriage of hyperdrama and the World Wide Web, with their mutual foundation in hypertext' (Deemer, 1996). In his view, hyperdrama should be presented and read as hypertext – in the manner of a closet drama – rather than solely performed on stage. Schnierer (2001) heavily draws on Deemer, considering him one of the most prominent hyperdrama practitioners. Like Deemer, he observes the general reluctance of an audience to leave a centre stage and therefore suggests hyperdrama should be received as a distinctly off-stage form of dramatic art.

1.7 Geoff Ryman, *253* (1996)

With *253*, an 'interactive narrative' published in 1996 on the internet, Geoff Ryman instigated a concept to be imitated by many a hypertext writer since the late 1990s: the concept of a journey through (hyper-)space. Ryman subtitles his hypertext 'Tube Theatre', despite largely adhering to a descriptive rather than dramatic style, thus placing it in an – albeit small – tradition of narratives revolving around public transport (e.g. *Linie 1*, a musical about the pre-Wende Berlin tram [1986], and, although to a far lesser extent, Alfred Döblin's *Berlin Alexanderplatz* of 1929). In a wider context, *253* alludes to distinctly 'London' novels like Michael Moorcock's *Mother London* (1988), Ian Sinclair's *Lights Out for the Territory* (1998) and Peter Ackroyd's *London: A Biography* (2000), most of which were published after Ryman's hypertext yet display a tendency among British writers to document and personify 'their' city as an organism structurally representable by maps.

Like Moulthrop and Larsen, Ryman provides an interactive map, which is organized in a linear rather than topographical fashion. Be that as it may, there is no storyline as such. In fact, the author is far more interested in his characters, their backgrounds, problems, and interconnections with one another than in plot and action. What the 'novel' really provides is a complex, interwoven network of individual character studies, with the looming catastrophe being used as a functional element of creating morbid, apocalyptic suspense. When Ryman first created *253*, it was specifically for the internet, in order to explore its possibilities for writing. A printed version followed, which cannot be called nearly as successful and effective as the hypertext, mainly because it does not have links.

The fable centres around the last minutes of a London Underground journey, set on 11 January 1995, and experienced from the point of view of 253 passengers. The date was of particular significance to the author because it marks the day when his best friend announced he would soon die of AIDS. In fact, the tragic ending did not enter Ryman's imaginative mind until he learned the sad news.

Each passenger of the seven-coach-long Bakerloo Line is described in precisely 253 words, both physically and psychologically. The order of reading about the passengers is left to the reader, and the most obvious way of proceeding is to click on links in each character study to jump to another character, who is in some way related to the previous one. Ryman chooses people of all age groups, social strata, nationalities, genders, sexual orientations and interests. The major focus herein lies on misleading appearances. Nobody is as they seem, which gives each character sketch the aura of a self-contained psychological narrative. What they all share is a set of recurrent themes and motifs, such as the grandparent theme and musings upon Margaret Thatcher's administration. Beyond the apparent mix of different, disconnected lives, various micro-dramas unfold, heightened by the powerful effects of links employed as an irony-evoking device:

Two characters two cars apart, Gary Collier and Amanda Stinton, are having an affair; Collier married, has told his wife he's leaving just as Amanda, single, has decided to end the relationship. They meet on the platform and exchange news, then stop, stunned. As Ryman says, you don't need links to put that mini-drama together: 'With a link, it's really in your face.' (Grossman, 1997)

The train is to crash at the end, which can be found by clicking on the 'final' node on the hypertext map. By providing the possibility or indeed the catastrophic inevitability of an ending, Ryman questions the antilinear claim of hypertextual storytelling. Another appealing element of *253* is the aesthetic effect of observing the passengers' very own thoughts. In learning about their innermost feelings, readers adopt a voyeuristic stance, which puts them in an unprecedented, powerful position of being able to virtually 'read' other people's minds. The experience is both positively and negatively surprising, as the reader frequently learns about the characters' tragic losses, terminal diseases or criminal records. The relatively low number of links provided by the author in each lexia is fortunate in that it prevents overwhelming resentments about being 'lost in hyperspace' and, instead, lends the hypertext a touch of finiteness and conquerability, which many other hyperfictions defy for aesthetic reasons. What makes the reading process particularly absorbing is Ryman's humorous, insightful, sympathetic and at times cynical voice. Evidently, every character sketch needs to have the potential to engage the readers' interest and cause them to continue. On the other hand, the author cannot expect the reader to complete all 253 lexias and therefore has to transmit a feeling of understanding the gist and purpose of the hypertext at any given stage. This is a challenging objective, which Ryman has managed to achieve.

Although Ryman's work does not come close to the academic popularity of other first-generation hyperfictions such as *afternoon* and *Patchwork Girl*, it has been reviewed and analysed by some critics. Schnierer (2000), for instance, refers to the concept of *theatrum mundi* suggested by the subtitle 'Tube Theatre', and reads *253* in dramatic terms, which is more than plausible given the preference to the *dramatic personae* over plot. Contrary to Landow's thesis that hypertext subverts the Aristotelian three unities, Ryman retains the unity of place (the train), time (minutes before the crash), and action: 'many characters are on their way to death . . . They either get off before the Elephant, or they almost certainly die' (Schnierer, 2000: 541). Schnierer also highlights the advantages of Ryman's hypertext version to the book version published in 1998 with regard to implementing the idea of antilinearity.

In her 1997 review, Grossman describes Ryman's *Tube Theatre* as:

an interactive version of Thornton Wilder's 'The Bridge of San Luis Rey,' which explored the lives of five people caught on a bridge when it collapses. But where Wilder had the freedom to roam through his characters' lives to explain their presence on that bridge at that specific moment, Ryman's self-imposed constraints limit his reach.

One of Ryman's major challenges is, notably, to pinpoint the significance of a character's biography, personal circumstances, social background and personality in only 253 words. He is fully aware that people sitting on a train cannot engage in physical action, yet their mental activity is highlighted, instead, 'in the form of small decisions people come to while they sit and think' (Grossman, 1997). Hence, it is the deductions made by the reader about the potential consequences of each character's reflections that make *253* an engaging read.

1.8   Bill Bly, *We Descend* (1997)

Bill Bly's *We Descend*, created in Storyspace and published by Eastgate in 1997, runs counter to common allegations made by hypertext critics as to the impossibility of writing a hypertextual crime novel (as Chris Willerton maintained at the 2000 Hypertext Conference in San Antonio, Texas). Largely sequential in organization, *We Descend* renders a thrilling murder case set in a medieval monastery. Subtitled 'Archives Pertaining to Egderus Scriptor', the novel alludes to one of his most famous novelistic forerunners, Umberto Eco's *The Name of the Rose*.

The hyperfiction's Foreword includes the author's principal concern of whether 'the gulf allegedly fixed between "linear" writing and hypertext' has ever been or may ever be bridged. He implements this notion by providing, on the one hand, an archive of documents which he claims to be an authentic archive of writings from widely separated periods of time, which repeats the conventional docuverse idea. On the other hand, the major part of the time dedicated to reading *We Descend* is inescapably spent on a linear narrative, a diary written by a monk, which contains the murder mystery. Of this document, the narrator only holds a copy, and he hastens to suspect that he is in fact drawing on a product of forgery.

The world of the frame narrative is set in the distant future. A scholar, the first-person narrator, broods over the fragmentary writings of an obscure figure known as Egderus Scriptor, who lived about a thousand years before him. The Scholar attempts to put all the writings of the archive into some kind of order, but before he can finish his work, the archives are confiscated. Another man takes over the research into them, as he is said to have provided anonymous glosses and annotations upon all the writings, including the scholar's very own.

Bly accounts for his decision to write *We Descend* as a hypertext thus: 'Given the multiplicity of voices in We Descend, it seemed the best way to present their stories was as hypertext, which also provided an apparatus for many layers of commentary and a way to cross-reference and link together related materials that might be separated by sometimes vast tracts of time' ('I Descend into Hypertext').

The major narrative features Edgerus Scriptor, a young scribe, who lives at the secluded Mountain House and witnesses a series of brutal murders, which point towards the existence of a bloodthirsty, ferocious beast inhabiting the rocky hills surrounding the monastery. He is entangled in a conspiracy led by his superiors. The killer is never found, and it remains open to question to what extent terror-stricken male psychology is capable of inventing fantasies of such a kind. Edgerus' major quest ends up being to save a historian who has been caught by the Good Doctor (the chief inquisitor), who tortures him regularly because the historian seems to know more than he is supposed to.

The most endearing element of Bly's hypertext crime novel is the fact that it defies a final resolution. The narrative breaks off as abruptly as it opened, which is due to the fact that the document is, like most others in the archive, a fragment. Given the almost unbearable suspense upheld throughout the fiction, this comes as an almost unbearable surprise. The reader's devotion to linear story-telling is thus ridiculed, and the reality of fragmentation appeals to the receiver's lethargy with regard to searching for truth. Truth is, according to Bly, buried in the totality of written documents, which all draw on each other, revealing single units of information rather than giving a holistic answer.

The spatiality of Bly's language graphically depicts the monastery like a prison to its inhabitants. Right from the outset, Bly sets the gloomy, medieval, gothic scene of a landscape that is strangely animate and menacing: 'When the sun goes down, the storms begin. Every night it is like this. The storms come in waves, one following another, as regular as breathing. This lasts all night. It is impossible to sleep' [*Storms & haze*]. Suspense, horror and terror in the conventional gothic sense pervade the narrative, and the surprising effect of abruptly breaking off the most enthralling passages of the thriller strikes the absorbed reader as downright intolerable. Robert Kendall comments that 'this evocative exploration of the slippery nature of knowledge becomes the hypertext equivalent of a good old-fashioned page-turner' [blib], thus insinuating the fact that neither the medium nor the fragmented character of the hypernarrative necessarily influences the aesthetic effect although it has to be said that the expression 'page-turner' is somewhat ill-chosen, as it also, inappropriately in this case, suggests closure.

1.9   Richard Holeton, *Figurski at Findhorn on Acid* (2001)

Richard Holeton ranks among the few writers who have taken the original concept of hyperfiction in the sense of graphemic centrality into the new millennium. In his traditional, Storyspace-based hypernovel *Figurski at Findhorn on Acid*, he uses colour and image sparsely and, if he does, mostly iconically and indexically. Colour-coding is applied to distinguish character (e.g. 'Figurski'), place (e.g. 'Findhorn') and artefacts (e.g. 'acid') in his combinatory titles, thus signalling hypertext's characteristic multiplicity of storylines. In fact, as Hinderaker (2002) puts it,

every possible combination and permutation of character, artifact and location – Figurski at Findhorn on acid, for example – comprises its own page.

> Readers of conventional fiction, beware: there are 147 scenarios in Figurski's brainchild, and not a single one can definitively be characterized as the beginning or end.

Graphics and photographs mostly illustrate elements mentioned in the text, as well as adding comic, surprising pastiche features to the novel (e.g. the Wing Tips online-shopping commercial, [*034*]). Some pictorial items are depicted without further subtitling, except for their sources, which lends the novel a slight touch of a hypermedia pandemonium (e.g. 'Collage with the Writer' [*047*]). It has to be conceded, however, that pictographic and photographic elements only occasionally carry their own, isolated meaning. In the majority of cases, they are rather employed intersemiotically to underline previously established concepts.

The quadripartite macrostructure of time, character, place and artefacts gives the hypertext a foundation upon which its navigation unfolds. The three central elements (character, place and artefacts) subdivide into further triads, thus augmenting the emphasis placed by the author on the figure three. The reader learns about the multiplex interrelationships of the underlying narrative elements by following the various navigational opportunities they offer. By pressing the return key, the reader embarks on a default path, which initiates him or her to the implications of the title, before it starts *in medias res*, with the first dialogue between Figurski and a member of the Findhorn New Age Community.

Beginning with the element 'time', the reader is presented with a timescale of historical and biographical events that convey the contrived and ambiguous sense of reality of the narrative. This reality is determined by a complex blend of seemingly unrelated, random subnarratives: science-fiction and fantasy, issues surrounding pigs and pork ('Spam'), robotics, Boy Scouts, the Vietnam and Gulf Wars, drugs (LSD), New Age spiritualism, celebrities and television chatshows.[4] In the course of the reading process, it becomes clear that many features are interconnected via psychoanalytically conceived associations, which, more often than not, surface in surrealistic, traumatic, utterly nonsensical actions on the part of the protagonists. The real-life story unfolds over a period of several years, starting in 1993, directly succeeding Figurski's release from prison, as he finds a crated 'Mechanical Pig' on a beach near Findhorn, Scotland, unaware of its material and historic value, and of the fact that two malicious antagonists are feverishly tracking the antique. The realistic narrative ends in December 2000, i.e. shortly before the publication of the hypertext. This date marks the final meeting of the main characters to re-assemble the previously discarded original of the ubiquitous Pig, designed and built by Guillermo Rossellini of Venice in 1737, and its nineteenth-century emulation, the parts of which they have equally distributed among themselves. The virtual reality story continues, however, until 'Stardate 0012'. It starts 'some time in the 21st century', when aliens land at Findhorn and 'organize[] human experience into 9 major directories containing 354 nodes and 2001 hyperlinks'

[*Findhorn 3.x*]. Again, the figure three features strongly, signalling the infinity of a new cyber-Trinity. Other instances of numerical symbolism include globally applicable number codes used to obtain LSD, with all cross-sums resulting in a multiple of three.

Starting with one of the three major characters, the convict Frank 'Many-Pens' Figurski, The No-Hands Cup Flipper Nguyen Van Tho, or the journalist and double-crossdresser Fatima Michelle Vieuchanger, is perhaps the most insightful approach, as the reader learns about the characters' biographies, their motivations and, most importantly, their obsessive relationships with the Mechanical Pig. The three protagonists compete to take possession of this proto-robotic automaton and its physical and virtual emulations, whose symbolic and subconscious significance is only gradually revealed to the bemused receiver. Upon their final encounter in 2000 at Findhorn, they inadvertently 'merg[e] into different components of the same character, taking on aspects of one another's personality' [*3.2.01*]. In what follows, all three are presented on the Holodeck, in an ultimately permutative stage, swaying between egos and alter egos, between actual and model identities. Figurski becomes Ted Streleski, on whose murder case he modelled his own, Nguyen transforms into his master cup flipper, Eugene Zanger, and Vieuchanger experiences the bewildering feeling of physically turning into a man.

Much of the novel is written in dialogue rather than narrative. In some lexias, the speakers' names are given as in a drama script; in others, the reader has to perform a lot of guesswork to fathom out who is speaking at what stage. To create further comic effects, Holeton sporadically uses dialectally transcribed language, imitating, for instance, Scottish youth slang and pronunciation ('Useta be a lot o' the drugs and new-dee-tay there' [*1.02.01*]). Other text types include electronic mails sent between characters, quotes and chapters from other books, as well as a vast amount of intertextual references to films (*Pulp Fiction*), songs (*The Wall*), and various kinds of scientific, journalistic and imaginary literature.

2   Second-Generation Hypermedia

2.1   John McDaid, *Uncle Buddy's Phantom Funhouse* (1992)

Although described as a 'hypermedia novel' by McDaid himself, *Uncle Buddy's Phantom Funhouse* comes close to an entire literary, scholarly and artistic legacy, left by the recently deceased, or rather vanished, and therefore intrinsically paradoxical protagonist, Arthur 'Buddy' Newkirk. The read me file, which readers are advised to consult before moving on to the hypertext proper, contains further enigmatic information, given in the form of a letter addressed to the reader by the fictitious company Merck and Ladre, specialists in electronic law. The letter states that the inheriting reader once knew Mr Newkirk, 'probably as a family acquaintance referred to as "Uncle Buddy" ', but the chances are that he or she may have forgotten this person, due to 'lapses of memory' or other 'divergences' of an unspecified nature.

The perhaps most striking feature of this hypermedia novel is the fact that it undermines its own claim for synchronized data encryption, in other words uniformly digital encoding. Unlike any other hypertext, the CD on which it is saved comes with two separate music tapes, which are supposed to be played while reading the hypertext. Furthermore, the box in which the media items are distributed contains a printed and photocopied short story (*Tree*) by Arthur Newkirk including the mock proofmarks and accompanying letter of an editor. One could thus speak of a multi-hypermedia piece of fiction, which not only implements postmodernist and poststructuralist theory, but deconstructs itself on yet another level, by detachment rather than synthesis of inter-semiotic elements.

The central navigation device is the title-giving 'Funhouse', i.e. the property left by the protagonist, which represents a navigational map, or 'palette', and remains, in a minimized version, visible on the screen throughout. Upon visiting the various rooms pointed out on the map, readers find themselves immersed in a wide array of different intersemiotic text types, comprising, for instance, feigned conference announcements, an academic journal, email correspondence, cartoons, photos, lyrics, a deck of tarot cards, a hyperbolic, hypertextual parody of Pavić's *The Dictionary of the Khazars* (entitled *Fictionary of the Bezoars*), and a screenplay by Newkirk, entitled *Sooner or Later* from the year 1982, which features a number of physics students.

This meta-hyperdrama, as it may legitimately be called, takes itself *ad absurdum*, in that it has no serious plotlines, but rather stands out for its elliptical, fragmentary qualities, as the author has omitted entire scenes. Most textual elements are used, in Peirce's terminology, symbolically or indexically, i.e. they do not share any or only some semantic features with other textual elements.

It is not only by its title that *Uncle Buddy* alludes to John Barth's postmodern short story *Lost in the Funhouse*, which features an adolescent boy, who fantasizes himself into a semi-fictional funhouse and loses himself among 'the endless replication[s] of his image in the mirrors'. The reader virtually loses him- or herself in the vast array of pseudo-realistic documents, which are nonsensical and ludic in nature and thus distort the fond expectations of the funhouse visitor. The quest for a manifestation of Uncle Buddy remains futile, although the reader's imagination is activated to such a degree by the documents he or she reads that the 'phantom' of Uncle Buddy becomes even more vivid in the mind than if the very person were indeed present in the text. And indeed, all we learn about Newkirk is his love for a female poet called Emily (his 'Beatrice' figure, revealed through his emails and articles) and his membership in a band called The Reptiles, for whom he has composed extensive lyrics.

Robert Coover praises *Uncle Buddy* as 'the most ambitious hyperfiction yet attempted by a single author' (1993: 11). Keep *et al.* (1993–2000) pick up on the psychological individualism conveyed by the hypertext, putting it in the context of the realist novel and its 'fascination with interiority and psychological verisimilitude'. Rau (2000b) points in her review of *Uncle Buddy* at the subversion of Landow's wreader ideal. Neither are readers at any stage during the reading process in a position to complete the jigsaw spread out before their eyes, nor can the symbolic 'death of the author' be confirmed at any point. On the contrary, the Necropolis path leads to the symbolic death of the reader, as it does not offer any possibility of returning or diverging from the prescribed, linear reading path. Nor, however, does this element of apparent closure translate onto the whole text. The fact that some reading paths are password-protected is a further point in favour of Rau's argument.

2.2   Deena Larsen, *Marble Springs* (1993)

Marble Springs, Deena Larsen's feminist, narrative hyper-poem (as it is categorized by the author herself and her publisher Eastgate), was made solely for Macintosh, using HyperCard. Alongside Stuart Moulthrop's *Victory Garden*, it is one of the earliest successful attempts to base a hypertext on a pictorial navigation map and, indeed, one of the first Eastgate hypermedia products. To a greater extent than Moulthrop, Larsen emphasizes the importance of visual art in supplementing scripted text, and may thus be regarded as a borderline case between hypertext and hypermedia, although visual and auditive material are used mainly for illustrative, iconic purposes. In other words, most of the images and tunes complement and mirror semantic information given in the written text rather than establishing independent, additional elements of meaning. Unlike McDaid's *Uncle Buddy's Phantom Funhouse*, where various semiotic systems are deliberately juxtaposed to represent independent meaning and therefore support the underlying idea of searching through archives, *Marble Springs* uses audiovisual material decoratively to enhance the journalized style of the writing. The illustrations, which capture the reader's eye to a degree that clearly distinguishes *Marble Springs* from *Victory Garden*, were made by Kathleen A. Turner-Suarez. *Marble Springs* consists of 35 pages and approximately 600 links. Encouraged by many non-Macintosh-based readers, Larsen put a demonstration version on the internet.

Marble Springs may be considered canonical in its own right in that it follows in the tradition of geographically grounded historical novels such as *Spoon River Anthology*, *Winesburg, Ohio* and *Cold Mountain*. *Marble Springs* poeticizes the stories of women who helped to build the American West in the nineteenth century. Although called a 'narrative poem', it may rather be conceived as an archive of lyrical, narrative and factual texts assembled to give an authentic picture of times gone by. Prior to writing *Marble Springs*, Larsen undertook a great deal of research into the history of a derelict Colorado mining village of the same name. She was particularly interested in documents written by and about refugee women from Ireland, China, and American slavery. Each poem is attributed to one of Marble Spring's former denizens, and their multifarious interrelationships are realized through hypertext links. Thus, as the author points out, *Marble Springs* conjoins reality and fiction and may well reveal to 'students and history buffs' (introduction booklet: 3) the history of the American West. The hypertext is conceived as an open-ended educational co-product and invites readers to add new text links, buttons, trails, character cards and connection cards.

The tragedy lurks beyond the peaceful surface of the user interface, as the text never ceases to imply the eventual failure of trying to turn an unyielding mountain region into a thriving industrial town. Houses are given the metonymic function of reflecting the memories of earlier inhabitants. These memories are activated by clicking on icons or labels on the hypertext map, which, quite unlike similar maps in other hypertexts, actually does fulfil a reliable navigational role. Doc Nancy, for instance, the local midwife and resident in the mountains surrounding Crystal River Valley, tells the story of many women whom she helped to abort illegitimate children (cf. *Vera Drake*), as it was 'better than living with shame' [*Doc Nancy*]. The introduction takes Doc Nancy as the very example of how, by now, 'primroses have taken over the streets, rising up through gaping boardwalks' [*Marble Springs*]. Billie Rose, a Dublin-born women, defied poverty and starvation, 'forged herself a new character', 'sailed for the new world' [*Settling in*] and married a local miner in Marble Springs. Finally, Mrs Matthew Cole, representative of the better-off in the valley, leads the church choir while, at the same time, secretively hiding 'baby preventatives' [*Rules*] and severe alcoholism. Larsen's attempts to capture the simplistic language of the valley dwellers, which, even so, does not lack in natural imagery and lyrical qualities, are largely successful, and she does not fail to impart an aesthetic impression of nostalgia by mentioning ancient objects such as 'travellers' trunk', 'sateen ribbons', 'curlicues', 'pocketwatch' and 'woodstove'.

In terms of macrostructure, cards (lexias) display either short narrative poems about individual characters or connection maps, which form associative links between characters. Like the patches of a quilt, each card is a unified pattern in itself. The links connecting the cards transform the pieces into a whole (Larsen, 1992). The author sees her work as a meta-hypertextual, 'direct comment on structure and connections, so the structure is made abundantly clear, as well as commented on within the poem' (*ibid.*, pp. 61–2). She goes on to explain that:

> *Marble Springs* is an orderly network, which shows its connections through maps, a directory, character connections, group connections, place connections and connections within poems themselves. Again, the structure of *Marble Springs* is brought forward and made obvious so that the reader will focus on the relationships and the ways this hyperpoem explores connections. (*ibid.*: 72)

In terms of navigation, it is left to readers whether they want to use the 'table of contents' method, the 'map' method, the linear 'next card' method, or a 'connections' approach, which takes them from one character or venue to another. Larsen's characters are designed such that they cannot be fully understood or put in context until they are contrasted with other characters. Navigational strategies are thus used as a distinctly poetic and narrative element.

Marble Springs owes its uniqueness to a high degree of 'wreaderly' interactivity. Readers are invited to write notes in the margins and on blank character cards, thus extending and re-writing the work. Book icons take the reader to a bibliography of intertextual references. The author remarks that, '[w]ere this connected to Xanadu, the reader could go directly to those sources. I included these sources so that readers interested in writing their own stories for Marble Springs would have somewhere to turn' (1992: 46). In other words, Larsen ventures to make concrete the openness of the web, the ultimate 'frontier', to the contemporary reader. Its aesthetic appeal, however, owes less to its interactivity – which falls far short of elaborate projects such as Guido Grigat's *23:40* – than to the diligence and realism of its visual presentation. For a pre-World Wide Web hypertext map, the one used by Larsen depicts a surprising amount of detail, such as single buildings, rivers, a railway line, a graveyard, and a legend explaining the symbols she uses. The map is interactive, taking the reader directly into the homes of mining families or institutions of public interest. In my (subjective) view, *Marble Springs* succeeds in imparting a distinct sense of nostalgia and empathy with its characters, thus stimulating a potential research interest in the reader.

2.3   Guido Grigat, *23:40* (1997)

Guido Grigat's *23:40–das kollektive Gedächtnis* ('23:40 – The Collective Memory') is a prime example of second-generation hypermedia in that it takes advantage of the internet's communicative possibilities. It is a prototypical collaborative hypertext in that it gives full authorship to its 'wreaders', who may post their contributions directly to the website. Their lexias subsequently appear as part of an ever-changing hypertext clock, which changes its lexias every minute, displaying the contribution which has been appointed to that particular time.

Unlike other collaborative hypertexts, *23:40* has been in operation since 1997 and is still inviting contributions from readers who understand the German language. To contribute, users simply write their texts into the box provided, also stating the exact time at which they wish it to appear. The texts are posted like an email and promptly published.

Simanowski (1999c) reviews *23:40* in comparison with a similar hypomnetic work, *Das Generationenprojekt* (Hasecke, 1997), which, pursuing a 'bottom-up' historical approach, invites 'wreaders' to contribute their personal accounts of historic events that happened in twentieth-century Germany. In another publication, Simanowski (2004) discusses *23:40* as one of the three most representative collaborative writing projects in German collaborative hypermedia, the other two being Carola Heine's *Beim Bäcker*, which discontinued to invite contributions in December 1998 and is therefore not included in this canon, and Alvar Freude and Dragan Espenschied's *Assoziations-Blaster*, which will be

discussed shortly. Simanowski remarks that, in *23:40*, the author collaborates
with the programme. In fact, the programme 'instructs the reader to become
an author, it occupies the author's name, and it creates, together with the
author, the deeper meaning of the text' (2004: 89). Grigat himself assumes
the function of programmer-editor, leaving the major aesthetic efforts up to his
contributors.

Whether or not Grigat's self-evolving hypertext is of high aesthetic value
from a poetic point of view is open to question, mostly because of the plurality
of its writers and their equally pluralistic approaches to poetic expression,
which in some cases appears entirely prosaic, in others poetically overstruc-
tured. That said, the text draws its wide appeal among readers and users less
from textual and writerly authority than from the mere fascination it arouses
in participants about the possibility of actually becoming a wreader and partaking in a shared, creative written event. The project is innovative and, more
compellingly than most other hypertexts, implements the idea of true multiple
authorship and the 'empowerment' of the (w)reader.

2.4 Dirk Günther and Frank Klötgen, *Die Aaleskorte der Ölig* (1998)

Dirk Günther and Frank Klötgen's German internet-based hypertext *Die Aaleskorte der Ölig* was originally created for the 1998 Pegasus Competition, organized by the German broadsheet *Die Zeit*, which awarded it the First Prize.
For the first-time reader, *Die Aaleskorte der Ölig* may well fall under the category
of cybertext as the programme appears to take over control of the 'film' once the
reader has chosen his or her particular point(s) of view. Upon several readings,
however, the reader gradually gains control over the underlying mechanisms.
He or she becomes the director of a filmic story, whose perspectivity is in his
or her hands. At the end of each 'film', or rather 'commented slideshow', the
authors suggest revisiting the text from a different set of perspectives, as there
are 6.9 billion possible versions available.

Die Aaleskorte der Ölig is a novelty because it places the reader in the position of
a scriptwriter, who chooses the pictures and plot for a film. Twenty scenes and
points of view have to be selected prior to 'watching' the film, i.e. reading the
plot fragments and observing the pictures. Every scene can be viewed from the
point of view of the eel, the child-narrator, a woman called Ölig, the fishmonger
Hohmann, or the neighbourhood children. The reader clicks his or her way
through the plot. Only after a few run-throughs does the reader understand
what the story is about. It describes the last minutes in the life of an eel, which
is about to be beheaded by Hohmann, the fishmonger, and sold to Ölig.
Depending on the chosen viewpoints, more or less information about each
point of view will be revealed: of the eel, who tries to think of ways of escaping
death; of Hohmann, who routinely goes through the process of killing the
animal; of Ölig, who buys the fish because her doctor suggested it as a healthier
alternative to meat, yet is horrified by its slipperiness and her own responsibility for its death; of the neighbourhood children standing by and frolicking

whenever a fish has been caught; and, not least, by the child-narrator, the most obscure of all the characters, who tells the story from a neutral point of view. From him we learn about a somewhat perverse sexual relationship between the fishmonger and his female client, with the phallic, castrated (beheaded) eel representing, in a psychoanalytical reading, the male penis and the female clitoris.[5]After all, the Romans tellingly referred to the animal, which was considered the epitome of culinary (and, by the same token, oral sexual) pleasure, as *rex voluptatis*.

Die Aaleskorte der Ölig follows an aesthetics of disgust and revulsion. The story is deliberately kept banal, and the largely symbolically employed, photographic images often display revolting scenes such as rotten food, blood, distorted faces, genitals and slippery fish. The language is similarly mundane and colloquial. Upon repeated reading, however, a far more profound subtext is revealed. Continuing a psychoanalytical reading, the Ölig character represents the motif of the Electra complex. According to Simanowski (1999a), the female protagonist sees in the eel the phallic desire for her lost father, symbolizing a postponed marriage. What seems more plausible to me, however, is her neurotic need to compensate for having been sexually abused as a child. Her inability to withdraw her order, along with her sadistic pleasure in watching the 'dance' of the fishmonger's penis and the moribund eel, conveys her yet unassimilated aggression towards and revenge for male sexual violence. Her fear of repeated abuse by the phallic eel becomes evident in her insistence upon company on her way home.

From a metamedial perspective, *Die Aaleskorte der Ölig* celebrates the reincarnation of the linear in hypertext. In offering a plethora of different sequentially organized plots, it defies the usual craze surrounding antilinearity, and thus reminds the reader about hypertext's actual reception-oriented quintessence: 'What makes hypertext hypertext is not non-linearity but choice, the interaction of the reader to determine which of several or many paths through the available information is the one taken at a certain moment in time' (Deemer, 1994).

In addition to emphasizing this element of choice, *Die Aaleskorte der Ölig* lays bare the affinity between hypermedia and film, adding the element of reader control. The similarity with 'choose-your-own-adventure' stories is intended. However, the authors undermine the 'willing suspension of disbelief' experienced in such projects by ways of disillusioning images, perverse imagery, and the banality of everyday life.

2.5 Alvar Freude and Dragan Espenschied, *Assoziations-Blaster* (1999/2000)

Alvar Freude and Dragan Espenschied's *Assoziations-Blaster*, an internet-based collaborative writing project available in English and German, is radically different from other collaborative writing projects in that the software programme, not a human being, acts as project leader or editor. The 'machine', an element which positions the text in close relationship with cybertext, is 'the only element that definitely "knows" all the segments in the text pool' (Simanowski, 2004: 87). Therefore, the empowered 'wreader' has 'absolute freedom' as author. The programme creates all the links ('Assoziationen'), partly through a random generator. The crucial problem with this technology is that links are solely based on morphological resemblances. Nevertheless, the novelty of *Assoziations-Blaster* lies in the programme's capacity to develop the structure independently from its authors. Collaboration thus occurs at programme level.

Assoziations-Blaster parodies the Faustian endeavour among hypertext enthusiasts of using infinite associative chains to find the essence of truth. 'It ridicules the notion of truth in random, mechanical, and intentionally silly associations. What really matters in this project is blasting open the connections between both texts and their writers' (Simanowski, 2004: 87–9).

Assoziations-Blaster is a prime example of self-referentiality. Individual words are used as associative triggers, which link to each other automatically. Contributions are stored in a database, which keeps a list of key words and matches them with the contributions. The machine operates in such a way as to ban readers from progressing unless they add more texts themselves. While a chronological order of reading the contributions is impossible, the reader jumps from one associative link to another. At first glance, *Assoziations-Blaster* seems to convey the ultimate interconnectivity between cognates, words and ideas. Nevertheless, what looms much larger is the limitation that emerges from such an apparatus. Simanowski (2004) mentions *Assoziations-Blaster* as one of the three most representative examples of internet-based collaborative writing in German, and discusses it in depth in his book *Interfictions* (2002b). The work-in-process was awarded a prize at the 1999 Ettlinger Wettbewerb für Netzliteratur and has, since it became available in English, been met with increasing international acclaim.

2.6   M. D. Coverley, *Califia* (2000)

M. D. Coverley's *Califia* was published in 2000 by Eastgate and is only available on CD-ROM for Windows. It may be regarded as one of the classics of hypermedia, as it combines a literary riddle with an interactive pastiche of music, images, animated graphics, text and photography. The reader has to make use of all semiotic codes available to capture the full sense of the story. Thematically, *Califia* is thus related to a long tradition of literary and cinematographic representations of characteristically North American, but also England-originated treasure hunts, such as Robert Louis Stevenson's *Treasure Island* (1883), Jack London's *Burning Daylight* (1910) and *Smoke Bellew* (1912), B. Traven's *The Treasure of the Sierra Madre* (1935; adapted to film in 1948 by John Huston) and, taking a particularly fitting, gender approach to the Californian gold rush, novels by JoAnn Levy, such as *Daughter of Joy: A Novel of Gold Rush San Francisco* (1999) and *For California's Gold* (2001).

The narrative is set in mid-nineteenth-century California, at the time of the gold rush. Augusta Summerland, a present-day first-person narrator living in Los Angeles, takes the reader on an epic two-dimensional treasure hunt, a hunt for gold, the 'Treasure of Califia', as well as a hunt for her past. The Treasure is said to be buried in the Southern Californian hills, 'but, through foul play or a California mixup, knowledge of the actual location was lost' [*to Read*]. Augusta embarks on her quest with her friends Kaye Beveridge and Calvin Lugo, and readers can choose which of those narrators, or rather sources of information, they would like to join. Augusta describes the strategy of the joint venture, which reflects Coverley's writerly programme, thus:

> Here, we bring together the legends, photos, maps, and documents that lead us to believe that there was a good reason for generations of Californians to keep searching for the secret treasure. So far, the gold has eluded us, but the project continues. [*to Read*]

Accordingly, the story is arranged as a diary, mixed with photographs of Augusta's family and ancestors. The use of visual materials is mostly indexical, as the images reflect semantic information given in writing, but also carry their own idiosyncratic features that move beyond the written text.

Augusta's account of *Califia* consists of four linear journeys, leading north, south, east and west. Calvin provides realistic materials for navigation (maps, docudramas and diagrams), and Kaye supplies mythical information surrounding her family, astrology, the ethnic spirituality of the Chumash Indians, and historical legends. The ultimate aim is for readers to compile the information they obtain in such a way as to 'discover more than we [the narrators] know' [*Join Us*].

The author takes a feminist approach to the history of California. This is borne out by her title, which refers to the name of a legendary Amazon warrior queen, who, according to the text, gave the state its name. Coverley draws on the destiny of Native Indian women. Furthermore, the fact that she offers and indeed tempts the reader into alternatives to sequential reading has been described by Carolyn Guertin as 'a feminist anti-history of navigation where the nomadic reader steers by dead reckoning' (2000). The story reveals that Augusta's mother, Violet Summerland, suffers from Alzheimer's Disease, a symptom comparable to the state of being 'lost in hyperspace'. Augusta considers it her duty to follow up her mother's memories as long as traces of them exist. However, the disease causes her to express herself in a very private, largely associative, encoded language, which, indicative as it is of her isolation, refers to the underlying risks of excessive internet research.

At an advanced semantic level, *Califia* reflects meta-hypertextually on aspects of the medium that stand in relation to previous manifestations of hypertextuality. In the course of the reading experience, the reader learns about historical and ethnic methods of navigation. Another metatheoretical feature is the colossal size of the text, which, in conjunction with frequent allusions to astrology, insinuates the infinity of hypertext with regard to production and reception. The fact that the character-narrators search a wide range of physical 'sites' and 'documents' suggests the analogy of a web search, taking place in metaphorical cyberspace. At yet another level of meaning, the modern frenzy about Hollywood stardom is implied by the never-ending search for material wealth.

Despite the bewilderment of the reader with respect to the sheer plethora of information, images, maps and possible trails, Coverley manages to generate and sustain a high degree of suspense and curiosity. A treasure hunt is bound to evoke memories from childhood, as well as exerting its emotive powers on the imaginative reader. The prospect of such a hunt is normally associated with a premonition of evil and danger, heralded through eerie forebodings, strange characters, or the wayward topography of the surrounding landscape. The explorative appeal of the hypertext is supplemented by evidence of scholarly expertise, specifically concerning ethnology, which meets the expectations and interests of an educated, academically oriented reader. What adds to the fascination of reading it is the illusion of realism, which the author manages to create by using authentic-sounding names, and mentioning real locations and historical circumstances, as well as giving an account of genuine aboriginal traditions.

From an aesthetic point of view, *Califia* appeals to the ears and eyes of its readers. The photographic and pictorial images are compelling for their beauty and potential to arouse feelings of nostalgia and pleasure in the beholder. Some lexias trigger sequences of folkloristic guitar music, which adds a slightly sentimental, exotic touch to the visual experience. Furthermore, the diligence with which Coverley has compiled her materials showcases the author's artistic talent and skill and thus defies common complaints made in relation to poor visual representation.

Califia has been extensively reviewed and analysed by a number of hypermedia experts, including: Guertin (2000), who draws attention to its way of construction and deconstruction of ethnic dementia, its 'aesthetics of forgetting'; Koskimaa (2000), who compares and contrasts *Califia* with the computer game *Myst* to convey the differences between hyperfiction and virtual reality – namely the dominance of the written word in the context of other, surrounding semiotic systems (which have to be 'read' in their own ways as well) in the former, as opposed to a reduction of (written) text to 'just one category of effects' in the latter; Hayles (2002), who points out to readers the fact that Coverley's work is metahypertextual in that it emphasizes navigation and trans-semiotic signification as a way of reaching the 'hidden' linguistic and ethnic treasures underlying the actual treasure hunt, rather than following conventional narrative; and Odin (n.d.), who once again stresses the synchronically and diachronically multi-layered, multi-sensory semiotic techniques employed by Coverley to convey stories of loss experienced by the dispossessed and exploited Chumash Indians as their land was virtually swept away by the builders of the Californian metropolis, Los Angeles.

2.7   Stefan Maskiewicz, *Quadrego* (2001)

Stefan Maskiewicz's dialogic hypertext *Quadrego* was written for and awarded the First Prize at the 2001 literatur.digital competition, organized and funded by T-Online and the Deutscher Taschenbuchverlag (dtv). It was created for the internet using HTML and JavaScript. In its thematic focus, it follows narratives like Edgar Allen Poe's 'The Tell-Tale Heart' and 'The Black Cat', and William Faulkner's *The Sound and the Fury*, as it embarks on a journey through the mentally diseased consciousness of an unreliable narrator – or speaker, to use a term more suitable for *Quadrego*. It could thus come under the term 'psychological' narrative, although it largely consists of dramatic dialogue. One may well argue that *Quadrego* comes close to Schnierer's concept of hypertext as reinstating eighteenth-century closet drama.

Maskiewicz explores the mental condition of a girl suffering from Multiple Personality Disorder. His major innovation lies in the exploration of hypertextual reading strategies so as to make them resemble the rituality of competing voices and identities within one mind, a type of multiple schizophrenia. The GUI serves as a two-dimensional stage for the four egos ('Quadr-ego'), who are engaged in an argument. The reader activates the conversational turns via mouseclick. Whereas some responses seem to refer clearly to what was said directly before, others seem to be uttered incoherently. The resulting mix of sense and non-sense, of logic and irrationality, is intended by the author to convey a maximally authentic picture of the symptoms of Multiple Personality Disorder.

Maskiewicz opens his hypertext with a prologue that, due to its tragic outlook, invariably attracts the reader's interest. It introduces 'a little girl who learns to live under her brother's brutality and dominance. But one day she realizes that she can free herself. The path to liberation is impeded by her brother's violence and her love for him. Her conscience starts taking possession of her' [*start*; my translation]. The hypertext 'starts' (there is only one possible path at the beginning) by revealing Iris's alias No's (the name the girl chooses for herself) desperate interior monologue, which has an arresting effect on the readers making them want to read on.

> ... and suddenly they were there. They appeared out of the darkness of her tainted soul. They came without a warning and settled down – in her head – and became louder. A deplorable state. Forced into a corner of her own mind, crouched, freezing and ... [*start*; my translation]

What follows is a convoluted, multiple dialogue between No's internal voices, whom she gives the names of her abusive brother (Tom), her friends Iris and Rolf, and herself. The 'characters' in her psychodrama express their opinions about each other and, in the *Quadrego* lexia, embark on a discussion that resembles the partially disjointed conversation fragments of a chatroom. The climactic reading process moves towards the absorption of the reader into the hypertext. As No becomes increasingly entangled with her own schizophrenic conflict, she 'invents' a new identity, Georg, who functions as the reader's mouthpiece. This unexpected turn of the 'story' is tantalizing for the reader, who increasingly identifies with, but at the same time tries to escape from, No's psychosis. It comes as a relief to choose the link 'MPD', which gives a sobering, demystifying turn to the otherwise alarming development of the reading experience.

Aesthetically, *Quadrego* owes its major visual appeal to Maskiewicz's artistic skill. The writer, who is a fully trained visual artist and art teacher, makes it clear that in his hypermedia artwork, visuality ranks high. Content is paralleled in formal intricacy and an elaborate linking pattern, which clearly symbolizes No's psychosomatic condition. An element of semiotic complementation between writing and pictorial representation is Iris's – a telling name – changing eye colour, which iconically reflects her shifting identities. Paralleling the turns of voices, the contorted, colourful photographic images of the four egos change their eye colour at regular intervals, thus enhancing the effect of random personality transitions. The visual effect is such that the portraits seem to smoothly undergo gender transformations as the reader's eye wanders along them. As a matter of fact, all portraits are based on one picture of the author himself, which Maskiewicz has managed to modify to such an extent as to make some look distinctly feminine, and others clearly masculine.

Quadrego has been widely discussed and analysed by critics, as well as used by a variety of literature teachers. Online reviews have been written, for example by Roberto Simanowski (2001b, 2001d, 2002a), and didactic interpretation questions can be found on the 'Bildungsserver Mecklenburg Vorpommern'.

2.8 Zeitgenossen, *Yatoo* (2001)

Zeitgenossen are a team of Viennese writers, whose real names are Ursula Hentschläger and Zelko Wiener. *Yatoo*, a piece of so-called 'audio contact art', was one of their pilot projects, involving vocalized rather than written language. In this respect, *Yatoo* forms an exception in my hypermedia canon, for it offers no written language at all but rather experiments with the synergies of roll-over graphic animation and de-sequentialized oral love poetry. The online version of this poetry cycle features a stylized, futuristic visual setting reminiscent of the interior of an overdimensional spacecraft. In the foreground, a tiny human creature in a salamander-painted space suit is depicted, who is set against an enormous, sublime landscape featuring digitized, moving geometric constellations. The impression evoked by this visual arrangement may be described as a neo-Romantic cyberspace 'painting', or piece of digital art, where the human individual finds himself confronted with an overpowering scenery that combines the phenomenology of virtual reality with a new approach to orally transmitted poetry. This supports Clayton's (2003) thesis that postmodernism and Romanticism are, on the whole, related literary movements.

Yatoo is short for 'you are the only one'. The hypertext toys with phrases like 'I love you so much', 'I won't leave you alone', 'I will suffer from you', 'I want you to escape', read out in turns by a female and a male voice, as the reader activates sound and image simultaneously by rolling the mouse over stars consisting of symmetrically organized geometrical shapes. As the shapes are activated, they change colour and form, releasing one of the above words at a time. There is only one way of triggering the original sequence of words – by hitting identical shapes in a certain order. Therefore, the first reading experience equals a jigsaw, a game, a play on words, augmented by a transmedial interplay of various semiotic systems. The mathematical logic of the geometric shapes diametrically opposes the emotional message delivered by the spoken language in the 'poems'. Visual material is therefore employed symbolically, as it does not share any semantic features with the other semiotic elements conveyed by the text and, rather than complementing verbally revealed information, undermines the emotive nature of the love poems.

Yatoo has received a thorough review by Roberto Simanowski (2002d), who follows both the male and the female side through to the end, discovering that, upon the close of each poem, the star closes and starts again from scratch. He further points out that the stars are organized so that the male shapes enclose the female ones, both protectively and restrictively. Linguistically, Simanowski explains that the words of the poems follow the rules of Constraint Poetics, i.e. they are subject to structural restraints as can be found in palindromes and lipograms. In *Yatoo*, these structural restraints are transferred to the receptive side. As mentioned earlier, the love poems are only traditionally meaningful if the words are activated in a prescribed order.

3   Third-Generation Cybertext

3.1   Michael Joyce, *Twilight, a Symphony* (1996)

Available for Macintosh computers only, Michael Joyce's second major hyperfiction, *Twilight, a Symphony*, is, at the same time, a prime example of hypermedia and one of the first and few quasi-cybertexts produced by Eastgate Systems. It represents a borderline case, which adds elements of machine autonomy to a rich hypermedia design, on both an aesthetic and semiotic basis. It intersperses textual lexias with photographs, operating largely symbolically, i.e. independently of preceding or succeeding text spaces. Furthermore, *Twilight* contains sound files, mostly triggered by activating a new lexia, which function as brief, emotive signals of an underlying atmosphere (e.g. chirping crickets, music used as accompaniment for a number of textual lexias, and streaming video clips, which open up yet more symbolic layers of meaning to the already intricately interlaced textual and intersemiotic patterns). So do the different kinds of graphemic representation, including various font types and instances of pasted handwriting, both alphabetical and numerical. The infinity and evasiveness of meaning, which figure prominently in *Twilight*, are further reinforced by a lexia entitled [*Meaning*], in which the author quotes from Harold Pinter's letters to Peter Wood (1958):

Meaning begins in the words, in the action, continues in your head and ends nowhere. There is no end to meaning. Meaning which is resolved, parceled, labeled and ready for export is dead, impertinent, and meaningless.

In terms of subject matter and intertextuality, the author maps out his socio-critical and literary reference frame right from the outset. On the entry page he refers explicitly to Milorad and Jasmina Pavić, trapped in wintery Belgrade at the end of the Bosnian War. He quotes from a personal letter by Milorad Pavic, the writer of *The Dictionary of the Khazars*, which – as I mentioned before – may be regarded as one of the twentieth century's central proto-hypertexts. Pavić writes:

> In this moment we live hardly, without bread and heating, so please, pray for us. But I am still publishing my books. The title of the last is 'Forever and a Day'; it is a play. But I do not believe we could perform it here; theaters are not performing in Belgrade this winter.

Although the narrative framework does not explicitly refer to the war in the former Yugoslavia or indeed to any other war, it clearly focuses on matters of life and death, with a strong emphasis on the latter. The 'Twilight' of the title is taken from a 'Twilight Doctor' of the westward storyline, who provides euthanasia for those who desire it. He forms the hub around which the 'concrete' story revolves. The first-person narrator, a former reporter called Hugh Colin Enright, reveals himself as a man who has become estranged from his wife and 'childnapped' [sic] his infant son. In his hiding place, a holiday resort, he meets a couple of Polish refugees. In the westward storyline (see below), Hugh reappears, ten years later, as the partner of the then terminally ill Polish woman (Magda), who seeks help from the notorious Twilight Doctor in committing suicide and thus finding relief from her pain. He decides to assist her himself, and the greater part of the text builds up the tension leading to the tragic yet redeeming moment. As it turns out, Hugh cannot bring himself to help her die, thus breaking his promise and upsetting her greatly. The reader skips between tragic episodes of last-minute togetherness and the narrator's solitary musings, in which a wide array of seemingly incoherent philosophical concepts are revealed to the reader in a manner reminiscent of late Woolfian and Joycean stream of consciousness:

> ... and sometimes thoughts came like thunder or there was never a disjunctive – or really only sometimes memories of flesh given over to something other than biomass once in Cambridge mass this sort of hardwired synaptic flash is called introibo ad altare if you work for it syntax generates storms ... [*biomass*]

The novel discontinues abruptly, with the words 'out of memory' [*out of memory*] and 'An unfinished novel' [*Pleasant Lake*], as though a sudden fit of amnesia had befallen the narrator, which he uses to suppress undesirable recollections. The notion of Magda's death, however, pervades the hypertext throughout, thus building the readers' expectations up to the tragic, albeit foreseeable event, and returns with every new reading path.

The four topographically conceived storylines, or 'arcs', go, according to the author's Foreword, 'east toward life (though in the past)', 'west toward death (though in the future)', south, or down, to the beginning of the story, 'in something approximating the present moment of the shifting text', and north, or up, to 'something like dream or mind, a set of sometimes fragmentary, sometimes speculative linkages' [*our story so far*]. Joyce further explains the story's underlying macrostructural paradox, that the story starts at its own end, and even beyond the end of other stories contained within the hypertext. By explaining the intricacies of its macrostructure on the [*our story so far*] lexia, which every thorough reader is likely to read to obtain a general picture of the thematic background, Joyce implies that this hypertext indeed resembles Borges's *The Garden of the Forking Paths* in that it interweaves numerous layers of human consciousness and philosophical thought, such as concrete and virtual reality, historicity, metaphysics, mortality, existentialism, coincidence and temporality.

A key macrostructural idiosyncrasy is Joyce's 'floating island' – in 1996 – as yet unprecedented navigation tool. Appearing on the screen as a separate desktop item, it represents a separate indexical 'space'. It contains four directional arrows, which virtually implement Bolter's idea of topographic reading, as they help readers move through the arrangement of text boxes ('spaces') as outlined in the Roadmap. The Roadmap can be accessed by clicking on the question mark button on the same icon. Furthermore, a 'pop tool' opens and closes text spaces, and a bi-directional arrow replaces the backshift key function for going backwards.

Upon reading the hypertext, however, it dawns on the reader that the underlying structural principles as well as the seemingly transparent navigational devices are indeed more problematic and opaque than expected, as the four arrows do not reliably point in the aforementioned conceptual directions but operate on a highly arbitrary basis. The theme of coincidence, which permeates the whole text, is thus reflected in its structure. Mostly, only one of the four directions can be chosen, sometimes even none, which then causes the reader to fall back on other navigational means such as the bi-directional arrow (see below), which again does not necessarily lead backwards but often on to other semiotic elements like photographs, which open up new semantic dimensions. Similarly, upon having read the [*our story so far*] screen, the reader is taken to the following lexia in a randomized fashion, as the text (which may thus well be termed an approximate hybrid between hypermedia and cybertext), and not the reader, chooses different starting points.

Twilight has been praised by critics not only for its structural subtleties, but for its lyrical, musical qualities (e.g. Barron, 1995; Renshaw, 2000). Other critics have highlighted the author's progress compared to his first hypertext classic (Tosca, 1999). With regard to formal qualities, the elegiac tone of the lyrical narrative is heightened by word repetitions as well as low, sombre, at times dipthongal assonances, combined with rounded vowel onsets and voiceless glottal fricatives, as exemplified by the following passage from [*here*]:

> Having been here once here now once again. One could actually reach and touch where in the air there before the eyes the center of the body had been bound by bone staves, heavy kettle of innards slung below corseted bellows; reach where once a winged shoulder moved at eye level . . .

Joyce's aesthetically thought-out style lends the narrative its distinctively meditative, pensive, poetic quality, which makes the reading process an emotionally engaging undertaking.

3.2   Mark Amerika, *Grammatron* (1996)

Grammatron by Mark Amerika is one of the first attempts to employ the internet's transmedial potential in order to create a hypermedia piece of literature. Like *Twilight*, it is a precarious borderline case positioned somewhere between hypertext, hypermedia and cybertext as, although making use of animated graphics and streaming audio, its central symbolic semiotic system is script. Graphics and sound serve decorative, but also semiotic purposes, generally underscoring the impression of reading 'in cyberspace'. On the other hand, *Grammatron* pioneers the empowered 'writing machine', as the author himself calls it, in that some parts of it show pre-programmed, almost filmic sequences of lexias, which cannot be navigated via mouseclick.

Grammatron is indebted to narrative theory. It explores the possibilities of narrative in the Digital Age. It portrays alternative worlds, in which stories are created for an immersive, networked environment. It questions traditional narrative in terms of composition, publishing and distribution, and argues, instead, for digital dissemination. It depicts the body as liberated in hyperspace, but, on the other hand, does not fail to point out the dangers looming beyond the user interface – the existence of 'anarcho-nomads' [*Thing*], threatening to take advantage of other programmers' ideas to usurp power, wealth and control.

In a 1998 online review, Karin Wenz, one of Germany's leading hypertext and New Media experts, emphasizes Amerika's endeavour to create *Grammatron* as a set of instructions suggesting appropriate ways of reading hypermedia narrative. She discovers four distinct narrative levels, which resemble those in a computer game and, ironically, the structure of a North American creative writing course. A supplementary fifth level is provided, which is formed by the theoretical part 'Hypertextual Consciousness'. The reader transgresses those levels to gain insight into the depths of cyburbia, a city in cyberspace called 'Prague-23', 'a beautiful new city modeled after the beautiful old city of the same name. It was one of the few places where people flowed freely through the streets and even had an active café, club and party scene' [*scene 505*].

Abe Golam, the central character, is a 'legendary info-shaman, cracker of the sorcerer code and creator of Grammatron and Nanoscript' [*Abe Golam*].

He represents the implied author-in-cyberspace himself. In creating Gramma-tron (a cyber-narrative) and Nanoscript (a new language for cyberspace), Golam was inspired by his muse Cynthia, who has since left him. Longing for her to return, Golam idealizes Cynthia – a typical cyborg – like a materialized digital goddess: 'model-perfect body, tall and thin with all the right curvatures, [she] came equipped with a world-class smile that would turn any other living creature into a melting puddle of digital residue' [*cyn*]. Amerika's frequently insinuated cyber-eroticism alludes to Dery's theory on cyber- and machine sex, 'orgasmatrons' and 'teledildonics' (1996), published only one year before the release of *Grammatron*. Cybersexual imagery recurs frequently throughout *Grammatron*, both pictorially and verbally, and may be regarded as a crucial aes-thetic tool for retaining the attention of the reader.

Amerika outlines the linguistic programme behind his hypertext in *Gramma-tron* itself:

GRAMMATRON uses the language of desire's own consciousness to disse-minate the potential creative power that resides within the vast electro-sphere. Meanwhile, the electrosphere as a whole is composed of an endless recombination of alphanumerical imagery that discharges itself as an ever-morphing terrain of linguistic microbits threaded together in such a way so as to form the true signatures of all Digital Being. [*signatures*]

As the inventor and master of Nanoscript, Abe Golam sees himself as the 'poet laureate' of this code. To illustrate this point, Amerika opens his work with a pun surrounding the words 'écriture' and 'a creature', and the genesis of an impersonated machine (cf. Jackson's *Patchwork Girl*): 'I am ... I am a machine ... a writing machine' [*interfacing*]. As Wenz (1998) rightly observes, Amerika draws on the surrealistic art of *écriture automatique*, a key precursor of literary hypertext.

From an aesthetic point of view, *Grammatron* is a highly readable hypertext, far more so than many of its Storyspace and HyperCard precursors. Lexias are kept at a minimum length, and the language created by Amerika is pervaded by rhetorical self-mockery ('fluffy butterfly-flakes', 'glazed donut eyes'), neologisms ('electrosphere', 'trendoid', 'cyburbia', 'creepoid'), netspeak ('maxed out', 'backspaced', 'voice-mail message-icon'), and fantastical para-doxons, which are both comical and thought-provoking. Many of these ele-ments, including their underlying parodistic potential, place *Grammatron* in the tradition of the science fiction novel, TV series and film, such as William Gib-son's *Neuromancer* (for its cyberspace setting and cyborg characters) and Dou-glas Adam's *The Hitchhiker's Guide to the Galaxy* (for its satire on 'real' life). The title-giving, poststructuralist focus on language is reminiscent of feminist science-fiction novels of the 1980s, for instance Joan Slonczewski's *A Door into Ocean* (1986) and Sheila Finch's *Triad* (1986).

Critics have praised *Grammatron* as 'sophisticated' (Chaouli, 2001: 65), and, since its first web release in 1997, the *Grammatron* website has been on display in more than 20 art shows, including the Ars Electronica Festival, the International Symposium of Electronic Art, the Whitney Biennial of American Art, and the Virtual Worlds 98 in Paris. It was reviewed in *The New York Times, Die Zeit, Reuters International* and *Time Digital*. In all, it has become one of the most widely accessed digital art sites on the World Wide Web and is frequently read and discussed in hypertext seminars around the world.

3.3   Stuart Moulthrop, *Hegirascope* (1995/1997)

'What if the word will not be still?' are the opening words of Stuart Moulthrop's dynamic, meta- or anti-theoretical 'web fiction' *Hegirascope*, first released in 1995. An extended, visually enhanced second version was launched in 1997, which will be the object of my discussion in this chapter. The current version incorporates 175 pages and more than 700 links, which are only partially visible and controllable. According to the author himself (1997), most pages:

> carry instructions that cause the browser to refresh the active window with a new page after 30 seconds. You can circumvent this by following a hypertext link, though in most cases this will just start a new half-minute timer on a fresh page.

The best starting point is, as Moulthrop suggests, to either 'dive in' or navigate via an index page to the most significant sequences.

Hegirascope comes under the label of cybertext because it leaves the ultimate control over the reading process to the underlying programme. Timed links make the lexias change without giving the reader a chance to take control via mouseclick. Notably, Version 1.0 refreshed its pages after only 18 seconds and was thus far more challenging to read. One could therefore argue that, with Version 2.0, Moulthrop takes a step backwards, reducing the power of the machine to the advantage of the quick reader. In fact, if one reads the lexias at normal to quick speed, the impression of being faced with a cybertextual machine may not even occur. The intention behind this move was to give more weight to content and language, which was, in Moulthrop's case, a provident thing to do, as both his style and treatment of subject matter are worthy of close reading.

  Sarcastically, Moulthrop mocks aspects of hypertext theory and culture such as the alleged empowerment of the reader, as well as the many recurring catch-phrases and quotations with which hypertext readers and researchers are normally bombarded. Via quasi-Socratic fictional dialogues as well as monologous passages, Moulthrop takes hypertext and New Media criticism *ad absurdum*. Vannevar Bush with his visionary *Memex* idea, foreshadowing the capacity to store and infinitely access human knowledge in its entirety, and Marshall McLuhan, with his largely television-focused concepts, are his favourite targets. Others include Jürgen Habermas, and political American warmongers such as Curtis LeMay.

Moulthrop humbly points out that 'much of what [he] was doing in "Hegira-scope" was indeed just playing', which is believable only to the extent that he was indeed playing, but with serious intentions. The title itself, which alludes to the Arabic word 'hejira', Mohammed's flight from Mecca to Medina, and, on a figurative level, an escape from danger, contains a hint of pessimism in relation to the main subject matter: the internet and its implications for the seduced surfer. And indeed, the author confesses that 'there's at least one very scary story unfolding in the midst of all that channel-surfing' (Simanowski, 2000b).

Hegirascope may be read, as suggested by Aarseth, as a parody of hypertext (1997: 81), or even of the World Wide Web itself. Evidence for this is provided in many places throughout the text: Moulthrop not only mentions but virtually stages the zapping of television channels via the onomatopoeic 'zick', his narra-tive is convoluted to the brink of cognitive exhaustion, and speed and quantity replace calm and diligence: 'We can expect a billion Web pages by 2000. Some of them will even be worth reading' [*Epigraph*].

At the centre of Moulthrop's work lies a narrative which, due to its lack of coherence in character, setting and plot, is strongly reminiscent of prototypical postmodern novels such as Thomas Pynchon's *Gravity's Rainbow*. Matevoy's picaresque dreams mingle with Gina's terror upon observing a dead body; other characters appear out of nowhere, such as Hattie and Pirate Queen, hold-ing conversations. Among the most recurrent motifs are dreams and voyages, which are – for good reasons – frequently used metaphors of surfing the web.

Unlike Jacques Servin's *BEAST*, *Hegirascope* is physically readable, despite the relatively quick changes in lexias. What is more, the fact that the lexias appear on a large screen and are concise and legible enough to be scanned with ease gives the reader a feeling of mastering the reading process rather than being completely subjected to the machine's usurping power. Every lexia is framed by four text links, which lead the reader on to other theories and post-modern personalities. As a matter of fact, the author avoids links within the text but places them in the margin. Moulthrop's intelligent poetic style causes the text to be pleasant and stimulating to read, confusing though it may be in its entirety. The willing perceiver feels encouraged to look up previously unfami-liar theories and biographies, which adds a touch of academic prestige to the work and clearly shows Moulthrop's vocational and writerly claim.

The academic character of *Hegirascope* is reinforced by lists of references displayed in some lexias. They give account of the author's commitment to academic study and convey a high degree of authenticity and realism to the fic-tion. The rigidity of the text itself is a clear indicator of Moulthrop's scepticism towards blind web fanaticism. At the end of each narrative strand, the screen grows either black or white, signalling the end of colour and, on a symbolic level, the loss of all so-called knowledge upon the downfall of the machine.

Simanowski (1999b) focuses in his extended essay on hypertext aesthetics on one particular section of *Hegirascope*, which promises to recount a dream placing the reader above human civilization. In reality, however, this empowering dream is deconstructed by the shortage of time allowed to read the lexia, which swiftly switches on to the next one, thus forcing the reader to press the 'back' button to return to the target lexia. In this respect, Simanowski understands the text as a double reconstruction, of both the reader's semantic expectation and the assumed power he or she has over the reading process.

Another, exhaustive review of *Hegirascope* has recently been published by Shuen-shing Lee at *literatur-digital*. Lee investigates the use of hyperlinks and colour codings as 'instances that exhibit the fluidity of digital materiality' (2005) and demonstrates how '*order* is buried in the *disorder* of the apparent "narrative confetti"' (*ibid.*). In doing so, Lee ventures the bold thesis that, in analogy to Victor Shklovsky's claim of *Tristram Shandy* being 'the most typical novel in world literature' (Shklovsky, 1991), *Hegirascope* is 'the most typical hypernovel in digital literature' (Lee, 2005).

3.4   Jacques Servin, *BEAST* (1997)

Jacques Servin's *BEAST* is a transitional phenomenon. It makes use of hypermedia technology in such a way as to exploit different semiotic systems semantically, in different combinations, transitional stages, and competitive situations, and it does even more than that. As a matter of fact, the system renders the readers almost powerless, as the cybertext exposes them to continuously transforming, interacting semiotic systems. It is never possible to finish reading a lexia, as the cybertext programme determines the speed at which lexias will be superimposed by others, regardless of what kind of pictorial or textual material they contain. It is thus hardly possible for the reader to work out any coherent sense. The prevailing sensation is that of confusion, bemusement, amusement and challenge. Readers are indeed requested by the 'beastly' programme to compete with it, to take control by closing down and restarting it, only to lose themselves again in the entangling array of dynamic text, image and sound.

In a psychoanalytical reading, the 'beast in man' (cf. Zola's novel of 1898), which is represented by the text, alludes to human instinct-driven behaviour, to the Freudian 'id', which is only controllable by the 'ego' provided it confronts it with the 'super-ego' (as expounded in Freud's 1923 publication *The Ego and the Id*). In Servin's cybertext, the 'successful' in the sense of 'socially acceptable' interplay between those three elements is taken *ad absurdum*, by giving full control to the machine, which assumes ultimate power over human will-power. Alternatively, a structuralist, or rather anti-structuralist, reading pinpoints the inherent absurdity of the 'message-for-the-message's-sake' idea as maintained by Jakobson (1960), which dominates a large proportion of contemporary web art that denies extratextual and extramedial denotation. Understood in this way, one may detect an allusion to the Greek Laocoon myth, in which a sea monster is sent out by Apollo to kill the prophet Laocoon (and his sons), who has warned the Trojans (the name is now used to designate a powerful computer virus) against the enigmatic wooden horse. In a radical mythopoetic reading of *BEAST*, the receiver of web art in general, or hypertext in particular, may hence be viewed as the victim of Servin's monstrous cybertext, which is sent as a double warning, yet whose destructive symbolic power is dramatically misunderstood by the unsuspecting target readership.

Upon entering *BEAST*, the reader is presented, or rather bombarded, with a series of small windows containing quotations from fictional, philosophical and expository texts. Purely pictorial windows complement the text lexias, although it is highly questionable whether or not their symbolic content reveals any relevant extra information. The picture lexias are accompanied by distinct sound sequences, which are reminiscent of Wagner's *leitmotif* idea. In addition to the information overload, readers are confronted with repeating system messages requesting them to take immediate action in order to prevent the machine from crashing.

The crucial message behind Servin's seemingly random arrangements is a critique of the web and its treatment or, for that matter, lack of content and aesthetics, as well as technology's takeover. The author primarily criticizes the web's 'utter transience of attention' and its support of commercialism. By allowing readers to feel in control and, subsequently, subjecting them to the system's caprices, Servin draws attention to human indifference to processes of human commodification, and growing inertia in the face of a decrease in the need for concrete human action.

BEAST has generally been met with great critical acclaim. Mark Amerika, for instance, reviews it in 'The Book and the Beast' (1998), emphasizing its transsemiotic intertextuality, as Servin uses quotes 'from Benjamin to Benn', mixing them with images taken from various popular magazines and with snippets of programming language 'hacked' from a variety of Windows systems. Literally, the title refers to a 'monster java applet' that arranges the components of the cybertext into a capricious performance of programming text that unfolds before the reader's eyes, who is thus made into a puppet, another element of this on-screen vaudeville show. Amerika includes a short statement by Servin himself, who explains his programme as follows:

> While [BEAST(TM)] [sic] highlights the ugliness of computer technology, it also leads the user to see the harmony in it, since the profusion of images, warnings, sounds and tyrannical acts on the part of the system have an ultimately pleasing rhythm . . . The user is inducted into understanding his or her own complicity in this state of affairs. (Amerika, 1998)

With respect to *BEAST*'s distinctive cybertextuality, Christiane Heibach calls it 'one of the most elaborate projects of its category, where image, text and sound interact hypermedially' (2001: 34, my translation).

3.5 Urs Schreiber, *Das Epos der Maschine* (1998)

Urs Schreiber's Java-based internet opus *Das Epos der Maschine* epitomizes like no other hypertext the paradigm of cybertext, featuring the control of the 'machine' over its user both practically and (meta-)theoretically. As the title suggests, *Das Epos* regards itself as a poem of epic dimensions, i.e. a conglomerate of poetry and narrative which operates as a symbol of an entire national or, as in the case of the internet, virtual paradigm. In other words, Schreiber bravely positions his cybertext in the tradition of the great ethnic and religious epics (e.g. Homer's *Iliad* and *Odyssey*, the *Nibelungenlied* and Milton's *Paradise Lost*). By the same token, *Das Epos* follows the tradition of concrete poetry, which critically and playfully reflects on language itself as well as its inextricable determination by the medium in which it appears. *Das Epos* is a joint venture. Text and programming were done by Urs Schreiber, the graphics by Kai Jelinek and Cesare Wosko, the photographs by Claudia König, and the sound by 'Die with Dignity'.

Das Epos operates via animated script, image and sound. Its key element is autonomously moving text, which appears, vanishes, expands, diminishes and wanders across a highly interactive user interface. It does so virtually of its own accord, as reader interaction controls textual performance only to a certain degree. At times, script melts with image, which conveys the major semiotic property of digital media, the shared underlying code. The visual experience occurs against the audio backdrop of the sound of an electric guitar, playing distorted sequences of recurring, monotonous sinus curves, superimposed with a synthesized knocking, evoking the impression of being surrounded by heavy machines. The overall image is that of a quasi-gothic, electronic macrocosm, which, unlike science fiction and cyberpunk literature, does not endeavour to imitate reality but rather to take the effects of linguistic, auditory and visual symbolism to an extreme. On the whole, various semiotic levels are juxtaposed in an indexical fashion, partly complementing and representing each other, partly conveying independent aspects of meaning.

The author provides a set of instructions as to what elements can be activated via mouseclick, for example grey areas, which can be made to appear and disappear, and framed, underlined or otherwise marked passages, about which the author does not convey any information except for the fact that they may be activated. Schreiber requests 'SUCHEN Sie, manches ist versteckt' ('Look out for hidden elements'), thus revealing the partly playful character of his work.

Although the cursor does trigger certain mechanisms and developments in the presentation of text, it activates operations that are out of the reader's control. So it happens that, upon mouseclick, diverse text sequences are opened, while in a different place on the same screen, another script line appears, meanders, and disappears before the eyes of the bewildered perceiver. The overall impression is that of a text-based dream, of subconscious currents, incoherent, illogical and arbitrarily conjoined. As in Matthias Goldmann's *Schreiben auf Wasser*, text is presented in a state of flux, which is, after all, a major propensity of language and meaning itself, particularly in the digital medium. As opposed to Goldmann, however, Schreiber challenges the reader's aesthetic nerve by going beyond conventional enlightenment expectations of visual harmony, musical consonance and cognitive logic.

Das Epos was awarded a special prize for the creative use of media techniques at the ARTE them@ literature competition. Simanowski describes its aesthetic appeal as 'of peculiar beauty, a beauty of the technological, which does not fail to communicate its deeper sense' (2000a, my translation). Despite or, paradoxically, because of its affinity to technology, Schreiber's language is highly poetic. He achieves an interplay of syntactic overstructuring and an expressive mixture of biological and technological lexis, thus mingling two – in a traditionalist understanding – irreconcilable features. The human-machine synthesis does not lead to an entire transformation of the experiencing third-person narrator. However, the above passage clearly alludes to a somewhat paradoxical personification of the de-humanizing machine, which feeds on human body fluids, in a similar way as it is depicted, for instance, by H. G. Wells in his pioneering science-fiction novel, *The War of the Worlds* (1898). Hence, Schreiber's cybertext joins a number of literary traditions on both a textual and subtextual level.

3.6 Kate Pullinger, *The Breathing Wall* (2004)

Kate Pullinger's recent cybertext *The Breathing Wall*, first presented at the 2004 trAce Conference in Nottingham, undermines any theories of reader-response criticism which presuppose the reader's intention as a major guiding principle in the construction of textual meaning. Like Bill Bly's *We Descend*, it is one of the very few hypertexts defying the allegation that the detective story has never really entered hyperfiction (see Chapter 3.1.8). And indeed, *The Breathing Wall* departs from the rules of the conventional thriller by leaving the solution of the mystery not to the reader's intention-driven, cognitive interplay with the plot, but to his or her very physical condition at the time of reading. The programmed 'machine' does in fact take control over significant stretches of the text. Particularly in the 'daydreams', large amounts of textual material are presented to the reader as a sequence of filmic text lexias, which do not give readers an opportunity to choose their own speed of reading but appear and disappear at a pre-programmed pace. Readers can move from subchapter to subchapter within a daydream; however, they lose control once the text film has started. A more controversial case of generic categorization is the Hyper Trans Fiction Matrix used for the dreams, which responds to the vegetative system of a breathing organism which does not need to be human in nature. It is in fact the dreams which make *The Breathing Wall* one of the most interesting and forward-looking examples of cyberfiction. It may, as it were, be considered a pilot example of 'physio-cybertext'.

Generically, *The Breathing Wall* may be described as a neo-Freudian gothic detective novel, which combines a conscious, realistic level with an unconscious, supernatural world in much the same way as does the American film romance *Ghost* (directed by Jerry Zucker and released in 1990). The cybertext consists of two key components: a hypertext-based, largely sequential narrative, organized into five parts, or 'daydreams', and a set of 'dreams', which reveal the protagonist Michael's nightly conversations with his deceased girlfriend Lana. The story opens with Michael, who has been in prison for six months over allegations of having murdered Lana, a crime which he did not commit, yet for which he cannot provide a satisfactory alibi. The hypertext story reveals Michael's frustration over his hopeless situation. In his (waking) dreams, Lana speaks to him, giving him clues as to what really happened. She suggests that he should consult his sister Florence, her best friend, who, despite her suspicions, decides to help her brother. She finds out that Lana was killed by her own father in one of his psychopathic fits. The last daydream is set after Michael's release, as he converses with Lana at the cemetery, under a cherry tree. Whereas the hypertext sequence serves to reveal the gist of the detective story, the essential detail can only be obtained from the dreams, the reading of which requires utter patience, calm, and the appropriate breathing rate and depth.

Bizarre as it may sound, the speed and intensity of information transfer during Michael's 'dreams' is entirely dependent on the reader's respiratory mechanism. The breathing rate is measured by means of a run-of-the-mill microphone, attached to a headset and placed directly underneath the reader's nostrils. The software used to transfer the measured data to the computer is called Hyper Trans Fiction Matrix, and was especially created for Kate Pullinger's project by the German software programmer Stefan Schemat, whose responsibilities were, according to the credits, 'hypnotic lyrics, programming, sound & vision of the dreams'. Babel created the hypertext, on which the 'daydreams' are based, and the background sound to them. Whereas the sound in the 'daydreams' serves purely decorative purposes, the 'dream' voices, read by Mufrida Hayes and Harry Capehorn, are in fact crucial to understanding the dialogues between the two main characters, as no written information is revealed in their subconscious conversations.

The Breathing Wall owes its attractiveness to a variety of things. Visually and auditorily, a lot of effort and attention to detail went into creating an enticing user interface. Background images, colours and sounds change frequently, giving the work a synaesthetic aura akin to film. However, verbal language remains the decisive medium of information retrieval. Reading and listening are the two major receptive activities undertaken by the perceiver. Nevertheless, for experienced and unexperienced readers alike, the most important aspect is the overriding physical impression of finding their respiratory apparatus in harmony with that of the protagonist, thus establishing a previously unknown degree of identification. Michael is told by Lana to 'sleep', 'breathe', 'feel [his] lungs' and 'dream' [*Daydream 2*]. These instructions are meant for him as well as for the readers in order to intensify their reading and listening experience.

At the time of writing this study, only very few reviews of *The Breathing Wall* were available either in print or online. One exception is Picot's review (2004) at *The Hyperliterature Exchange*, who coins the term 'hyperventiliterature' for Pullinger's work. At the aforementioned trAce Conference, the large number of people wanting to do a test session and buy a copy of the CD-ROM shows how great the acclaim was (and may be in future), at least among hypertext and New Media experts.

Chapter 4

Literary Competence – Conceptual Adaptations

1   Constructivist Influences on Literature Teaching

Human beings can only comprehend what they have made themselves. This is why the
world exists and why the world, as experienced by human beings, has to be the way it is,
precisely because they have made it this way.
(Schmidt, 2002: 152, my translation)

This chapter marks the beginning of the second part of this study, which is concerned with the constructive side of hypertext. It investigates the philosophy of constructivism in terms of its significance as the prevailing learning theory of our day[1] and, thereafter, outlines conclusions which can be drawn for an extended, hypermedia-centred concept of literary competence. Chapter 4 provides the pedagogic background to Chapter 5, which will report the findings of a hypertext-based, literary action research project aimed at implementing contemporary educational philosophy.

Coined in the eighteenth century by the Neapolitan philosopher Giambattista Vico, constructivism has, in the course of the twentieth century, pervaded almost all academic disciplines (von Glasersfeld, 2002: 29; Ensslin, 2004: 308).[2] Its major implications, however, were already formulated and discussed among philosophers of Greek Antiquity – particularly pre-Socratians such as Xenophanes (570–475 BC), Alcmaion (approximately 530–500 BC), Democritus (460–370 BC) and Heraclitus (540–480 BC), as well as by sceptics across the centuries. What they had in common was their defiant attitude towards the positivist chimera of absolute truth.

To offer an alternative, they understood all knowledge to be relative and subjective, if not absurd in itself: '. . . we cannot know what every object really is or is not like' (Democritus; quoted in von Glasersfeld, 2002: 9 – my translation). Reinforced by the Enlightenment philosophers Hume, Berkeley and Kant as well as by Darwinian evolutionism, this fundamentally rebellious idea, which threatened to overthrow the prevailing dogma of conventional empiricism, was revisited and refined by Jean Piaget from the 1930s onwards and, as of the late 1960s, by Jerome Bruner.[3] It finally led to radical changes in the outlook on developmental psychology, in that knowledge came to be seen as the result of cognitive processing, which was felt to be part of human adaptation to and of environmental structures. In this context, Piaget used the two complementary concepts of accommodation and assimilation. Accommodation is, in his view, the adaptation of the environment to the human subject, whereas by assimilation he understood the exact opposite: adjustment to one's environment. Both phenomena are in fact essential for the 'human organism'[4] insofar as they enable it to reach an approximate understanding of its construct of the world, which ultimately depends on the individual's aims in life. This idea, which Popper (1963) refers to as *instrumentalism*, regards knowledge as a means to an end. Human beings will only learn what is of interest to them – either extrinsically or intrinsically motivated.

Hence, all human beings gradually adapt to the world and, at the same time, adapt the world to themselves in their own particular ways, depending on their specific potentials, skills, abilities, inclinations, characteristics, situational dispositions and opportunities. They have to find individual ways through the 'jungle' of obstacles, which consists of the 'objects' (Latin for 'what has been thrown in the way') with which they are confronted in daily life. Therefore, von Glasersfeld (2002) uses the term *viability* to describe the human ability to make things feasible and plausible, to modify them to their own benefit, and, ultimately, to survive physically, mentally and spiritually.

Radical constructivism, a coinage of Ernst von Glasersfeld (see Reinfried, 2000), is associated with the names of Humberto R. Maturana, Karl Popper, Francisco J. Varela, Siegfried J. Schmidt, Heinz von Foerster, Ernst von Glasersfeld and Paul Watzlawick. It is, in itself, a metatheory (Werning, 1998), which seeks empirically to undermine blind belief in the objectivity of science and the interconnectedness of power and truth. Its essential claim is the subjectivity of all scientific evidence, which conventionally conforms to and thus reinforces hierarchical, centralistic and dualistic Western thought. Radical constructivism regards human beings as *autopoietic systems* (e.g. Varela, 1979; Maturana, 1980; Maturana and Varela, 1980), which are organized by the principle of *operational autonomy*.[5] Although interacting with their environment to guarantee their own survival, they are neurally disconnected from it and act independently – each in his or her own way.

Before the cognitive turn in psychology, philosophy and linguistics, which first started in the mid-1940s and gathered force in the 1960s and 1970s, literary education across Europe was seen primarily as an ideological vehicle, in a moral as well as a nationalist sense. In a dogmatic way, it aimed to prepare learners for their future roles in society, stereotypical though they were. In Imperialist and Weimar Germany, for instance, the *Nibelungenlied* and other heroic epics were given primarily to boys to read, whereas the exclusively domestic, yielding image of the Wilhelminian woman was spoon-fed to girls by means of serialized 'Backfischromane' such as Emmy von Rhoden's *Der Trotzkopf* and Else Ury's *Das Nesthäkchen* (Wilkending, 2002: 48). Correspondingly, the growing book market in Victorian England was ideologically instrumentalized to promote enculturation and the development of appropriate linguistic style in young readers. To help them – boys and girls alike – become members of a 'textual community' (Stock, 1983), medieval and Arthurian literature, as well as Sir Walter Scott's historical novels, with their ideal of chivalry, of 'good manners and breeding', were understood to make particularly suitable reading (see Sir Walter Scott's *Essay on Chivalry* of 1819). By means of popular literary forms such as serial novels and children's book adaptations, chivalric literature was functionalized to help create and preserve cultural memory and collective national identity – especially in order to mark the contrast between 'English heritage' and what was perceived to be the historically inferior, dangerously progress-oriented American culture – through its deeply rooted tension between myth and history (Müller-Oberhäuser, 2002: 25–34).

By the same token, the late nineteenth century saw the beginning of a tradition in England, spearheaded by eminent scholars like Matthew Arnold, F. R. Leavis and Denys Thompson, according to which English ought to be considered *the* educational subject, not only for the purpose of developing a unified and unifying national identity. The central status of English as a subject in its own right was accounted for, for instance, by the beliefs that the appropriate use of the mother tongue is a prerequisite to civilized living, and that literature provides a plethora of material, the familiarity with which leads to wisdom via enjoyment (Allen, 1980: 8).

In response to emerging popular culture in the 1960s, Thompson, one of the major educationalists of that day, saw the role of the English teacher 'in terms of countering the effects of a mass society ... at a time when human values [imagination, sympathy, understanding and tolerance] are not upheld' (quoted in Allen, 1980: 9). Thompson believed in the importance of 'experiencing' literature and, most of all, literary language, 'the most deeply effective form of language', which 'shapes the habits of mind and feeling which determine a man's capacity for living' (*ibid.*: 9).

In following up the idea of literature as personal experience, Thompson drew on theories developed as early as the 1930s in the USA, where progressive educationalists like Louise Rosenblatt opposed the predominance of New Criticism with her so-called transactional theory of the literary work. Rosenblatt maintained that reading was essentially exploration, i.e. aesthetic experiences that had 'both social origin and effect' (Pike, 2003: 61) and that were performed by the reader as a 'form of intense personal activity' (Rosenblatt, 1976: v). Thompson's approach, however, diverges from Rosenblatt's in its quasi-utilitarian outlook on the 'effectiveness' of reading. The postulation of 'effectiveness' was, at the time, informed by the emergence of communication theory and linguistic pragmatics. Upon closer examination, however, Thompson's view that 'literature is the best route to good communications – that is, practical uses of language' (quoted in Allen, 1980: 9) was ultimately directed towards the development of moral values, his keyword for which was 'growth'. In so doing, he partly subscribed to the conventional understanding of literature as a vehicle for ethical education.

Adopting a more sociological, psychological position, Rosenblatt's approach may be regarded as an early forerunner of reader-response criticism, which did not come into full swing until the 1960s and led, about two decades later, to the decisive turn in educational theory towards individualization and learner-centred curriculum planning.[6] As a matter of fact, it was as early as 1966 when a child-centred view was first foregrounded on a large scale and with a considerable effect, at a seminal education seminar in Dartmouth, USA. Harris (1980: 20) summarizes the results of this conference in terms of there being a:

> general movement in at least the theory of education towards a child-centred and outward-looking and away from a subject-centred organization of the curriculum ... Again and again, successful teaching is seen as focused in the child himself, in his attitude to learning and in his growth as a mature person.

At the beginning of the twenty-first century, constructivist philosophy, complemented, in the field of literature, by the tenets of reader-response criticism, may be regarded as the predominant paradigm in educational theory and practice. It has two basic principles: First, the relationship between the subjective organism and its environment ('milieu'). According to Maturana and Varela (1998), the milieu cannot be objectively known. It differs from the empirical world, which influences the individual by means of perturbations. Individuals perpetually re-construct their reality in a sensory, affective and cognitive way, on the basis of interaction with the empirical world. It is transformed functionally, according to personal interests. Hence, deep learning, which, as opposed to surface learning, helps integrate new data with existing knowledge structures in a meaningful way, can only occur if the learner is able to identify the personal relevance in a learning object (Biggs, 1979).

Second, constructivism focuses on 'understanding the learning subject' (Werning, 1998: 40 – my translation), who is characterized by three attributes: structural determinacy, self-referentiality and non-triviality. Structural determinacy can be explained in terms of the human organism determining autonomously how it is going to deal with its immediate environment. External stimuli, i.e. cognitive information, will only be embedded in the reality structures of an individual if he or she has emotional or functional reasons for this to happen – in other words, if the information is subjectively regarded as relevant. Hence, the 'structure' of a living organism decides selectively on its objects of perception.

Individuals are self-referential in that all their mental, verbal or physical actions, in varying degrees of intensity and transparency, give account of their personal structure. Human subjects find themselves in continuous interaction with their experienced environment, yet always act in a manner that relates back to their own needs and interests.

Finally, living human organisms are non-trivial because, rather than acting and re-acting according to simple cause-and-effect mechanisms, they are essentially unpredictable. Human self-understanding is historically determined. Therefore, the structure of human perception and reality is highly flexible and changes permanently in response to its changing environment. Werning describes this phenomenon in terms of 'structural dynamics' (*ibid*.: 40). In other words, human beings are not like the 'black box' of behaviorism, which claims that responses (output) are predictable given certain stimuli (input). Contrarily, humans perpetually reflect on their actions and make decisions in alignment with their present environment as well as their current physical and mental disposition.

To draw consequences for literary education, pedagogues should try to stimulate 'the complex affective and cognitive systems ... which operate in accordance with their own logic' (*ibid*.: 40). As every individual is structurally determined, students cannot be expected to respond with equal enthusiasm to learning objects stipulated by the curriculum or provided by the teacher. Therefore, learners need help in identifying the potential significance and personal relevance, in Reich's (1998) words, the 'transparency' of the learning object. This awareness-raising process needs to be complemented with a variety and openness of teaching methods, which meet different learning styles and interests, for example egalitarian classroom discourse, encouraging students to rethink their own concepts and attitudes, and learning activities that will stimulate 'activists', 'theorists', 'pragmatists' and 'reflectors' (Honey and Mumford, 1982), as well as facilitating top-down, bottom-up and sequential learning styles (Stanton and Stammers, 1990).[7] With respect to non-triviality, a constructivist classroom should encourage 'variety and individuality' (Werning, 1998: 40). As the internal structure of the human organism changes incessantly, and, furthermore, hardly any group or classroom community is homogeneous, there has to be room for unexpected contributions, suggestions and reactions, as well as creative individualism. Such an integrative didactic approach implies, according to Werning, 'inviting learners to question, evaluate, elaborate, refute, reconfirm etc. their own constructions of reality' (*ibid*.: 40 – my translation). By means of peer and tutor feedback, learners are made to develop a critical attitude towards their existing and newly acquired cognitive structures.

From a literary vantage point, the most influential figure in educational constructivism has been Siegfried J. Schmidt. Based on an explicitly non-positivistic point of view, Schmidt (2002) has designed a constructivist approach to literary theory, which he calls *empirical*. According to this theory, the central objective of learning and teaching is a procedural literary 'system' rather than an objectified literary 'body'. Schmidt derives the term *empirical* from a new understanding of literary theory as a science, which, by definition, has to make explicit its epistemological, linguistic and literary principles.

In this theoretical framework, he sets out to explain Maturana's (1980) theory of autopoietic systems, which cognitively develop through the observation of oneself and other organisms. Cognition is regarded as a life-long process, which cannot be described in terms of an ultimate and unalterable categorization of the observed objective environment. Instead, it is considered an ongoing, dynamic procedure, triggered by the observation and processing of new information and by integrating it with pre-existing knowledge structures.

Schmidt refrains from any kind of objective categorization within general human cognition. On the contrary, cognition is, in his view, essentially subjective and self-determined, as each individual system develops its own categories and representations. As a result, cognitive processes are entirely subject-determined and, therefore, cannot account for any kind of objective environment. Hence, reality as a generic, objectifiable concept does not exist, but can only be understood as a conglomerate of subjective descriptions and representations, which, in turn, cast more light on the observer himself than on the phenomena he or she observes. 'Humans can only know what they have created themselves' (Schmidt, 2002: 152 – my translation), which is why 'the world' as we like to call it is always the world of an individual and can only reflect his or her temporary, highly dynamic and flexible dispositions.

Consequently, what an empirical approach to teaching literature ventures to do is to foreground the individual and to take into consideration the distinctive needs, motives and interests of the surrounding society – in other words peer groups as they are situated in highly individualized and contextualized, often even overlapping structures. Every human being is a co-product of genetics, society and education. As far as the latter two are concerned, this implies that humanity is guided by historically grown conventions, generated through societal experiences. These conventions are chiefly reflected by language, which again is the basis of interaction and coordination (*ibid.*: 153). Interaction being the prerequisite of communication, Schmidt adopts Maturana's redefinition of language: rather than regarding language, in Saussurean terms, as a self-contained and fixed system of signs, or (as pragmatists like Hymes, Austin, Searle or Grice did) as a means of communication, the biologist Maturana sees language as a system of orientational behaviour, which forms the basis of consensual behaviour between linguistically interacting systems (Maturana, 1982: 73).

Each language system is therefore a self-contained network of *denotations*, which cannot be defined on a quasi-objective basis, as was traditionally done by logical positivists like Russell and Frege or by semioticians of the Saussurian tradition, but are essentially observer-determined. Similarly, from a constructivist point of view, the long-established term *reference* does not stand for the process of linguistically relating to concrete or abstract phenomena in an objective reality, but to some socially acquired type of orientational, linguistic behaviour, based on individual sensory perception, which serves to construct analogous informational structures within the cognitive systems of communicating organisms.

Finally, to draw a connecting line to the relation between the human subject and literary text, *literary meaning*, which had long been considered a teachable or even objectifiable textual property, was redefined in the constructivist educational paradigm, in analogy to the reader-response paradigm shift in critical theory. 'Literary meaning' came to be seen not only in the context of the time in which the text was written or the situation in which the writer is said to have been, but chiefly within the highly complex cognitive context of the reader, who will never read the same text twice but rather perceive, understand and process different aspects of the concrete written body differently each time he or she tackles it. Meaning, hence, has to be considered as a highly ramified network of situationally determined contextual relations, a multiple concept depending on the number of communicators, situations and temporal data derived intra- and extratextually.

For an empirical way of teaching literature, this implies a departure from the spoon-feed approach towards 'empowering' the learner-reader. (N.B.: I am using the Landowian term deliberately to demonstrate the relevance of Landow's claim with regard to learners' needs. It has been highlighted previously that reader empowerment, which Landow associates with (w)reading hypertext, is a dangerous simplification if not distortion of the empirical and cognitive nature of reading nonlinear texts.)

Understanding literary content underlies individual construction mechanisms, which are both intentional and holistic and involve a multiplicity of cognitive processes and epistemic subsystems (see; van Dijk, 1980; de Beaugrande and Dressler, 1981; Groeben, 1982). Consequently, among the crucial skills that students of literature need to develop is the ability to identify and verbalize their own subjective representation of contextually variable literary meaning: where they derived it from, what linguistic and stylistic means of the text illustrate their concepts and, finally, what other potential representations they deliberately neglected, and for what reasons. Activities supporting the evolution of such skills may be performed either autonomously or jointly, in open discourse. Evidently, in an exploratory hypertextual learning environment, such activities are easy to implement, as hypertext by its own nature undermines the possibility of arriving at a unified reading. Possible implications for a constructive hypertextual learning environment, which is designed in such a way as to address the aforementioned need for learner empowerment, will be examined in Chapter 5.

2   Aspects of Literary Competence

Every performance presupposes competence.
(Greimas, 1985: 357)

As maintained by Storrer (2002), hypertext as a macrostructural principle (with an emphasis on expository, as opposed to literary, hypertext) does not require a new concept of textuality. What it needs is, rather, an extended concept that takes account of the distinctive cohesive qualities of textual networks, lexias and links, as well as the trans-semiotic implications of hypermedia. According to Barthes, every image, every film, advertisement, song, in short, every perceivable element of our environment, has semiotic qualities and can be 'read' like a text. As mentioned previously, text is understood in this study primarily in terms of alphanumeric, scripted text, and other semiotic systems will be investigated only to the extent to which they supplement and complement script. Nevertheless, when it comes to developing a hypertext- or hypermedia-'proof' concept of literary competence, as is done in the remaining sections of this chapter, those issues have to be taken into consideration. So do the issues of mediality, navigation and communication, which, in a hypertextual environment, radically differ from a traditional print-based environment.

The origin of the 'competence' concept dates back to Chomsky's idea of linguistic, or grammatical competence, which he understands as the intuitive knowledge of an ideal speaker-listener about the rules of a language, and which he juxtaposes with 'performance', the actual manifestations of competence in speech. In Chomsky's view, competence is innate to every human being of normal physical and psychological disposition. Having linguistic competence equals the ability to form an infinite number of sentences from a finite set of grammatical rules. In Chomsky's view, which has been refuted by cognitivists and constructivists, this innate linguistic competence effects that, during early childhood, human beings 'choose' one or more language systems from a universal stock of inborn linguistic parameters, depending on which language community or communities they are most frequently exposed to. Because of this so-called Language Acquisition Device, which operates in conjunction with various hypothesis-forming processes, children can, according to Chomsky's nativist theory, acquire any natural language.

The concept of competence was adopted and further developed from the 1970s onwards, particularly by cognitivists in the tradition of Piaget on the one hand, and social scientists and constructivists on the other. The central debate revolved around the question of whether competence development might or might not be associated with social interaction and the participation in communicative processes (Bruner, 1977; Vygotsky, 1934/1986; Habermas, 1995). According to Piaget, competence acquisition succeeds processes of assimilation and accommodation, which are performed autonomously by learners in the construction and reconstruction of reality. In opposition to Piaget's intrasubjective, self-regulating assumption, subjective competences came to be seen as the result of intersubjective, communicative competence, which, in turn, can only emerge on the basis of communicative processes (Sutter and Charlton, 2002: 134). Consequently, the teacher's function is, in Vygotsky's interactionist view, that of an expert who implements his or her knowledge in collaboration with the learners. Knowledge acquisition equals sharing activities rather than internalizing individual cognitive structures (Sutter and Charlton, 2002: 141). Expert and peer feedback, which Nunan (1991: 87) refers to as 'conferencing' and which he contextualizes in terms of discovery learning, are seen as essential elements of the learning process. Collaborative learning involves the following steps (Collins *et al.*, 1989):

1. Modelling on the part of the expert
2. Individual encouragement on the part of the expert

3. Scaffolding and fading, i.e. gradual withdrawal of the expert for the sake of learner empowerment
4. Articulation of newly acquired and learned knowledge structures on the part of the learners
5. Learner reflection.

Contemporary educational theory subscribes to a combined approach, which is informed by both approaches described above. *Sensu* the tenets of 'interactionist constructivism' (Sutter, 1999), subjects construct cognitive structures both independently and in interaction with other individuals.

Following from and opposing Chomsky's (1965) notion, I shall, in what follows, discuss three different approaches to *literary* competence. First, Culler (1975), a structuralist indebted to Chomsky, presupposes a finite, complete set of rules contained within the literary system of a human being. Every human being owns an 'implicit understanding of the operations of literary discourse' (Culler, 1975: 114), which may be understood as *acquired* knowledge of literature, including, for instance, tropes, themes and genres. In other words, Culler cannot help departing from Chomsky's radical approach on account of the truism that knowledge of literary structures can only develop gradually with a growing experience in reading fictional and poetic texts or, for that matter, observing dramatic forms on stage. This dynamic, diachronic notion of competence corresponds with Hymes's (1971) organic concept of communicative competence, which draws on Piaget's stages of cognitive development rather than Chomsky's synchronic concept. Hymes deviates from Chomsky in that his concept of competence is strongly influenced by the communicative function of language rather than the idea of language as a system of rules. Communicative competence not only contains grammatical competence (vocabulary, grammar, phonology, orthography and discourse knowledge) but includes pragmatic aspects such as interactional skills, cultural framework, illocutionary functions and sociolinguistic variations of human discourse.

Another dividing feature between Culler and Chomsky is the Chomskyan distinction between linguistic universals and specific idiomatic knowledge, whereas for Culler, literary competence is universal (for all languages). Like Chomsky, Culler emphasizes literature as a rule system, disregarding the individual 'use' component.

I contend that literary competence, which is a multiple concept comprising a set of distinctly operating subcompetences, is both learned (through formal teaching) and acquired (through natural exposure). In opposition to Culler, I argue that literary structures are just as dynamic and use-related as linguistic structures. Furthermore, there is no such thing as a universal set of literary rules, or a maximally competent literary subject (in analogy to Chomsky's ideal speaker-listener). Literary conventions are historically relative phenomena, which are, from a diachronic perspective, continually extended, modified and subverted to varying degrees in individual language communities. Similarly, literary forms are permanently developing, evolving, appearing and disappearing, processes which have to be observed by learners and 'experts' alike, so as to enable them to compare and contrast formal variations.

Hubert Ivo (1971) developed the concept further. His approach was informed by demands predominant during the late 1960s, namely that young people should acquire skills that will facilitate their orientation and proactive participation in their particular socio-cultural environments. This demand should be addressed particularly in the literary classroom. Ivo distinguishes between critical and poetic competence, which, as he maintains, should be reflected in teaching objectives. Under poetic competence, Ivo subsumes three aspects: understanding poetically encoded texts, understanding poetic encoding and the ability to sojourn in fictional worlds. Poetically encoded texts are, in Ivo's view, texts in which language is superimposed with secondary structures which deliberately deviate from standardized usage. To identify such deviations, readers need to have acquired knowledge of standard forms and usage. Therefore, understanding poetically encoded texts is an acquired, largely unreflected skill which can hardly be taught formally but rather evolves through repeated exposure to poetically encoded texts. Understanding poetic encoding takes learners a step further as it confirms them in what they can do already. Provided learners are able to identify poetic language, the chances are that they will soon be able to identify 'irregular', poetic structures and patterns and name them according to their form and function. Finally, the ability to project one's own consciousness into fictional worlds for a limited period of time, and thereby experience previously unfamiliar situations, helps to develop the ability to regulate one's own life and routines prospectively.

On the other hand, Ivo's concept of critical competence comprises the ability to reflect critically on literary texts, their fictionality, reception and effects and the ability to analyse contemporary literary communication processes and their message about historical and social issues. The problem that Haas (2001) sees in this approach is a tendency towards generalization, which threatens to neglect the emotional componence of the learner. Haas further points out that, following Ivo, during the 1980s the emphasis was on critical, and during the 1990s on poetic competence. Based on Ivo's subcategorization, Haas (2001) suggests an entire taxonomy of literary (sub)competences:

1. By *literary competence*, Haas means the ability to connect to a text affectively and cognitively. In my view, the choice of term is rather unfortunate as it may cause confusions with the superordinate term 'literary competence'. I will thus call this aspect of literary competence *receptive-interactive competence*.
2. *Emotive competence* is to Haas a vital aspect, which draws on the latest findings of neurolinguistics and brain research. It encompasses any ability to respond to a text emotionally in terms of identifying oneself with it to a certain degree upon reading it. Performative evidence of emotive competence may be any spontaneous response to reading, such as the expression of emotions, empathy and sympathy with characters, which are also manifestations of emotional intelligence.

3. *Creative competence* refers to creative productivity that manifests itself in reaction to what has been read and learned about a text. Haas sees in this aspect an elementary human need to interact and interfere with objects, to change them and experience oneself as a 'co-author' in the artistic process.

4. *Emancipatory competence* comprises three aspects of the learner's autonomization process: the ability to make independent decisions as to how to deal with a literary text, the ability to immerse and lose oneself in an aesthetic text and thereby gain a distance from everyday life, and the ability to solve psychological, interhuman problems on the basis of previous reading experience.

5. *Projectory competence* is closely related to emancipatory competence in that it means the ability to mediate between the fictional and the real world in order to deduce concrete action plans for everyday life.

6. The concept of *aesthetic competence* corresponds to Culler's idea of being able to identify the poetological structure of an aesthetic text, to analyse stylistic and formal elements in order to arrive at an interpretation and an attempt to comprehend authorial intentions and strategies on the basis of linguistic and organizational evidence.

7. *Critical competence* manifests itself in the learner's ability to read, understand and evaluate a text critically, under ideological, socio-political and ethical criteria. Evidently, to achieve this level of competence, a considerable amount of background information is required, which may be reserved for advanced readers, yet can be provided to a certain extent by teachers in the form of informational input.

For my current investigation, which aims predominantly at advanced learners and readers (see Chapter 5.4) yet presupposes unfamiliarity with literary hypertext on the part of the learners, I shall take a closer look at specific aspects of literary competence which seem appropriate for advanced, post-A-level learners (approximately 19 to 20 years of age). At this stage it needs to be conceded that Haas's taxonomy has considerable shortcomings, especially with regard to the extended mediality of contemporary concepts of literature, which he fails to take into account. My first emphasis is thus on *creative competence*, particularly in relation to the role of writing, which requires highly complex cognitive and motoric skills. There are no phonetic, physical or physiognomic aids that may be used by the sender to indicate certain nuances of meaning. Similarly, writing requires detailed knowledge of various text types and their underlying structural and stylistic conventions. Therefore, inexperienced writers have to learn how to reflect critically on language, style, and the organization of knowledge in order to create a piece of writing that will be understood in the intended way (bearing in mind that, in a hypertextual paradigm, unintended readings may be the writer's main intention, which further complicates the composition process).

The significance of writing in literary pedagogy has increased over the past few decades, particularly with regard to cognitive processes and the construction of human knowledge. Since the advent of electronic text processing programmes, writing has been revolutionized in that it has come to be seen as a process rather than a product. In this regard, Flower and Hayes (1981) propose a three-stage model, which presents writing as a complex process that involves drafting, writing and rewriting. They distinguish between four basic, constantly interacting elements: planning (content and structure), converting concepts into language, self-monitoring and re-visiting. Ong (1982) further asserts that writing restructures consciousness, which allows human beings to rearrange their semantic networks. Especially the *creative* engagement with text helps prevent writer's blocks and establish a momentum of *flow*[8] (Csikszentmihalyi, 1990; Paefgen, 1999).

Among the advantages of *collaborative* writing projects is the fact that individual decisions are encouraged yet have to be aligned to those of others, which supports the development of social competence by means of joint ventures as well as compromising and converging ideas. In this respect, Smith and Kollock (1999) consider a triad of interaction, communication and coordination to be the essence of student collaboration.

Hypertext structures may be regarded as providing an ideal framework for collaborative creative writing, as they are flexible and expand infinitely (see Nielsen, 1990). Study into research-oriented hypertextual collaborative writing has been done by Trigg and Suchmann (1999), who describe a Note-Cards project. They come to the conclusion that hypertext is appropriate for collaborative writing because it allows 'the coexistence of multiple overlapping organizations of information' (*ibid.*: 46), which is particularly useful 'if authors are in the process of progressively reorganizing their work' (*ibid.*: 51). Furthermore, they emphasize the possibility of annotating authoring and editing activities. Finally, collaborators feel urged to adapt discursively to previously unfamiliar medial structures, which opens up possibilities of reciprocal dialogic learning.

3   Media Competence in Literary Studies

> *Digital literature requires authors to have multimedia competence.*
> *(Simanowski, 1999b: 4)*

My second emphasis is on *media* in the sense of *hypermedia competence*, which is not listed in Haas's catalogue but is indispensable for hypertext pedagogy. As Groeben (2002) points out, the term 'media' refers to technological means of communication on the one hand and their implications for processes of socialization and the development of individual personality, identity and world pictures on the other (160). Similarly, media competence is, according to Baacke (1999), Theunert (1999) and Sutter and Charlton (2002), a pluralist concept, which includes aspects of understanding, operation, implementation, production, critical evaluation and reciprocity (Dewe and Sander, 1996).

Understanding media requires linguistic, semiotic, logical and sociological knowledge, which enables recipients to reconstruct semantic structures of media phenomena. Of particular importance for developing receptive strategies is theoretical and practical media knowledge. The practical side, i.e. operating media, implies a variety of psycho-motor skills such as reading, writing, technical knowledge, and what, in the field of New Media, has come to be described by the buzz phrase 'ICT skills'. Implementing media necessitates experience with everyday psychological phenomena such as the implications of learner autonomy. Producing media warrants a wide range of technical skills, knowledge about media production and distribution and aesthetic awareness, which are needed for both effective media design and cogent argument. In order to be able to comment critically on media phenomena, individuals need to possess normative knowledge about social values as well as the ability to question acquired concepts rather than taking them for granted. Finally, the reciprocity of media usage implies the ability to communicate and collaborate through media.

Groebel (1997) discusses media competence from the teacher's point of view, who has to be able to implement media so as to facilitate autonomous learning. This requires not only technical know-how on the part of the teacher, but, more importantly, factual knowledge about distinct media qualities, semiotics, production, and the critical evaluation of sender–receiver relationships, particularly as regards digital media and manifestations of virtual reality.

Adopting a diachronic perspective, Tulodziecki (1997–1998) follows the history of media pedagogy since the beginning of the twentieth century. Taking international discrepancies into consideration, the overall development started with an attitude which sought to preserve traditional forms and protect national, largely book-centred heritage from an invasion of innovative media such as film and television. This attitude was soon revised, as film and later television gradually became accepted as art forms in their own right (in the case of film) and as important catalysts of Western democracy and capitalism (in the case of television and Hollywood film). Almost instantly, this also led to various critical approaches (e.g. by Foucault, Althusser and Barthes), which have sought to deconstruct the media as subliminal carriers of mainstream ideology.

With regard to hypertext pedagogy, operating and understanding the medium are the two most problematic, as well as most intimately related aspects, which almost necessarily generate a media- and self-critical, 'deconstructivist' stance in the reader, especially with regard to the palpability of textual, intertextual and meta(hyper)textual semantics. Similarly, the New Media, especially the internet with its nonlinear forms of organization, require a variety of specific reading and interpretation strategies, not to mention a plethora of technical skills when it comes to producing media texts. In relation to this, Daiber (1999) and Simanowski (2002c) emphasize that antilinear narrative, which may be regarded as the essence of hypertext, is largely constituted by the existence of hyperlinks and that consequently, in a New Media paradigm, literary hermeneutics needs to be extended by adding the hyperlink as a seminal analytical criterion.

With this in mind, and by drawing on Bernstein's (1998) linking patterns (see Chapter 1.1), Wenz (2000, 2001) identifies three main hypertextual reading styles: the reader, the zapper and the player. Wenz (2001) maintains that readers who are accustomed to zapping television channels are most likely to translate that strategy into reading hypertext. Accordingly, readers who often play computer games will apply more explorative, exhaustive reading strategies in their intention to find out about the scope of a hypertext, its layers and boundaries. Inexperienced hypertext readers, on the other hand, will most likely transfer their habitually linear reading styles to hyper-documents and thus spend a lot of time reading them thoroughly and comprehensively.

The *desideratum* of meta-media knowledge holds true in particular for literary hypertext, which generally instrumentalizes the lack or simulation of navigational aids (maps, dynamic content pages, history lists, search engines) for aesthetic effect. Furthermore, hypertext authors mostly leave the scope and level of networking complexity unaccounted for, thus leaving the reader uncertain as to the length and difficulty of the receptive process. Textual meaning – if there is any – is only in the minority of cases discernible or indeed reliably inferrable. Therefore, readers have to be more pro-active and autonomous in terms of constructing textual coherence than they would be in tackling a conventional print text. What is more, user interfaces vary such that, as a matter of fact, every hypertext presents a different medial form in its own right, the operability of which needs exploring before any serious reading can occur in the first place (Flender and Christmann, 2002: 219). Thus, reader expectations are bound to be broken from hypertext to hypertext, which, paradoxically, constitutes an expectation in itself.

As Kuhlen (1991) asserts, hypertext in particular demands a new form of competence, which depends on both theoretical and practical knowledge and skill. First, hypertext is essentially dialogic, i.e. conceptualized in such a way as to enable system-user interaction and multi-user cooperation. The possibility of actually contributing to an already existing literary work, or rather work-in-process, requires a higher degree of creativity on the part of the reader than in a completed, self-contained print medium. Needless to say, familiarity with run-of-the-mill internet functionalities such as using a mouse to click-activate electronic processes as well as a keyboard to actually type in one's own written contribution is a prerequisite to handling hypertext in the first place. Second, narrative hypertexts in particular defy any sense of delimitation. Instead of demarcating boundaries, the reader is left uncertain as to the mere physical extensions of the text. Even if the number of lexias is in fact countable, which is the case in software-based, offline hypertexts like the Eastgate product range, this does not mean that any reader will ever manage to visit all of them, let alone experience every possible plot. Given an inexperienced hypertext reader, this is bound to result in uncertainty and frustration. As Schnierer (2003: 94) puts it:

even a closed hypertext, however, does not have to have limits visible to the reader. Readers new to hypertext are usually disturbed by texts whose size cannot be established. Invisible textual boundaries initially work in much the same way as non-existent ones, even though they do delimit the reading process eventually.

Third, hypertext represents content in a nonlinear format. This does not necessarily imply, however, that each node contains one self-contained episodic plot section. On the contrary, 'hyper-' poetic licence very often prevents readers from 'adding' episodic knowledge of the narrative to form a coherent whole. Nodes frequently raise ideas without developing them any further. Neither do they provide satisfying answers to questions arising during the reading process. Especially when perceived in a nonsequential order, the non-paragraphic nature of nodes becomes strikingly and often painfully obvious to readers, whose major task is to form their own mental plot from their individualized reading sequence, which changes upon every revisitation of the hypertext. Problems such as 'cognitive overhead' (Conklin, 1987: 40), disorientation ('getting lost in hyperspace', see Edwards and Hardman, 1989) and 'informational short-sightedness' (Conklin, 1987: 40) are generally caused by associative browsing mechanisms, which are considerably more randomized in literary than informational hypertext, as the reader does not read with a specific informational aid in mind. As I discussed earlier, such 'indeterminacy' (I use the term deliberately to allude to Iser's concept) forms an essential part of hypertext aesthetics. Therefore, its effects on the reader must be taken as necessary elements of the hypertext reading experience. Cognitive overhead, disorientation and informational short-sightedness arise from hypertextual poetic licence. Coherence is deliberately undermined by the elision of cohesive markers or other means of helping the reader form a uniquely reliable, coherent mental model of the text.

Instead, on a macrostructural level, the hyperlink serves as a major cohesive element. From the vantage point of the reader, this requires a continual decision-making process, which becomes increasingly random if the chosen path does not exhibit any logically structured sequence of events or if it does not provide answers to hypothetical questions that motivate the reader's choice. From the perspective of the hypertext author, links are conventionally used to illustrate connections between ideas. These connections have to be most transparent and intersubjectively predictable in factual hypertexts. Authors of literary hypertexts, on the other hand, tend to subvert the transparency of interconnectedness deliberately to achieve certain aesthetic effects. However, most literary hypertexts are situated on a continuum between those two poles. Thus, the linking of character names to lexias which provide direct or indirect characterizations is a widespread structural device, which is used, for instance, by Ruth Nestvold in *Cutting Edges, Or, A Web of Women*, by Stefan Maskiewicz in *Quadrego*, and, as the dominant navigational device, by Geoff Ryman in *253*. Linking names to characterizations or biographical background is, in fact, one of the few commonly applied strategies that aid the reader in making sense of the text and creating an at least partly cogent mental model of the relationships between characters.

The main difficulties with links are decisions relating to their number, distribution, transparency and location. These decisions reflect the writer's idea of textual synthesis, involving the level of complexity and playfulness, as well as the question regarding which lexias he or she considers to be key. Such lexias may be worked into loops, which cause the reader to revisit them on a frequent basis. As Duguay (1999) points out, decisions pertaining to linking strategies present an additional challenge to conventional decisions, which are mostly to do with the inclusion and elision of information, as well as their spatial arrangement.

In sum, what the user needs in order to tackle hypertext effectively is an extended media competence profile, which takes into account the distinctly low level of macro- and microstructural predictability and conventionality of the textual genre. Such a profile needs to exhibit specifically versatile receptive and productive strategies, as well as the ability to create coherence more independently from surface structure clues than in the case of linear print text. That these skills can indeed be learned by repeated exposure and regular practice, which help users develop procedural and receptive strategies, has been shown by numerous empirical studies (summarized in Hammond, 1993).

Yet another decisive component of hypertext, which comes into play particularly with second-generation hypermedia, is the interplay between different semiotic systems. William Blake, one of the pioneers of intermediality, combined word and image to produce complementary levels of meaning. Vaughan (1999: 27–8) writes that his:

> own position as being equally gifted in both [media] enabled him to explore the interchange in a unique manner. For with him painting was not simply the illustration of poetry, or even its rival. It was a counterpart, a genuine other half. Indeed, one might see the relationship as that of two voices singing a duet.

Most hypermedia artists pick up this convention and explore it by adding sound, animation and film in multifarious ways. Hence, hypertexts cannot be 'read' and interpreted solely on a graphemic basis. The competent reader has to take into account those various interacting symbolic levels, their weighting in the context as a whole, and the extent to which text in the traditional sense is supplemented or complemented by other semiotic systems.

To sum up, in order to develop a hypertext-specific form of media competence, learners need to:

- become aware of the potentially discouraging effects caused by associative browsing, which I consider the most common manner of navigating other than sequential proceeding

- develop accessing and reading strategies which take account of such adverse effects and integrate them into their reading experience, which eventually results in an aesthetics of revis(itat)ion (see Chapter 1.5)
- incorporate considerations of hypermedia synaesthetics in their interpretive strategies, i.e. they need to be sensitized to the aesthetic interplay between various semiotic systems in order to include it in their interpretation of hypermedia artefacts
- develop an awareness of the vast diversity of linking types and strategies, which form the foundation of a distinctly hypertextual reading experience, and take them into account when interpreting hypertexts
- enter the paradigm of 'productive reception' as the foundation of aesthetic pleasure, for which the physicality of hypertext, which, due to its virtual nature, can only be of an abstract kind, only serves as the building blocks or the 'raw material' for individualized, autonomous understanding (Kuhlen, 1991: 43).

In conclusion, to fit into a hypertextual paradigm, literary competence needs to be revisited. In the age of hypermedia, literary competence must be perceived to include creative interaction with the New Media, collaborative projects, and productive transformation of knowledge (subject-oriented). Add the recent developments in the realm of cybertext, and one has to include the willingness to give in, at least partly, to the stylized control mechanisms of the empowered machine and to 'play along' as human constituent of a remotely controlled performance. Given that hypertext, hypermedia and cybertext are based on a variety of symbolic levels, which continuously create new forms of representations, it may hence be argued that it is 'necessary for users to develop new areas of [literary] competence' (Heibach, 2004: 49). Literary education cannot content itself with the conventionalities of verbal art, but has to incorporate aspects of multimodal, as well as 'code' education. Finally, the nature of the *medium* itself has to be taken into consideration on a synchronic, diachronic and contrastive basis.

Chapter 5

Hypertext in the Literature Classroom

1 Psychological Implications

It appears that arbitrarily imposed semantic nets may not be adequate to overcome personal ones or at least not directly map onto learners' knowledge.
(*Jonassen, 1991: 164*)

This chapter focuses on psychological research into the potential of hypertext structures with regard to human cognition and learning, as well as theories about hypertext pedagogy. It provides a survey of projects that have employed hypertext in the literary and creative writing classroom, and discusses the upsides and downsides of hypertext as a teaching object and method. Finally, it reports the findings of an action research project using hypertext to help students develop literary competence in an extended sense, as outlined in Chapter 4.

As mentioned in the previous chapter, constructivism has had a considerable role to play in opening up pedagogy to new technologies, which were and still are promising to support the development of learner autonomy. In this respect, hypertext as a tool for organizing and structuring information has, since its first heyday in the early 1990s, become of particular interest to cognitive and educational psychology. Following up Bush's idea of a memory expander operating by association (1945/1975), psychologists and early representatives of Artificial Intelligence research held the euphoric yet largely hypothetical view that hypertextual structures resembled human neurons and thus corresponded with the associative networks of human memory (Fiderio, 1988; Jonassen, 1989). Therefore, it was assumed that, if hypertext knowledge bases were to be organized to reflect an expert's or teacher's semantic knowledge structure, learners would adopt these structures over time (Jonassen, 1990: 142; cf. Shavelson, 1974). This theory came to be known as the cognitive plausibility hypothesis (Jonassen, 1986). The confidence with which it was propagated was based on the neurological observation that neuronal activation increases the strength of 'important' nodes in contrast to other, less important ones, which are, as a result, weakened. Given this insight, cognitive psychologists assume that more frequently revisited information is retained longer and more readily accessible than less frequently rehearsed and retrieved material (e.g. Dell, 1986; Dell *et al.*, 1997). The validity of this assumption, as well as its relevance for the design and revision of learning material and curricula, have been supported by a number of studies (e.g. Jensen, 1996, 1998). Nevertheless, the conclusion made with regard to hypertext learning, namely that hypertext structures facilitate and improve learning efficiency, proved to be more problematic than it appeared to be at the outset.

The cognitive plausibility hypothesis was based on the fact that human neurons are made up of intricately interconnected dendrites and axons, which account for our associative capacities. As Norman (1976) confirms, learning operates in terms of constructing new structures through generating new nodes and interconnecting them with each other and existing nodes. Learner knowledge is thus reorganized in such as way as to accommodate new information. Consequently, it was assumed that web structures, with their variously interconnected nodes, are likely to be more easily processed than conventional linear structures, and might therefore facilitate learning. On the basis of Schema Theory (Rumelhart and Ortony, 1977), psychologists considered those analogies highly useful, particularly with respect to mapping expert cognitive structures onto semantic maps, which could then be used as powerful, empowering learning templates (cf. Jonassen and Mandel, 1990; McKnight *et al.*, 1991).[1] Furthermore, it was believed that providing instant, multilinear access to information via associative links rather than logical linearization might further increase learning efficiency. With regard to retaining information via hypertext, however, this hypothesis could not be verified. McKnight *et al.* (1990) performed a series of empirical studies comparing learner performance (accuracy of memory and processing speed) with linear text and hypertext. The result (*ibid.*: 16) was that:

> in general, subjects performed better with the linear-format texts than with the hypertexts. The linear formats led to significantly more accurate performance and to significantly less time spent in the index and contents.

The authors' overarching conclusion is that 'more claims have been made on hypertext's behalf than the experimental evidence has been able to support' (McKnight *et al.*, 1991: 120). In fact, in terms of epistemology, hypertexts may be considered of similar or even lesser value than books (Whalley, 1990), an observation which, according to Jones (1989), also holds true for incidental (unintentional and unconscious) learning.

Notwithstanding the above-mentioned results, experts agree that hypertext is indeed a powerful tool when it comes to the major intellectual activities practised in educational institutions, namely storage, rapid information retrieval (particularly when using search engines and topic-related portals) and browsing, as well as easy control and manipulation of cognitive material, which includes note-taking and annotation facilities (Marchionini and Shneiderman, 1988; Leggett *et al.*, 1990; McKnight *et al.*, 1991). Therefore, today the most widely held view maintains that hypertext structures should serve learners to gather rather than acquire information, the latter of which is perceived to be more effectively done by means of linear, logically structured documents.[2]

Furthermore, as Duffy and Knuth (1990) argue, the degree to which hypertext structures can enhance deep learning is largely due to 'the pedagogy of the professor rather than . . . the database'. Hence, hypertext as a pedagogic tool has to be organically incorporated in a carefully planned syllabus, which, as will be shown later in this chapter, integrates conventional teaching approaches with a constructive use of the technology. The following section outlines some major pedagogic approaches undertaken so far with respect to implementing hypertext in the literary and creative writing classroom, thus providing the research context in which my own empirical approach (Chapter 5.4) is placed.

2   Hypertext as a Tool in the Literary and Creative Writing Classroom

Hypertext allows for a move away from the monologic towards discrepancies.
(Morgan and Andrews, 1999: 89)

Lack of interest and knowledge about digital forms of literature other than 'paper under glass' can be found in many teachers of literature, which is often due to a lack of hypermedia competence, confidence and the willingness to experiment with non-printed forms of writing. Similarly, the fact that hypertext has not been canonized in terms of being explicitly suggested by the National Curriculum adds to a general sense of suspiciousness and uncertainty. Nevertheless, many an innovative teaching approach has been taken by progressive pedagogues and learning psychologists with a view to exploring the didactic potential of hypertext in the literary and creative writing classroom.

Only a few years after its first emergence in the mid-1980s, literary hypertext was 'discovered' by educationalists, who started to investigate Bush's and Nelson's technological concept of interlinking and accessing documents associatively in terms of its potential for teaching literature and writing skills. The general educational benefits to be gained from classroom hypertext applications, which served literary educationalists as a point of departure, are summarized by DeWitt (1999: 118):

- Hypertext gives students a new, powerful tool for accessing and creating knowledge.
- Hypertext can help students make connections between seemingly unrelated ideas.
- Hypertext promotes organized and integrative thought.
- Hypertext encourages collaborative learning.
- Hypertext gives students easier access to their own writing.

The major argument among researchers was that hypertext stands in harsh contrast to traditional writing, as well as to the objectives of traditional writing instruction. Similarly, major emphasis was placed on hypertext's capability of organizing, saving and transmitting information. Following up on these obser-vations, a number of educational theorists and practitioners in literary studies, namely Joyce (1988/2002b), Howell (1990), Delany and Landow (1991) and Landow (1992/1997), pioneered research into hypertext's potential for the literary and creative writing classroom. Particularly in the early hypertext community surrounding George Landow at Brown University, there was wide-spread enthusiasm about the:

> multivocality, open-endedness, multilinear organization, greater inclusion of nontextual information, and fundamental reconfiguration of authorship, including ideas of authorial property, and of status relations in the text. (Landow, 1994: 36)

Putting this euphoria in the context of educational constructivism, Landow (1992/1997: 163) emphasizes learner autonomy and responsibility, while Kaplan and Moulthrop (1993: 264) assert that hypertextual composition tech-niques can be performed 'in a much richer context than the typed or word-pro-cessed essay can provide'. Hence, for a writer to be successful, he or she has to be familiar with a set of techniques that illustrate media competence.

Landow's most widely quoted projects include *The Dickens Web* (Landow, 1992), the *In Memoriam Web* (Landow and Lanestedt, 1992) and *The Postcolonial Web* (Landow, 2005), which are collaborative educational products containing critical readings and essays by both students and lecturers of literature. Some of them are open, web-based systems, and scholars from around the world are encouraged to contribute to their growing structure. Another co-authored pub-lication by Landow (Delany and Landow, 1991) is the volume *Hypermedia and Literary Studies*, which locates hypertext and hypermedia issues in the context of the humanities. As well as outlining hypertext projects and systems established at Brown University, this essay collection provides instructions on how to link literary works and looks at specific curricular programmes and strategies.

Another literary educationalist to embrace hypertext as a new teaching environment is Lanham (1989, 1993), who politicizes the pedagogic role of hypertext in literary studies by arguing that the new electronic environment is indeed compatible with it, as it 'democratizes the world of arts and letters', and, *ergo*, 'value structures, markets ideological as well as financial and theoretical, will be reassessed' (1993: 23). In response to this, contends Lanham, the realm of literary studies will have to be adapted in such a way as to 'accommodate [it] to the electronic world in which that world will increasingly deal' (*ibid.*: 23).

To refer back to the beginning of this book, let me once again mention Joyce (1988/2002b), who proposes a binary distinction between exploratory and con-structive hypertext. Taking this distinction as a starting point, we can identify essentially two widespread didactic methods of applying hypertext in the lit-erary classroom, which are, at least so far as creative writing is concerned, gen-erally kept separate from each other.[3] First, hypertextually organized websites are employed for information-gathering and learning to read a variety of text types on the internet. In this sense, reading equals what Joyce terms 'exploring'. Literary websites that facilitate this kind of web-based learning include 'paper-under-glass' collections such as *Project Gutenberg*, *The Perseus Digital Library* (Crane, 2005) for classical, medieval and Renaissance literature, and the comprehensive *Voice of the Shuttle* website (Liu, 2005) for philosophical writings. They further include critical commentaries on canonical works, such as Barnes & Noble's *SparkNotes*, and websites providing information about individual authors and their works. Among the most comprehensive, pedagogically oriented of these hypertexts are, for instance, *Triangulating Shakespeare* (Marx, 2002), *The Thoreau Project* (Calliope Inc, 2005) and Christiane Paul's Eastgate Hypertext *Unreal City: A Hypertext Guide to T. S. Eliot's The Waste Land* (1995). Finally, there are hybrid phenomena like *The Victorian Web* and *The Dickens Web*, which are created and explored by learners on the one hand and provide both primary and secondary research material on the other. In this respect, Landow's 'Webs' fall only partly into the category of exploratory hypertext.

Second, on the constructive side, there are creative and expository writing workshops, which set out to encourage students to write their own aesthetic and critical texts, either individually or in collaboration with part of or the whole class. Tools that are reported to have been used for such projects are, in quasi-chronological order of their origination, HyperCard for Macintosh (since 1987); Notecards (since the late 1980s); Aquanet; Trellis; Dexter; SEPIA (Bolter, 2001: 38) and, since the popularization of the World Wide Web in the early 1990s, various versions and adaptations of HTML, as well as Java and JavaScript, which can nowadays be circumvented elegantly by means of web-editing software like Frontpage, Flash and Dreamweaver.

Inspired by constructivism and what they regard as 'a scarcity of contextual studies on hypertext and writing' bringing together theory and practice, DeWitt and Strasma (1999: 4) have published a compilation of essays reporting on empirical teaching projects investigating 'the practical application of hypertext theory within the contexts of our writing classroom' (*ibid.*: 5). The authors describe qualitative studies investigating pupils and students of various age groups engaging in hypertext and hypermedia writing activities. Bearing in mind that the rapid evolution of HTML editors and other computer software has made older applications like Storyspace, HyperCard, Guide etc. obsolete, the majority of the projects are, on a methodological basis, no longer up to date. Be that as it may, the volume provides a highly relevant footing for my case study in that it contains essential research undertaken in the area of free, and creative rather than expository, academic writing. Research done by McKillop and Myers (1999), for instance, leads the authors to question earlier claims that composing processes in hypertext may generate more democratic structures and freedom among learners. Instead, their findings suggest that it is, in fact, the role of the teacher and of traditional narrative structures that becomes stronger, as the students struggle to find a meaningful pathway through hypermedia space.

Further concern is voiced by Saul (1999), who reports conflicts arising from what I would identify as a lack in media competence, which interferes with and disturbs the actual objectives of teaching writing. Clearly, learners who are not familiar with a New Media environment take time to become acquainted with the software as well as with the concepts surrounding hypertext authoring. Hence, coordinators of hypertext seminars have to take into consideration temporal restrictions on the teaching of extra-technological subject matter.

Norton *et al.* (1999) contend that making decisions concerning ways of linking documents is one of the greatest difficulties students encounter in collaborating on hypertext. The authors develop a 'hyperphoric grammar' for hypertext references, and a punctuation system that is aimed to help students and teachers to describe and negotiate hypertext structures, allowing them to plan and name relationships between text before linking them.

Another essential study is provided by Strasma (1999), who suggests that using nonelectronic hypertext is a useful or even essential part of creating electronic hypertext. Equally significant is Gary Ryan's (1999) exploration of quasi-Socratic, 'epistemic discourse', which his students transferred into the computer medium, using hypertext tools to represent the essentially fluid, procedural nature of writing.

Having outlined the major research previously undertaken into literary hypertext pedagogy, I will, in what follows, take a closer look at hypertext's motivational potential, and discuss the ways in which it may positively influence learning. To obtain a realistic basis for mapping out my empirical research project, I shall revisit a number of claims made by hypertext theorists about psychological implications of this literary media genre. As it turns out, particularly with respect to hypertext pedagogy, a variety of misconceptions need to be demystified and rectified in order to arrive at a working basis for any didactic decisions.

3   Hypertext, Motivation and Learning

> *The combination of technology and constructivism, however, offers possibilities undreamed of until recently.*
> *(Cunningham et al., 1993: 45)*

To consolidate the theoretical and practical dimensions of hypertext and contextualize them with regard to the requirements of the constructivist classroom, I dedicate a considerable portion of the following section to debunking and rectifying some major misconceptions about the psychological and epistemological implications of hypertext processing. I do so with a view to providing a realistic image of hypertext as an object and instrument of developing literary competence. Furthermore, to address one of the central tenets of constructivism and strike a balance between areas of potential difficulty and utility, I investigate hypertext's specific motivational potential and the ways in which it may have a positive impact on student learning.

My overall approach is based on the widely held and empirically under-pinned assumption that *intrinsic motivation* stimulates deep learning, i.e. learning that is long-term and therefore more efficient than surface learning, which is often facilitated by extrinsic motivation. More specifically, intrinsic motivation occurs inside learners and is stimulated by personal relevance, enjoyment, interest and curiosity. It helps learners to realize that the learning activity in question will assist them in obtaining personally valued accomplishments, as well as in integrating themselves with the world and with other people (Deci and Ryan, 1985; Chance, 1992). Extrinsic motivation, on the other hand, is cre-ated by external stimuli, in other words positive reinforcements, or rewards, which include material (money, gifts) as well as abstract (good marks, atten-tion, love) tokens. Extrinsic motivation is associated with the behaviorist learn-ing paradigm initiated by Watson (e.g. 1912), Pavlov (1927) and Skinner (e.g. 1953), which is mainly concerned with individuals' responses to given stimuli rather than their interests or cognitive dispositions and processes.

Among the 'myths' put forward by 'evangelical' believers in hypertext's psy-chological efficiency is the question of reader empowerment. In contrast to many early enthusiasts, who consider hypertext readers as 'wreaders' (e.g. Landow, 1992/1997), i.e. (co-)authors, empirical studies on hypertextual reading patterns have found that literary hypertexts are in fact highly 'con-trolled environments' (Wenz, 2001: 44), which are more likely to impede than to facilitate learning, as they do not increase but reduce the single reader's free-dom. This is mainly due to a lack of web views, content pages and other naviga-tion aids, as well as the aforementioned subversion of mutually supplementary bottom-up and top-down processing, aspects which readers have to bear in mind and get used to when embarking on their first hypertextual experiences. According to Douglas (1992) and Dobson (1999), the most typical reactions are surprise, confusion, frustration and even agitation. These are partly due to obscure, disconcerting linking structures, and partly to the fact that many hypertexts have a cyclical structure (cf. Bernstein, 1998), which makes the reader return to the same lexias over and over again. As Douglas (1992) points out, readers of complex hypertexts typically lack 'any tangible sense of a macro-structure which could give significance to the elements they encounter[ed] in each individual narrative segment'. A further observation Dobson (1999) makes is that the more time a reader spends on one hypertext, the higher the pace of reading, which subjects explained in terms of unrest and impatience. This response runs counter to the experience of reading linear texts, which is characterized by an increase in immersion and attention over the same period of time. Hence, considering the relative inferiority of the hypertext reader, alternative motivational means need to be found to increase accessibility.

Second, we have to revisit the cognitive plausibility hypothesis (Jonassen, 1986), which assumes that web structures resemble human cognition and there-fore facilitate learning. As discussed in Chapter 5.1, empirical findings do not support this claim. In fact, linear texts are more suitable for building new cognitive structures, whereas hypertext structures are perceived to be useful mostly for information retrieval, manipulation and storage, as well as for developing strategic and organizational skills.

Third, while hypertext does in fact offer new ways of reading and writing, this can only be useful if novice readers and writers know when to use which (reading) strategy. Particularly, linear reading needs to be encouraged, as hypertext readers tend to read superficially, in terms of browsing and searching. Thus, to prevent lethargy and surface learning, a didactically applicable hypertext needs to be organized in such a way as to invite new and, ideally, also close readings with every revisitation.

A final misconception is Bolter's (1992) simplifying assumption that links are essentially manifestations of Iser's semantic gap. Bolter (1992: 24) argues that:

> [w]hen Wolfgang Iser and Stanley Fish argue that the reader constitutes the text in the act of reading, they are describing hypertext. When the deconstructionists emphasize that a text is unlimited, that it expands to include its own interpretations – they are describing a hypertext, which grows with the addition of new links and elements.

It has to be objected that Iser and Fish understand the semantic gap metaphorically. Whereas semantic gaps are left open to be concretized by the reader, links are manifest and, above all, manually inserted by the author. Furthermore, visiting a link in a literary hypertext only rarely provides satisfying answers to the questions arising while reading lexias. As Aarseth (1997: 83) rightly explains, here we are dealing with a 'confusion of two different levels – between Ingarden's "real object" and "aesthetic object", that is, between physical reality and the construction in the observer's mind'.

Having said that, for hypertext we need an additional, third level of observation, which is situated between the manifest and the aesthetic object, or rather the mental representation of this object. In fact, we need to add the individual reading path, which constitutes the reader's physical and mental interaction with the text and forms the prerequisite of any mental representation(s).

Taking into consideration that, before the advent of the World Wide Web, text production, storage and publication took place in diverse media, which were also more often than not geographically disparate, it does not come as a surprise that the New Media requires a multiplicity of 'new' productive and receptive skills. These skills need to be seen in addition to recent innovations that have evolved in print-based literary pedagogy since the 1990s, largely initiated by constructivist learning philosophy, and mainly constitute a trend from teacher- and product-centredness towards learner-orientation and process-orientation. These relatively new paradigms have been implemented, for instance, by means of specifically learner-centred, creative rewriting experiments such as parodying stereotypical forms and topoi, inventing new beginnings, middles and ends, and genre transformation tasks (turning poems into narratives, narratives into dramas etc.). Such didactic approaches must, for their validity, be unconditionally embraced, as they invite learners to construct new cognitive structures from existing ones, largely by experimenting with and thereby appropriating the learning objects in question. Notably, such learning objects include, in the literary classroom, terminological, conceptual, formal, discursive, stylistic, strategic, interpersonal and communicative elements.

Clearly, empirical evidence suggests that some intrinsic qualities of literary hypertext put a high cognitive demand upon inexperienced readers, which may, unless appropriate pedagogic support is provided, result in resignation and negative learning curves. Therefore, it is crucial to carefully explore those intrinsic attributes that may have a positive motivational effect.[4] The brevity of lexias, for instance, needs to be mentioned. In the majority of literary hypertexts, lexias do not exceed the size of one page (or window). As short cognitive tasks are generally more willingly performed than long tasks, this feature may be considered an intrinsic motivational factor. That said, despite the microstructural motivational potential of text chunks, on a macrostructural level they can be demotivating, as 'culinary' readers may be disheartened by the fact that they cannot see any end of the story. To mitigate this concern, Landow (1992/1997) asserts that the shorter the lexia, the bigger the resulting text corpus, which may have a high motivational effect as learners quickly reach a stage of looking back on an already covered, large textual corpus – no matter whether they are exploring or constructing a hypertext. It has to be conceded, however, that great numbers of lexias infinitely complicate the organization process for the novice author. Consequently, learner-authors need to be told right from the beginning to organize their lexias by means of navigation maps or tree diagrams, such as those given in Dreamweaver, always bearing in mind that they may later hide or even delete them to enhance the specific hypertext-aesthetic effect on the reader.

In order to introduce hypertexts effectively to first-time readers, efforts need to be made to sequence the selection of texts in such a way as to meet those readers' levels of experience. Most (documented) hypertext projects have proceeded chronologically, putting hypertexts first that, in terms of complexity, would be more appropriate for advanced readers (e.g. *afternoon, a story, Victory Garden, Quibbling* etc.). More straightforward examples – in the sense of structural transparency, comprehensibility of scope and thematic clarity – that may more suitably be employed at an introductory stage include 'manageable', concise hypertexts such as Gavin Inglis's *Same Day Test*, Kate Pullinger's *The Breathing Wall* and Deena Larsen's *Marble Springs*. At an advanced level, structurally more demanding hypertexts could be combined with critical approaches, for example *Patchwork Girl* for (cyber-)feminism, *afternoon* for poststructuralism and deconstruction, *Grammatron* for science fiction and/or utopian studies, and *We Descend* for gothic and crime fiction. In such a way, hypertexts could be read and analysed in comparison with other 'canonical' texts of each literary tradition, for example Mary Shelley's *Frankenstein* for a diachronic approach to gender studies, James Joyce's *Finnegans Wake* or Milorad Pavić's *Dictionary of the Khazars* for poststructuralism, William Gibson's *Neuromancer* for science-fiction literature, and Umberto Eco's *The Name of the Rose* for ecclesiastic gothic and crime fiction.

I have previously argued (Chapter 1.4) that the concept of true (w)reader, or learner 'empowerment' via hypertext is only feasible in the case of collaborative reading and writing projects. Due to the fact that, on a communicative level, the two essential qualities of the internet are intertextual and inter-human networking (Heibach, 2003: 40), it is fair to assume that these qualities can have a bearing on hypertext-based collaborative learning projects, be they aesthetic or expository in nature. The internet invites multiple authorship and readership, which is realized in the form of geographically centred and decentred networks. One of their central psychological effects is the prevention of writer's block among those who struggle in situations where they have to produce individual pieces of writing. Simanowski's (2000c) concept of *social aesthetic* and Heibach's (2003) notion of *cooperative aesthetics* are, in this respect, particularly suitable to justify the didactic implementation of collaborative writing projects. Having said that, such learning networks cannot succeed unless a certain degree of geographically situated, face-to-face verbal discourse is granted. After all, as Bandura (1977), Vygotsky (1978) and Gadamer (1979) rightly contend, immediate social intercourse, i.e. face-to-face dialogue, or conversation, provides the necessary affective basis for students to learn from and inspire each other.

Provided that hypertext is used in collective projects, the motivational effects of joint reception and production have to be taken into account. As Turner (1974) emphasizes, so-called liminal situations are mostly experienced in groups, which represent a radical alternative to the solitary, individually confrontational aspects of daily life. The *communitas* feeling, as Turner calls it, arises from such shared activities as collaborative writing. This assumption may well be connected to Johnson-Eilola's (1994: 214–15) empirical finding that the hypertext form appears to allow diverging opinions within a group without causing conflict:

> In a collaborative hypertext the preservation of multiple voices – especially when *collaborative writing* indicates the maintenance of individual (but internally and externally connected) voices – might be one way in which students can make their own voices part of the conversation.

In other words, hypertext environments allow or even invite the simultaneous existence and equivalent representation of diverging opinions. In order, however, to prevent any dialectic stalemate, which may well occur if those opinions are fixed rather than dialectically developed in open discourse, a platform for learner discussion needs to be provided, which is most easily done in a traditional classroom environment.

Given appropriate guidance, hypertext readers develop a multiplicity of reading and interpretation techniques, which they may also learn to reflect on and emulate in their own writing. Wenz (2001) lists three basic reading strategies that have to be acquired by learners in order for them to be able to appreciate hypertext literature: browsing, searching and fragmented reading. These are closely connected to and developed in opposition to more conventional reading strategies used in related media such as books and other print media (e.g. linear reading, skimming and scanning), television (where zapping may be considered a pre-form of searching) and playing computer games (where browsing precedes exploring 'topographical' text space).

As previously written, hypertext's distinctive structural property is the hyperlink, which connects webpages (lexias) and gives electronic documents their distinctly relational character. The relationship between modular lexias can be described in terms of a continuum between aggregation, if documents are entirely separate and do not link to other pages, and integration, if documents are multiply interconnected to form a complex network (Raible, 1992). What is more, the fact that hyperlinks have to be planned and programmed by an author or a group of authors has a significant effect on the level of reader autonomy. Similarly, when we look at students as writers of hypertext, the link becomes a tool for them to practise summarizing and synthesizing texts, implicitly or explicitly, particularly when they are encouraged to name links in accordance with the contents of the target lexias (see DeWitt, 1999: 140).

A further, related point in favour of hypertext's motivational, autonomizing potential is the fact that readers bear responsibility for their own 'text' (as an either abstract, mental construct or a physical, written product), which is built on the basis of learners' individual backgrounds. By the same token, the role of the teacher is that of a resource, an administrator and a student, rather than of an aloof, dominant instructor (Sommers, 1985). At the same time, however, tutors still fulfil a seminal role insofar as they need to select appropriate teaching methods which align the selection of hypertexts, background theories and exploratory and constructive teaching methods with the demands of each individual group of learners.

The use of hypermedia is generally considered another motivational aspect of pedagogic hypertext, as learners can express their ideas in a variety of creative ways. What is more, learners are made to reflect on the intrinsic properties, constraints and possibilities of diverse semiotic systems and 'how they shape the form of narrative and affect the narrative experience' (Rimmon-Kenan, 1989; Ryan, 2004: 1). With respect to the purposeful and artistic combination of those various semiotic modes, McKillop and Myers (1999: 68) point out that 'critical theory in hypermedia means the juxtaposing of texts, images, and so on, to foster critique about the potential meanings of texts'. Put differently, authors have to bear in mind that hypertext criticism is, to a large extent, constituted by the engagement with textual diversity and the medial semantics it entails. This poses a major challenge to hypertext novices and their considerations as to how to convey a critical hypermedia attitude. The most difficult task for hypertext writers is, however, to envisage potential readerships and how the intended effects may be reached. After all, particularly in the case of complex hypertexts, it is virtually impossible to predict which path(s) readers may choose and which mental representations they may form during the reading process(es).

The points raised in the preceding discussion form part of a critical, quasi-enlightened attitude towards hypertextual phenomena, and should therefore be taken into account by teachers and learners of hypertext alike. Furthermore, they need to inform the organization and theoretical underpinnings of any pedagogic hypertext project, be it exploratory or constructive in nature – or indeed both. When embarking on such a project, tutors need to prepare their students with regard to the potentially frustrating elements of hypertext and, equally importantly, functionalize those (motivational) qualities that enhance reading, writing and learning in general. As Stanton and Stammers' (1990) empirical research confirms, hypertextual learning environments are suitable for different levels of prior knowledge. They encourage exploration and allow subjects to adapt material to their own learning styles (*ibid.*: 119). Further to these, flexibility, integrative potential, multimedia and interactivity are features adaptable to a variety of learning styles, provided they are employed in the context of carefully thought-out didactic approaches. Against the backdrop of all considerations made in this section, I therefore propose an eclectic teaching approach, which offers a mixture of old and New Media and teaching methods, integrating both traditional classroom discourse and independent student collaboration. How such an approach may be implemented is shown in the following case study.

4   Case Study

Da Kompetenzen immer nur an ihren greifbaren Äußerungsformen, also anhand von Performanzphänomenen dingfest gemacht werden können, stehen diese theoretischen Ansätze vor besonderen Meßproblemen.
(Habermas, 1983: 199)

In the above motto, Jürgen Habermas draws attention to the fact that competence can only ever become manifest in performance-related phenomena, and that trying to 'measure' these phenomena poses considerable difficulties to the researcher. Taking Habermas's advice (or rather warning) into account, this book concludes by offering a 'manifest' application of the previously discussed theoretical phenomena, and by taking a look at performance-related aspects of hypertext pedagogy. Having established the theoretical implications of literary hypertext in the light of contemporary educational theory and practice, I will thus continue with an applied approach to literary education via hypertext.

As a preliminary note, educational research is traditionally understood to be of a pragmatic, political nature, insofar as it is directed at improving learning and teaching standards. Therefore it generally seeks to inform curricular development (Kemmis, 1993:188). As we have seen in Chapter 2.3, recent changes in UK educational policies have opened up the syllabus to the New Media, which are still understood in terms of general ICT knowledge as well as media and moving image texts, i.e. television and cinema. Thus, essential reforms have already taken place which, for the first time, permit the usage of alternative literary media and demand new teaching strategies necessitated by (so far) *expository* forms of hypermedia composition and perception. However, literary hypertext has not yet entered the National Curriculum.

This case study ought to be seen in the context of educational constructivism, which sees learners as producing rather than receiving knowledge (Stenhouse, 1975; Hammersley, 1993). Similarly, teachers are conceived of as learners, as they draw conclusions from their own practice in order to improve their own teaching. Similarly, I do not set out to propose a catalogue of best practices for the reformist literature teacher but rather give an account of practical educational research that aims to test hypertext for its potential of facilitating the development of literary competence. The case study report reflects findings of a qualitative research project, which is of an essentially procedural character and ventures to describe student action in class. As previously mentioned, the report demonstrates an integrated approach, which combines aspects of literary stylistics with creative hypertext writing. Along with Cumming and Sinclair (1991:315), I understand 'integrated' in the sense of 'conventional instructional practices', which are 'enhance[d] ... through computer-based interactive media'. This approach stands in opposition to radically decentring approaches to networking students and instructors, which prioritize distance learning and therefore do not comply with classroom curricula such as the National Curriculum of England and Wales.

1   Motivation and Rationale

The 'Hypertext Project', as I will refer to it, draws on but also goes beyond previous theoretical and empirical research as outlined in Chapter 5.2. It represents the first practical implementation of constructivist literary pedagogy in a hypertext classroom. So far, the majority of pedagogic approaches have examined the impact of poststructuralist and hypertext theory on teaching hypertext rather than looking at the learner, who, after all, ought to be at the centre of pedagogic interest.

Hence, the major purpose of this section is to give an account of actual learning processes and student activities that happen in the context of implementing collective hypertextual authorship in a *formal* classroom environment. 'Formal' in this context refers to a specific didactic constellation, which includes aspects of venue and time, as well as teacher and student activities. Logistically, the same locality and computer set-up were used, to make the group feel familiar with external conditions throughout. The time spent by students on the project was fixed in terms of recurrence and duration. Furthermore, each session was organized in a similar manner and order: approximately 10 per cent teacher feedback, revision and recapitulation; 15 per cent teacher input; 20 per cent student application of new theory; 50 per cent student collaboration on hypertext; and 5 per cent student feedback. Used in this sense, 'formal' is also understood to facilitate constructivist pedagogy, as it establishes a clearly defined context, within which learners are enabled to develop new cognitive structures from tutor and peer input and, at the same time, to unfold their creative potential in critical reflection and discourse with peers.

My major research question was whether and how an integrated hypertext learning environment, which incorporates theory and practice, may help students develop certain levels of medially extended literary competence (see Chapter 4). I focused on three aspects of literary competence: *aesthetic competence* (Haas, 2001); *creative competence* with special emphasis on collaborative and organizational skills within a group; and *media competence*, i.e. hypermedia reception and production.

Project members were observed in terms of how they reproduced acquired and taught knowledge structures and developed literary competence from jointly dealing with information input in a digital creative writing group. As Habermas (1983: 199) suggests, there is, of course, a high risk involved in trying to deduce from student action or products (performance) aspects of their competence. On the other hand, only performance data are directly accessible empirically, which makes the retrieval of such data inevitable for the educational researcher (Hurrelmann, 2002: 309). To tackle this methodological dilemma, triangulation methods were applied,[5] which were to give an insight into the students' subjective self-assessment, as well as their actual output and classroom behaviour.

Another point of interest was the question of how students' attitudes towards hypertext as a literary mode and object of literary education would develop through regular exposure and perceptive as well as productive interaction with it. Motivational levels clearly have an impact on the extent to which deep learning takes place. Therefore, it was crucial to examine how literary hypertext might help increase intrinsic motivation and whether the use of hypertext for reading, writing and assimilating poetic structures can in fact be learned in such a way as to generate genuine aesthetic enjoyment.

The pedagogic and empirical objectives of the hypertext project are understood to interrelate and build up on each other. *In nuce*, they include (1) the implementation of hypertext in a formal teaching environment, with a focus on student 'constructions' and their learning activities during the project sessions; (2) an investigation of how the development of literary competence is noticeable in students; and (3) an examination of learners' levels of intrinsic motivation, which is perceived to be key for deep learning.

The project focused on both formative and summative aspects of student learning. Formative (procedural and developmental) aspects were observable during the sessions as part of classroom discourse, notably with respect to student collaboration, learning strategies and styles, instances of self-reflection, peer feedback, exchanging ideas, using new terminology, discussing writing strategies, awareness of learning processes and evidence of learner autonomy. Summative evaluations of student progress, on the other hand, were carried out by means of questionnaires and writing tasks at the beginning and the end of the project.

2   Methodology

To gain an insight into learners' attitudes, emotions and cognitive disposition, I adopt a qualitative rather than quantitative approach.[6] In so doing, I follow a trend that emerged in the 1960s in Britain as a counter-reaction to beliefs held previously that education was essentially a (social) science and should therefore make use of scientific research paradigms such as causal relationships, standardized research instruments and techniques (experimentation, verifying or falsifying hypotheses, product-orientedness, before-and-after tests), and statistical techniques (Hammersley *et al.*, 1994: 84). I share the view that only qualitative research can cast light on cultural and political processes involved in education (*ibid.*: 12), which is a vital prerequisite for curriculum development and interpretation. 'Quantitative' methods will be used only to the extent to which they supplement and validate qualitative findings, without, however, aiming at generalized conclusions. The characteristics of qualitative research as put forward by Hammersley *et al.* (*ibid.*: 11/50) can be summarized as follows.[7]

   Qualitative research explores the nature of a particular educational phenomenon, rather than testing hypotheses. It is therefore process- rather than product-oriented. Tests are carried out during and after each session rather than before and after the project, as is the case, for example, in quantitative, cross-sectional studies. There is, furthermore, a tendency to work with unstructured, uncoded data, which are raised by way of audio- and/or video-recordings, open-ended field notes, and interviews with prevailingly open-ended questions rather than categorical, tabular or fill-in responses. In terms of sampling, a small number of cases are investigated in detail. This is to obtain a complex profile of each subject rather than a general, broad image of a whole population. Qualitative research examines verbal and non-verbal behaviour, which is described with a view to gaining insight in the subjects' cognitive and emotional processes. In terms of research environment, natural settings are preferred, i.e. data is collected in familiar rather than artificial surroundings. The data is generally analysed inductively, to arrive at 'grounded theory', i.e. theory which is generated from data and thus grounded in the social activities it sets out to explain. Similarly, researchers largely refrain from hypotheses and assumptions before the study but rather restrict themselves to general and specific research objectives. Another important element is the involvement of the participants in evaluating and attributing meaning to their own behaviour. Hence, they are typically asked to interpret situations themselves and to reveal their own perspectives on particular aspects of the study.

   One of the most striking differences to quantitative research is that the researcher is seen as the main research instrument. He or she observes and listens, trying to establish rapport with the subjects, asking them to stay natural, mediating, negotiating, playing the part of social manager. Consequently, it is important to note that qualitative research is always a 'construction', 'because researchers must put their own selves into the research and interpret what they see or hear' (*ibid.*: 61). Validity is achieved through non-reactive methods (backgrounding the researcher and foregrounding students' responses and actions), respondent validation (acclaim on the part of the respondents), and triangulation.

Evidently, a major downside of qualitative research is that it cannot serve as a basis for generalizing conclusions. Findings should therefore not be unconditionally transferred to other cases, as they are highly individualized and situationally determined. Another concession is that qualitative research also has to rely to some extent on theoretical presuppositions. In our case, hypertext as a creative literary means is considered potentially useful for the literature classroom, and hence for inclusion in curricular planning.

The research methodology applied here follows the tradition of action research (Corey, 1949; Kemmis, 1993), which means that research is carried out by one or more reflective practitioners (administrators, teachers etc.) to improve their own (teaching) practice. Action research has four main characteristics: it is practical, collaborative, participatory and self-reflective. In other words, it goes hand-in-hand with the implications of qualitative research in that it focuses on the pedagogue's praxis; it involves subjects in the interpretation of their own actions; and it understands the researcher as a practitioner who investigates his or her own practices to draw practical conclusions. Correspondingly, I triangulate the case study methods, which involves mainly observation, survey (based on questionnaires) and interview (building on and supplementing findings of the survey to deepen the understanding of answers given in questionnaires and to establish rapport with the respondents). A research diary was kept to record all observations and considerations made during the research period and serve as a forum for self-reflection on the part of the researcher. Furthermore, student logs were kept to record individual learning outcomes.

Table 3 shows the interrelationships between pedagogic objectives, research objectives and research methods.

As previously mentioned, questionnaires were employed in the first and last project session to test students on exemplary aspects of aesthetic competence, and more specifically their familiarity with and ability to identify poetic forms, imagery and figures of speech, metre, rhyme, stanza and narrative perspective. Students completed them individually and subsequently discussed their answers in structured interviews with the researcher.

The development of creative competence was investigated in two ways. First, student products were examined on a weekly basis in terms of formal criteria: on a macrostructural basis, in terms of how they organized lexias into a hypertextual network by means of linking structures; and on a microstructural basis, in terms of how they used language and style to create an aesthetic piece of writing rather than what may be likened to a little-intriguing school essay. It has to be

Table 3   Pedagogic objectives, research objectives and research methods

Pedagogic objectives	Research objectives	Research methods
Test implementation of hypertext in formal teaching environment, with an emphasis on collective production	Description of classroom action taken by students involved in a productive hypertext environment	Observation, note-taking, filming classroom activities
Development of literary competence, especially aesthetic, creative and (hyper-) media competence	Obtain evidence of student learning in terms of developing certain aspects of literary competence	Questionnaires combined with before-and-after tests, learning log, combined with group feedback, analysis of student products in terms of a longitudinal study (comparison with earlier products), observation of classroom discourse (note-taking, tape-recording, filming)
Maximizing intrinsic motivation to facilitate deep learning	Elicit learners' motivational attitudes towards hypertext as an object of literary education and how they change upon repeatedly experiencing a productive hypertext environment over a certain period of time	Structured interviews based on previously completed questionnaires; learners' written evaluation

taken into account that the students were writing in German, which is not their mother tongue. Hence, grammatical and grave lexical errors were discussed and rectified in the students' presence and did not form part of the aesthetic analysis. Generally, however, students were given a maximum of poetic licence, which allowed them to use the language creatively and autonomously – to make it their own, as it were.

Second, the students were observed in terms of how they collaborated on a hypertext. In analysing my observations I will concentrate on Smith and Kollock's (1999) three major criteria of interaction, communication and coordination, which include the negotiating, compromising and converging of ideas.[8] Observation took place in the form of note-taking, tape-recording and filming classroom intercourse. The students were also asked in regular interviews whether and how they benefited from collective production of hypertext.

Media competence, and more specifically, 'hypermedia' competence as elaborated in Chapter 4.3 was examined both receptively and productively. On the receptive side, hypertext reading sessions were followed by individualized interviews, in which the students were asked about their first impressions, emotional reactions and reading strategies. Of major interest was how they coped with problems of cognitive overhead, disorientation and informational short-sightedness, as well as whether and why they did or did not enjoy the reading process aesthetically. At a later stage, account was taken of how the students made use of previously introduced terminology and input concerning linking types and structures. On the productive side, grouped activities were observed, with a special focus on how they organized the structure of their products and interrelated them with those of other groups.

Finally, didactic and research objectives must result in concrete didactic strategies. As mentioned above, an integrated, eclectic approach was taken to cater for a variety of learner needs and learning styles. To provide a collaborative learning environment, there was an emphasis on learner–learner interaction and discourse. The teacher-researcher gave informational input tailored to the questions in the before-and-after tests (e.g. sonnet structures, poetic imagery, metrical forms, narrative perspectives). Project hours comprised (hypertext) reading sessions, the induction of poetic forms and rules from examples discussed in class, and the application of newly learned rules and forms to one's own creative writing. The productive aim was to create a collaborative literary hypertext based on communal writing. To further facilitate intrinsic motivation, evaluation was in the form of peer, self- and teacher feedback, rather than formal assessment.

3 Context

The project spanned the first term of the academic year 2004/05 at the University of Leeds, UK. The classroom contained three computers, around which the small 'teams' (approximately four students each) arranged themselves. Although some students tended to be in the same team every time, there was no strict seating order, so team constellations varied according to individual preferences. Each of the ten sessions lasted two hours. The 13 participants were Level 2 students of various Modern Languages programmes (e.g. German and French, German and Spanish, German Elective, English and German etc.), who took part in the project as a voluntary extracurricular activity.[9] A project webpage was created to publish student products, in order to provide access to the hypertexts read in class and the project timetable (Ensslin, 2005a).

4 Implementation

The project syllabus was organized around eight proper seminar sessions, which were framed by two audit units, in which student performance was recorded by means of questionnaires, structured interviews and test stories. The seminar sessions were centred around specific aspects of narrative theory, hypertext theory, stylistic text analysis, and web editing. In chronological order, the topics were distributed as follows:

1. (Week 2) Introduction to the concept of hypertext
2. (Week 3) Introduction to literary genres
3. (Week 4) Introduction to collaborative authorship and Macromedia Dreamweaver MX
4. (Week 5) Introduction to narrative theory
5. (Week 6) Introduction to poetry (I): metre, rhyme, verse
6. (Week 7) Introduction to poetry (II): types of poems
7. (Week 8) Introduction to stylistics: tropes, figures of speech
8. (Week 9) Finalization of hypertexts

None of the students had encountered literary hypertext before, nor did they know the term 'hypertext' itself. Therefore, participants were first familiarized with the concept and some examples. They were given three hypertexts (Ryman, 1996; Inglis, 1999; Ehlert and Bauer, 2002) to read jointly in three separate, rotating groups (for an introduction to the benefits of communal reading, see Pike, 2003: 70). During the reading process, participants were asked to voice first impressions and make suggestions about the actual theme of the texts. Their comments were taped in separate groups.

After the reading period, the group sat together to exchange ideas and impressions, at which point I explained the concept of (proto-)hypertext. The students were then given copies of an authentic hypertext map, which was taken from Ehlert and Bauer's (2002) webpage. I used this example to illustrate the structural components of hypertext and provide a model upon which they could then base their own hypertext maps. For the subsequent, preparatory activity, they could choose from a selection of hypertext metaphors (e.g. 'labyrinth', 'patchwork quilt', 'Gesamtkunstwerk', 'game', 'spider web' and 'journey') as the starting point for their own associative (mind) maps (see Preece, 1976, for knowledge elicitation via free word association). The students had to label their nodes and links in terms of how they interlinked with each other (for pattern noting, see Jonassen, 1987, 1990). At the end of the session, I collected the products, scanned them and put them on the project webpage. For homework, the students were given a section from Kuhlen (1991) on hyperlinks, which was to be discussed in the following week.

Session 2 (week 3) was dedicated to literary genres. During the first 15 minutes, the students were asked to discuss what they had read about linking structures on the basis of the hypertexts they had read so far. The second major part of the session was used to introduce literary genres, which was done inductively. The students were given excerpts from Theodor Storm's poem *Die Stadt*, Arthur Schnitzler's drama *Reigen*, and Alfred Döblin's novel *Berlin Alexanderplatz*. In their teams, participants had to discuss how the three texts could be distinguished in terms of structure, content and language. In pairs, they transformed the texts into different genres, turning, for instance, *Reigen* into narrative prose, *Berlin Alexanderplatz* into verse, and *Die Stadt* into dramatic dialogue or monologue. The products were read out and commented on by the other team members. Afterwards, they were collected, corrected and put on the project webpage by the tutor. For homework, the students were asked to read a section from Landow (1992/1997) on collaborative authorship.

Whereas, in the two initial sessions, the students wrote with pen and paper, session 3 was used to introduce Dreamweaver software, which would, from that point onwards, serve as the main writing platform. The session started with a revision of the reading task, which focused on collaborative authorship and how it could be employed to help learners improve their literary and communicative competence. Then they went into their usual groups to tackle their first web editing tasks. After a period of testing background and font colours and sizes in Maskiewicz's *ColoRama* (2004), they were introduced to the basic applications of Dreamweaver: text editing, colouring, linking, as well as inserting images and tables. For homework, students had to read various excerpts from Genette (1980) and Stanzel (1984) to prepare for the introduction to narrative.

In session 4, the students were taught and experimented with narrative perspectives and aspects of focalization. Again, during the first minutes students were asked to recapitulate and discuss the homework reading. After that, they were presented with a number of passages from English and German novels. In their teams, they discussed the excerpts in terms of narrative situation and focalization. The results were consolidated in a succeeding plenary discussion. Then the students were asked to transfer what they had learned to their own writing. The Dreamweaver documents were opened and continued. The writing was again followed by peer feedback. For homework, the students had to read passages from Ludwig (1994) about metre, rhyme and stanza.

Session 5 was dedicated to introducing students to central poetic terminology and concepts, namely metrical feet and rhyme. To apply the theory, the teams were given a number of stanzas, which they had to analyse in terms of metre and rhyme. The results were discussed with the whole group. Then, the usual writing teams were formed, and students were asked to try to add to their hypertexts elements of verse. They were also requested to get into the habit of gradually thinking beyond the limits of their own 'private' hypertexts, to read what the other teams had written and link parts of their writing products to other documents, where appropriate. For homework, they had to research stanza forms and types of poems.

Between sessions 5 and 6 was a one-week half-term break, after which a revision of all theory covered so far was necessary. This was done in open classroom discourse. Students also reported their experiences with hypertexts they had read over the holidays. In a succeeding theory section, students learned about stanza forms and types of poetry. They were again given text samples for analysis and subsequently wrote their own poems, following the conventions they had just learned about. Unsurprisingly, most of them chose non-rhyming or humoristic genres such as haikus and limericks. The poems were then read to the other team members and integrated as new lexias into the existing hypertext network. For homework, they had to read definitions of stylistic features such as trope, metaphor, metonymy, simile, anaphora and epiphora.

In session 7, figures of speech and tropes were the focus. First, students looked at and revised previously written texts, helping each other to find better formulations and to correct grammatical errors. After that, they discussed the texts they had read for homework, with additional input and explanations given by the instructor. The teams were then given a number of short texts, which were full of rhetorical figures and imagery. Jointly, they had to find examples of the stylistic means they had been taught. Subsequently, they were asked to create lexias which contained text types that typically contain a lot of rhetorical features. The teams discussed what sort of texts that could be, and concluded that they would try fictitious conference speeches. It turned out that, statistically, they found metaphors, parallelisms and assonances particularly convenient for their purposes.

There was no preparatory reading for the final project session, as it served as an opportunity for project members to complete and further embellish their hypertext. Students were also asked to write a report on how their motivation levels had developed throughout the project.

5 Results

This section summarizes the results of the project, in terms of student action and discourse during the sessions, their written products, and an evaluation of the questionnaires and structured interviews conducted in the audit sessions. I will particularly focus on student action; aesthetic, creative and media competence; and intrinsic motivation.

Student action

With respect to collective reading, it could be observed that, after a period of general bewilderment, the students got used to the task. One of each group generally directed the mouse while the others discussed quietly and carefully what had been read and where to go next. Links in the text were easily identified, yet if there was a range of links to choose from, students were confused as to which one they ought to choose. The existence of hidden links was readily accepted, and students often explored lexias in order to find some. Emerging images and animations generally were perceived as entertainment and stimulation. The playfulness of 'browsing' held readers in a mixture of suspense, uncertainty and curiosity, and discussing individual and collective reading processes seemed to keep the level of personal frustration low. Some comments made by the students, however, suggested negative receptive effects, such as 'lost in hyperspace' or cognitive overload. That said, student discourse also suggested that these problems might be solved through joint reading strategies. In fact, despite the relatively large size of the reading groups (four per computer), the students managed to find effective and mutually supportive ways of reading together. There also seemed to be general acceptance of the fact that they had to compromise (see Smith and Kollock, 1999) on a reading path and, furthermore, that not everything could possibly be read within the given timeframe.

An interesting observation was that group members often adopted the role of a secondary narrator-commentator. They commented and hypothesized on previously read occurrences, expressing empathy or disagreement with the protagonist. Individual comments were either approved or debated by the group. In a discussion ensuing the hypertext reading session, students generally disagreed as to how 'empowered' they really were as readers, thus confirming many a critique of Landow's wreader concept. Some did not even think they could create their own story but felt rather entrenched in the complexities of the texts. Others, however, liked the way they could choose what they wanted to know more about. There was consensus that the collective reading process is a beneficial experience, as problems and questions can be discussed as they occur, which minimizes individual frustration levels.

When asked what, to them, the major advantages of hypertext are compared to books, the students mentioned navigational and selective freedom, interactivity, hypermediality, affordability, the absence of fixity and closure, and global accessibility. Some particularly enthused students agreed that hypertext was a more personal, (inter-)active and thus activ*ating* medium than the book. In terms of disadvantages, the most frequent complaint was, predictably, lack of closure.

The greater part of the sessions was dedicated to the collaborative creative writing of hypertext stories. It was observed that most students collaborated well in small groups, whereas a few others preferred to work individually. This is indicative of how sensitive a relatively large collaborative writing team is to different learning styles (e.g. Honey and Mumford, 1982): activists and pragmatists thrive on group work, whereas theorists and reflectors generally prefer individual tasks and learning from observing and reflecting on other people's experiences. Similarly, the 'individualists' in the group did not appear to benefit greatly from paired composition, nor did they form a good working relationship with their teammates. On the contrary, they produced more text in less time than others, who worked in little groups and, evidently, spent a lot of their time discussing ideas and formulations. Interestingly, the 'single' workers also showed a tendency to write texts that not only exceeded the length of an average webpage, but which were structured according to linear, logic principles of traditional print writing. The small groups, by contrast, seemed more capable of creating lexia-sized text chunks, which were often more experimental in terms of language and style than those of the individualists, as well as more easily linkable to other, existing lexias.

During the sessions, conversations within groups were lively. Tutor feedback was willingly received. The first stories, for instance, tended to be written in a rather matter-of-fact, reporting style, without any perspectival nuances or dramatizing elements such as direct speech. Having been made aware of a variety of narrative styles during the project, most participants used more varied and effective stylistic means in their later works. After each writing session, students readily read their texts to each other in their groups. Peer feedback was readily received and built into later drafts. Students also used the feedback groups to discuss what narrative perspectives could best be used to convey certain atmospheres.

Although all students collaborated on poems, they seemed to prefer writing short prose. This may be due to the fact that they were writing in a foreign language and were inexperienced in terms of rhyme patterns and connotation. Only one (individualist) student used dramatic dialogue in creating a whole scene, including entry and exit.

Linking was mostly done associatively. The groups discussed various possible linking strategies on a macrostructural level (e.g. the transition of characters from one story space to another), and then used existing textual clues to create connections to other students' pages. The resulting effect much resembled the change in text worlds as conveyed, for instance, in C. S. Lewis's *The Lion, the Witch and the Wardrobe*, where the children step into a magic wardrobe to suddenly find themselves in a fantasy world, which confronts them with a manichaeic and Darwinistic but essentially, however, Hollywoodian – world picture, much in opposition to their own familiar reality.

Finally, in all grouped activities, participants engaged in Smith and Kollock's (1999) three main communicative activities, interacting (with the machine and each other), communicating (verbally and non-verbally, by means of body language) and coordinating (in terms of planning and organizing grouped activities, as well as the production of text on a microstructural and macrostructural basis). More specifically, students negotiated their ideas, which mostly involved compromising and converging diverse concepts.

Aesthetic, creative and media competence

This section looks at the extent of development in aesthetic, creative and media competence. Particular emphasis will be placed on aesthetic competence, as it appeared to be the area that developed most noticeably.

Comments made by the students after each session and in the final audit were divided into four categories: analytical skills (aesthetic competence); language and style; media competence; and collaborative-creative competence. Summarizing the comments made by the participants, the main learning benefits with regard to aesthetic competence included raised levels of awareness towards narrative structures, increased knowledge of poetic terms and conventions, and increased skill in applying those terms to literary text analysis.

During the project, students verbalized recently introduced terminology only to a certain extent in describing their own writing, for example first- or third-person narrator, rather than personal, authorial or neutral. The fact that some of them had genuinely retained a variety of stylistic and poetic concepts and also knew how to apply them to literature emerged later in the academic year, when two of the project members, in a regular university seminar, started to analyse a poem in terms of metric feet and rhetorical figures without having been requested to do so, and with a visible degree of enthusiasm. When they were asked where they had learned those concepts, they replied that it had been in the hypertext project (rather than any other literature class).

Taking a closer look at aesthetic competence, some students commented in the final audit that they could still remember most of the terms and concepts that had been introduced. They also confirmed that they were able to use the terms and analytical skills in other literature seminars, where those skills were required, yet not formally taught. Their enthusiasm needs to be taken with a pinch of salt, however, as the summative tests performed by means of questionnaires indicated that not all of them had internalized the terminology and analytical skills to the degree they thought they had.

That said, comparing the first and the final questionnaires and interviews led to the overall observation that students' aesthetic competence, both theoretical and applied, had, on the whole, improved. Especially significant was the increase in factual knowledge about traditional literary genres and particular, structurally defined types of poems. In the first audit, only eight out of 13 named prose, poetry and drama as the three main literary genres, but none could name any acceptable subgenres in a systematic way. Some even confused them with periods of literary history or stylistic devices. In the final questionnaire, all students made the required distinction and most of them listed a considerable number of subgenres correctly.

Poetic forms were recognized more accurately in the second questionnaire than in the first. In the first audit, only one student could identify and describe the structure of a sonnet and a ballad accurately. Seven out of 13 either gave no answer or categorized the poems in terms of content (e.g. 'political', 'war'), whereas four could identify some patterns, such as certain rhyming patterns (rhyming couplets). In the second audit, three quarters of the students could identify and describe the structure of a sonnet and a ballad. One could even distinguish between a Petrarchan and an English sonnet.

Far less clear was the learning curve in relation to applying narrative theory. In the first audit, none of the students could identify a personal narrator, and only six mentioned the third-person narrative. Although, generally speaking, considerably more correct answers were given in the second audit, there was still a surprisingly high number of responses that were either uninformed, or evidenced that the underlying theory (perspectivity and/or focalization) had not been properly understood.

With regard to language and style, participants commented that their confidence in applying literary terminology, and their awareness about poetic diction and the importance of paradigmatic selection had increased, in particular in relation to stylistic conventions across literary genres. Focusing on student products longitudinally, it was evident that most students' writing style did indeed become increasingly eloquent and varied, although the degree of improvement varied considerably. Compared to the beginning of the project, they were more adventurous and willing to experiment and used more expressive and emotive language, as well as tropes, figures of speech and narrative techniques they had learned during the project. They also used more narratological terminology.

The development of creative competence was, according to most participants, stimulated through group work and the collaboration on creative text production. The mutual exchange of ideas was particularly emphasized, as it made students aware of the benefits of information interchange. Having said that, team skills of this kind are in fact encouraged and practised across the tertiary education sector in Britain, mostly by means of small group teaching and tightly scheduled activities with clear productive targets. Hence, most students were already experienced 'team players' when they joined the project. The novelty, however, was for most of them to collaborate creatively towards realistic deadlines and in a near-authentic web-publishing environment. Similarly, especially with respect to coordination and cooperation within a group, the existence and development of creative competence, realized through group work, was clearly recognizable during the project sessions.

Regarding media competence, most students confirmed they had learned how to use Dreamweaver to create webpages, edit text, link lexias and design webpages in terms of colour and illustration. Classroom observation confirmed that most students' level of hypermedia competence improved considerably, as they learned how to insert images and links in a Dreamweaver document, as well as editing text in the same software. They also became accustomed to reading hypertext in a group and on their own. Some confirmed that they were reading additional hypertexts outside project sessions, and that they would continue to do so in the future. Some even developed an awareness of how to 'prepare' a link such as to make it intelligible to the reader, and thus showed a clear understanding of the idea behind lexias.

Most students said in their logfiles and in their final interview that they had learned to use the basic functions of Dreamweaver confidently. Some students, whose typing and general IT skills were less advanced than those of others, received peer and tutor advice about how to use the mouse and keyboard, as well as a variety of web resources for particular research and terminology questions.

With respect to the combination of different semiotic systems, the teams considered various possibilities of combining and sequencing image and text. They particularly enjoyed testing colours, fonts and contrasts, and built their experiences into their writing products.

Intrinsic motivation

Going by attendance levels, intrinsic motivation fell towards the middle of the project (weeks 4 to 6), which was partly due to deadlines that had to be met for other seminars. From experience, there is also a tendency for extracurricular projects to be met with great enthusiasm, which tends to decrease among some participants as stress levels rise and activities have to be prioritized. Thus, it was not surprising that, in the second half of the project, attendance levels started rising again.

Intrinsic motivation was stimulated by the idea of sharing authorship with respect to creating and naming characters and choosing stylistic features, as well as aspects of tone, mood and register. The idea of web publishing initially caused concern and embarrassment, which were gradually replaced by greater confidence and even enthusiasm with respect to addressing a 'real' audience.

A particularly high level of intrinsic motivation was generated by linking to other groups' pages. This was partly due to the authorial possibilities but also the limitations and risks associated with combining and transgressing individual story spaces. Participants discussed those concerns and finally arrived at the conclusion that these risks were the necessary implications – and indeed welcome challenges – of having a collaborative hypertextual fiction network.

The transformation exercises were similarly stimulative, probably because a textual basis was given as a starting point, which the students could appropriate by processing and transforming it in their own ways, turning, for instance, verse into narrative, narrative into drama, and vice versa. Researching theoretical issues, on the other hand, was met with less enthusiasm, as it implied additional reading tasks at home. In fact, 80 per cent of the students did not do the preparatory or follow-up reading, which they explained in terms of high workloads in other, compulsory seminars, and difficulty in understanding the technical jargon. As a result, much of the theory that should have been acquired by ways of preparatory reading had to be covered in the classroom, which reduced the writing time. Having said that, theoretical information provided by the tutor was readily received, discussed and applied to textual analysis. Presumably, this situation would change if the project were an accreditable seminar, where the comprehension and oral presentation of previous reading would form part of the assessment.

A high degree of motivation was recorded when the project members used Dreamweaver and other software to edit their hypertexts. They visibly enjoyed creating and pasting images, using tables, experimenting with background colours, drag-and-drop linking etc. These activities also gave the tutor an opportunity and authentic context to sensitize students to internet plagiarism and aspects of copyright. They were made aware of strategies of avoiding plagiarism, through contacting site owners, as well as legally purchasing or creating one's own materials.

Both positive and negative feedback was given by the students on the pedagogic validity of an integrated approach, which marries formal classroom instruction with constructivist transformation exercises and a hypertextual production environment. Positive comments clearly outnumbered negative ones. This reflects the students' own view of their learning outcomes and motivation, particularly with regard to the creative aspects of the project. The fact that a couple of participants mentioned the theory component as one of the drawbacks of the project reconfirms this, as it were, *ex negativo*. On the other hand, four respondents said they appreciated the fact that they had to learn new terminology and theory. Hence, it can be concluded that the response of the group was rather mixed in terms of how the theoretical aspects were perceived.

6 Discussion: Didactic Consequences

In this section I will summarize the lessons that can be learned pedagogically from previous research into the hypertextual (literary) classroom, and compare it with the results yielded by the data from the student audits, the observations made about student responses to reading and writing hypertext jointly in the classroom, and suggestions made by the students at the close of the Leeds Hypertext Project. First and foremost, hypertext can be said to support constructivist objectives such as subject-orientation, process-orientation, learner autonomy, intrinsic motivation and deep learning insofar as it serves as an efficient tool for organizing, structuring, synthesizing, storing and making accessible information via learner-friendly templates, logically organized linking structures and navigational aids. Furthermore, the results of the case study support the assumption that hypertext enhances deep learning through collaboration, which again encourages the joint construction of knowledge, intrinsic motivation through immediate social discourse with peers, and peer as well as tutor feedback. What is more, learners bear responsibility for their own texts, which are published after undergoing peer-review, and are thus empowered and rewarded for expressing their ideas creatively and independently of any external motivational stimuli, such as assessment.

In terms of learning outcome, the answers given in the initial and final audit point to the fact that the project helped participants to improve their levels of aesthetic competence, albeit to varying degrees. At the end of the ten weeks, most students were confident in using the terminology that had been introduced and could apply it in stylistic literary analyses, whereas, at the beginning of the project, they had either not come across the terms or only remembered them very vaguely from their school years. According to the participants, this competence development could not have been acquired elsewhere, as it had not been the object of other university modules. This finding is significant insofar as it suggests high levels of intrinsic motivation and deep learning in view of the fact that no element of formal assessment was involved. As mentioned before, however, there were indeed exceptions, mainly in the area of narrative theory, which showed that students occasionally used terminology wrongly or unsystematically. This indicates that instructional detail and classroom discourse need to be refined mainly in those areas where theoretical nuances may distort the students' transitory concepts in the long term, for instance in the juxtaposition of Stanzel's and Genette's narratological theories.

From the distinct instructional environment that was chosen it can be concluded that, with regard to aesthetic competence or indeed any other area of learning and expertise, a hypertext environment may be considered a learning aid given that proper input is provided by the instructor and subsequently transformed by the students into personalized cognitive structures. As previous research confirms, tutor input may well be replaced or supplemented by tutor-guided student research, although this would seem suitable for an expository rather than creative writing syllabus. This is borne out by DeWitt (1999: 144), who stresses that hypertext's pedagogic potential is inextricably connected with a 'sound', systematic teaching approach, in which circumstances it also facilitates critical competence.

Student action, learning logs and final interviews suggest that, in the view of both participants and action researcher, their (hyper-)media competence and creative competence had improved in the course of the project. Most of them used Dreamweaver with increasing confidence and efficiency, which was borne out by the rising fluency in motoric movements when interacting with the medium, by the willingness of some students to teach less experienced peers skills they had acquired, and by the certainty with which they talked about their actions, using specific computer terminology. By the end of the project, the majority of participants knew how to create, link, colour-code and design web-pages in tabular format, as well as how to edit text. Only those students whose attendance levels were the lowest, who had never used the mouse on behalf of the group, or who had missed the Dreamweaver introduction uttered concern and uncertainty as to whether they would be able to use the software confidently without expert guidance. Participants' comments and behaviour explicitly and implicitly confirmed that creative, collaborative writing of hypertext improves creative competence, which by definition unites newly acquired with individual, pre-existing knowledge structures in a creative, meaningful way. Students further showed the ability to write concise and self-contained lexias and to link them with other students' texts in a previously agreed and macrostructurally coherent manner. This suggests that hypertext supports creative as well as media competence. Interestingly, however, some (mostly 'individualist') students preferred to take their texts home and finish them in a conventional, individual writing environment rather than in a hypertext classroom. Hence, it appears as if, at least for specific types of learners (theorists and reflectors), a mixture of collaborative writing in hypertext and individual composition is appropriate.

Motivational levels were considerable bearing in mind that the sessions were organized around theoretical input which, as we have seen, was not welcomed by all students. Furthermore, none of the participants were students of English literature and some even voiced their general lack of interest in literary analysis. As a general conclusion, therefore, collaborative hypertextual writing as a creative activity may have a high motivational potential if students are realistically challenged by technology as well as by the fact that they have to jointly create and transform literature, which is then to be compared and linked with the output of other teams. Possible associative connections between students' texts have to be found, which stimulates imaginative thinking and sets achievable targets for inquisitive reading.

To address a legitimate point of criticism, it may well be argued that, due to prior familiarity of some students with the researcher as well as their awareness that politeness and enthusiasm towards this project may lead to future advantages in other teaching contexts (e.g. other university modules or exams conducted by me), student responses may have been skewed towards optimism or even opportunism. It may be objected, however, that (1) the students were actively encouraged to express criticism of any kind; (2) they were repeatedly told that criticism on their part would not have any negative consequences with regard to their academic performance; (3) attendance levels rose again after the stressful mid-term period was over; and (4) the fact that participants had to dedicate an additional two hours per week to a project that was not accreditable to their university course did not seem to discourage them from regular attendance or from active participation. On the contrary, some participants commented that the knowledge they had acquired in the project sessions had come in useful in other university modules, and that they had started to apply non-linear structuring principles to other areas of study as well.

As the project results suggest, the extent to which students' style of writing develops depends on a variety of psychological factors. There was a tendency among students who enjoyed writing both in teams and individually to show the steepest learning curve. 'Individualists' improved more slowly, although their actual output was in general more prolific, and they produced longer and more texts than the team workers. Furthermore, it was revealing to notice that those participants who preferred to work in teams showed a higher capacity than the 'individualists' to think macrostructurally, in terms of interlinking the work of the three groups in accordance with a mutually agreed narrative concept. For a tutor it thus seems essential to recognize the various learning styles of the students and encourage those who seem inclined to work on their own to join other learners without, however, banning individual work entirely.

With regard to hypertext reception, a conclusion to be drawn from student feedback is that tutors should give learners questions to consider while they read, as well as a deadline which limits the reading time and allows a following discussion. Unless a reasonable timeframe is provided, students are at a risk of losing the scope of the learning task by getting lost in hyperspace and thereby forgetting about the reflective nature of their activity. Questions for reading teams could run, for instance: 'How does reading hypertexts (or this specific hypertext) differ from reading books?'; 'Do you feel more or less in control than when you are reading a book? Why?'; 'Can you identify the gist of the story? Do you consider yourself in the position of summarizing it? What are the difficulties in doing so?'; and 'What can we learn from reading hypertexts in terms of what writers do when they map out a story?'

Further prerequisites for a successful hypertext learning enterprise include (1) plenty of exercises for practising new terminology and theory; (2) at least one computer per pair of students, to avoid passivity; (3) exhaustive and accessible terminology lists and glossaries; and (4) assessment procedures, which supplement intrinsic motivation and thus further stimulate learning. Clearly, the last point runs counter to the objectives of this research project. With respect to curricular integration, however, it is valid (if not indispensable).

Finally, conjoining the implications of empirical psychological research into hypertext's effects on human learning with the findings of the Leeds Hypertext Project, I would conclude that hypertext cannot substitute for conventional lectures or formal classroom teaching (Allinson and Hammond, 1999: 54). Rather, it should be integrated into a traditional teaching and learning environment. Such an environment allows direct student discourse and the collective or individual transformation of conceptual input into the students' own mental disposition by means of free writing exercises. As we have seen, learning outcomes may be tested summatively at any stage during a course, thus giving learners further incentives to memorize what they have read and been taught. Lastly, as this chapter has shown, the addition of a medially extended, hypertextual, literary learning environment has a positive effect on levels of intrinsic motivation and hypermedially expanded literary competence, even with learners with (less than) average interest in literary studies.

Conclusion

The computer is not the enemy of the book. It is the child of print culture, a result of five centuries of organized, collective inquiry and invention that the printing press made possible.
(Murray, 1997: 8)

In an attempt to help canonize a literary media genre that has so far been largely ignored by school and university curricula across the UK, this book has explored the canonical potential of literary hypertext in two interrelated ways: by means of explorations, and constructions. An extended introduction explored a variety of diachronic and synchronic phenomena of hypertext and discussed, in particular, issues surrounding the convergence and divergence of hypertext theory and practice, specifically with regard to the disputed roles of author and reader, which have dominated scholarly discourse on hypertext over the past decade.

Based on Michael Joyce's (1988/2002b) concept of exploratory hypertext, the first part of the book was then dedicated to a hermeneutical analysis of a hypertext canon, which was compiled on the basis of a descriptive rather than prescriptive 'rule canon', a catalogue of evaluative criteria derived from existing hypertext practice and general literary and hypertext theory. That section was preceded by a discussion of major concepts of literature, ideologies surrounding canonicity and the causal relationship between the canon and the curriculum. The alternative hypertext canon, which is grounded in the principles of *avantgarde* canons (e.g. openness, innovation-orientedness, fluidity), contained examples from all three previously explained generations of hypertext, which were hermeneutically explored and analysed in conjunction with existing criticisms.

One major drawback that was noted while compiling the canon is the fact that a considerable number of closed hypertexts are only compatible with Apple computers, and can therefore not be accessed by the Microsoft community. This problem of 'exclusiveness', which discriminates against the majority of British people as well as Europeans, will have to be addressed by Eastgate Systems, the market leader in commercially traded, closed and peer-reviewed hypertext. For not only are hypertexts, by definition, a geographically 'colonialist' media genre (they categorically exclude underdeveloped, non-computerized nations far more than the book industry does), but the

Apple–Windows discrepancy rules out further, potential readerships outside the USA, a circumstance which has to be seen as one of the major reasons that (many) hypertexts have not been discovered more widely across the globe.

Drawing on and developing further Joyce's concept of constructive hypertext, the second part of this study ('Constructions') dealt with questions surrounding the construction of (literary) knowledge and skill and, in didactic application, the collaborative construction of literary hypertext. The central role of constructivism (the prevailing contemporary learning philosophy) was explored, as well as its implications for literary pedagogy. Another focal point was the concept of literary competence and the necessity to marry it with the demands posed by the New Media. With this in mind, I argued for a medially extended notion of literary competence, which, provided it translates into educational policy, will facilitate the inclusion of hypertextual forms in the National Curriculum. To give insight into the amount of research that has gone into literary hypertext pedagogy, a further section of 'Constructions' investigated empirical psychological and pedagogic research into literary hypertext, and concluded with a discussion of hypertext's pedagogic potential.

Finally, an action research-based case study report illustrated my idea of implementing hypertext in the literary classroom, using an eclectic, or integrated approach. The fact that the Leeds Hypertext Project was carried out in the tertiary rather than secondary educational sector was justifiable insofar as the (traditional) learning objects (literary concepts) were taken from a secondary school curriculum and combined with a technological approach that readily adapts to secondary teaching and learning environments. The relative success of the project, which was borne out by student comments (class discourse, non-verbal behaviour and feedback questionnaires) and achievements (selective aspects of literary competence revealed by written student output), proved to be due to increased levels of intrinsic motivation. A discussion of the data collected during the project weighed up the positive effects against potential problem areas, thus arriving at a set of guidelines for future practitioners.

By means of a theoretical discussion and practical application, it could be shown that, bearing in mind any possible reservations arising from the nature of the project and its empirical methods, integrating literary hypertext in a 'conventional' constructivist literary classroom heightens the effects of intrinsic motivation and deep learning, even in learners who would not call themselves particular friends of systematic literary analysis or computer technology in general. Similarly, what was previously explained as the development of hypermedially extended literary competence was borne out by the project results. Finally, the controversial concept of the liberated, empowered 'wreader', which has, in its original conceptual framework, rightly been rejected by many hypertext theorists, was proven to be 're-constructable', given that readers, or learners in this case, are given the opportunity to collaborate on a jointly produced and received hypertext.

To return to the questions posed at the beginning of this study, it may be concluded that including literary hypertext in the National Curriculum and integrating it with the traditional, constructivist literary classroom may indeed be considered a valid approach to making literature – the art of the written word – relevant for an increasingly hypermedia-oriented readership. As a prerequisite, however, we need to modify our concept of literature, literary competence and the literary canon itself. A significant move forward has already been taken by adopting alternative canons as well as the general, expository use of ICT into the National Curriculum. The epistemological and aesthetic quintessence of such modifications are, in a nutshell, a view of literature that goes beyond the technological confines of the conventional print media and embraces the computer medium as a site for creative, i.e. narrative, poetic and dramatic expression. The suggested hypertext canon may, due to its quasi-objective foundation in key aesthetic, literary-communicative criteria, serve as a valid starting point for integrating hypertext in English and/or bilingual literary syllabi.

Finally, by the beginning of the twenty-first century, our late postmodern society has become a highly diversified, instrumentalized apparatus, in which individuals are defined in terms of the diverse functions they can adopt in various social contexts. Furthermore, Western society offers an ever-increasing range of technologically refined media, which deliver a growing number of alternatives for their consumers, be they readers, viewers, listeners, users, players or even 'breathers'. By the same token, the New Media revolution has radically changed public discourse, verbal and non-verbal communication as well as the concept of text in much the same way as it will, to an increasing extent, change our notions of the forms and topics of literature. In the end, every scholar, teacher and student has to decide for themselves to which media they feel most inclined when it comes to the professional implementation of literature (as understood in this study) or media texts in general. Nevertheless, in an age of growing visuality, of truncating text-messaging and of new perceptive strategies, where text searches, Googling and scrolling replace line-by-line, close reading, particularly young people's development of literary competence needs to be nurtured. As the impact of the digital media on human cognition and behaviour cannot be ignored, literary education across all sectors needs to embrace both the creative and pedagogic potential of those media. Integrating literary hypertext, which is intrinsically bound to the computer and, in many cases, the internet (*the* medium with the fastest growing popularity), with a constructivist literature classroom unites the need to adapt to New Media technologies with the equally valid need to learn how to 'read' and 'write' creative literature. This will 'empower' learners in the sense of enabling them, via collective perceptive and productive text-processing activities, to develop a variety of different reading and writing modes, from which they can then select according to situational requirements.

Let me end this study with a note of consolation for those readers who see, in the face of the aforementioned tendencies, the book as an endangered literary species and, accordingly, this study as an iconoclastic undertaking. Quite the opposite is the case. I would like to emphasize that neither should nor will

Gutenberg's legacy ever disappear from the shelves of libraries or bookshops. Similarly, I would wish this study to be understood in the way it is intended, namely in advocacy of 'traditional' reading (as done with books). This kind of reading is indeed endangered by alternative 'browsing' methods which, unless used reflexively and selectively, may well replace close reading and textual immersion. In other words, this book is meant not as a propagation of a literary media genre which should, or will, upon entering curriculum and canon, substitute for literature in print. Much rather, literary hypertext ought to be viewed in terms of complementing the newly established variety of alternative, postmodern canons, not least because it endorses, *per se*, individuality, innovative spirit, metamediality, and the dynamic nature that so much characterizes literary creativity in the New Media.

Notes

Introduction

1. Bolter defines 'reverse ekphrasis' in terms of 'images [being] given the task of explaining words', which runs counter to ancient and Renaissance rhetoric, where 'the spoken word controlled the image' (2001: 56) and 'ekphrasis' was seen as a rhetoric skill, which meant being able to make an object (of art) come to life by means of words.
2. According to reports from *The Times* (14 September 2004), the *Glasgow Herald* and the *Daily Mail* (30 June 2004), the General Household Survey of June 2004, carried out by the Office for National Statistics, revealed that more people than ever are reading for pleasure (65 per cent as opposed to 55 per cent in 1979), and that book sales have risen by 19 per cent in five years.
3. The statistics were issued by NOP World and quoted in the *Independent*, 'Statistics of the Day', on 16 June 2005.
4. Evidently, Coover represents the situation in the USA, which seems in many ways more precarious than in central Europe, or Britain, for that matter. According to the National Adult Literacy Survey of 1992, about 44 million adults could neither write clearly nor fully understand what they read. What is more, over 20 per cent of American adults are considered functionally illiterate, i.e. they read at or below a fifth-grade (i.e. 11-year-old) level.
5. Despite the fact that hypertext research has, within its relatively short period of existence, come a long way, and a great number of scholarly studies across a wide variety of academic fields (e.g. literary studies, philosophy, psychology, communication studies and computer studies) have been published, literary hypertext has, to this day, not entered the National Curriculum; nor can it be regarded as an acknowledged field of academic study and teaching in the UK.
6. For hypertext, a medially extended concept of 'text' needs to be assumed, encompassing various semiotic systems such as image, script and sound, their 'codes' and their denotative and connotative interplay (Barthes, 1961/1977a, 1972, 1977b).
7. To preclude any misconceptions, the concept of hypertext adopted here does not correspond to Genette's, which dates back to the early 1980s. Genette (1982/1997) considers hypertexts to be second-order texts that are derived from pretexts (first order texts, or hypotexts), which they either transform (parody) or emulate. Virgil's *Aeneid* and James Joyce's *Ulysses* are thus hypertexts of the same hypotext, Homer's *Odyssey*.
8. There is an ongoing debate among hypertext scholars as to whether one should speak of antilinearity, nonlinearity or multilinearity. Similarly, individual conventions of terminological usage differ greatly, thus complicating academic

discourse. I therefore propose a clearly defined nomenclature, which does not marginalize any of the three terms but rather defines them as mutually complementary concepts.

9. MUDs are cyberspace sites in which users typically adopt the identity of an avatar (a virtual creature representing the user's alter-ego) to interact with each other synchronously, much as in a computer game. Originally, MUDs tended to be set in enormous old castles with secret rooms and passageways, trap-doors, monsters and other fantasy creatures and elements of magic. MUDs are also referred to as '3-D worlds' and 'chat worlds' (*Webopedia*). MOOs, on the other hand, are more focused on programming (setting up and managing) the 'objects' of a virtual playing environment, i.e. all animate and inanimate elements to be contained within that particular cyberspace site (Ackermann and Hartman, 2000).

10. For a detailed investigation of how console games may be integrated with the English literature classroom, see Zancanella *et al.* (2000).

11. The term 'generation' goes back to Hayles (2002), who remarks that first-generation hypertexts 'were more like books than they were like second-generation electronic literature, because they operated by replacing one screen of text with another, much as a book goes from one page to another' (37). I extend this terminology by adding a third generation to Hayles's binary distinction, the generation of cybertext.

12. Montfort's concept of interactive fiction refers to 'computer programs that display text, accept textual responses, and then display additional text in reaction to what has been typed' (2003: vii; see also Jerz, 2000; Short, 2001). Arguably, this form of narrative is indeed script-based and may therefore be considered under the heading 'hypertext'. Nevertheless, as Montfort's investigation suggests, interactive fiction needs to be considered as a genre in its own right, one which generates its own, fully fledged canon and therefore ought to be examined independently.

13. Bukatman's concept of Virtual Reality is largely a physical one, implying devices such as 'Datagloves, electronic bodysuits, 3D eyephones, and the simulation of 360° sound' (1994: 13), which help immerse the user in a virtual environment that resembles his or her 'real' environment yet is infinitely more malleable and versatile.

14. Cramer (2001) makes a valid point in distinguishing early idealist-utopian forms of hypertext from more recent manifestations of programme code poetry. Claiming that the potential of this kind of poetry has previously been underestimated, he draws attention to examples of Perl Poetry, which is essentially tri-functional: Perl Poems can be read as poems in English, as sequences of programming commands, and, once they are activated, as new poems in English, which differ from their original by ways of hypermedial representation.

15. Eastgate Systems is the most prominent and prolific American publisher of commercially traded, closed hypertexts (e.g. Michael Joyce's *afternoon, a story*, Stuart Moulthrop's *Victory Garden* and Shelley Jackson's *Patchwork Girl*). Such hypertexts are proprietary, peer-reviewed and sold via the internet platform www.eastgate.com. They are 'closed' insofar as they resemble the book in their materiality (they are sold on manifest data carriers), are independent of the evanescence of the web and, as a result, cannot be co-written by users in the same way as internet-based hypertext networks are (e.g. *Assoziations-Blaster*; *23:40*). Storyspace (currently version 2.0) is Eastgate's 'home-made' hypertext editing software, which was co-designed by hypertext pioneers Michael Joyce, Jay David Bolter and John Smith in the late 1980s.

16. Joyce limits his investigation to the structuring principles of expository and scho-
     larly hypertexts designed in traditional hypertext editors such as Apple's *Hypercard*
     and Eastgate's *Storyspace*. He does not express any particular interest in creative
     writing or, for that matter, the acquisition of literary competence through crea-
     tive writing in hypertext. Furthermore, logistically speaking, in 1988 Joyce did not
     have the same variety of sophisticated web editing tools to hand as we do now,
     which clearly limited his aesthetic choice.

1   Hypertextual Ontologies

1.   A comprehensive survey of Talmud annotation and its resulting 'dialogic recep-
     tion' is undertaken by Fendt (2001), who may also be referred to for details on
     proto-hypertexts by Sterne, Eco, Joyce, Queneau, Cortázar and Saporta.
2.   The novel may be conceived of as a rebellious genre *per se*, as it set out to subvert the
     established tradition of the romance by going beyond the thematic, spatial and per-
     sonal confines of conventional, shorter narrative forms and by making deliberate
     use of non-aristocratic settings, incidents and characters.
3.   Sterne explains the interludic structure of *Tristram Shandy* in terms of simultaneous
     progression and digression, two converse movements which, contradictorily, con-
     verge into a proto-postmodern textual 'machinery'. Wirth (2001) consequently
     regards the principles of hypertexts as 'radicalized Shandyism' (57), as it realizes
     digression as 'a radicalized, electronic form of digressive association rooted in 18th
     century aesthetics' (Wirth, 2000).
4.   Gendolla and Schäfer (2001) add to the literary pre-history of hypertext a second,
     technological dimension. Hypertextual software has developed from electronic
     text adventures through MUDs to so-called chatter bots (e.g. Weizenbaum's
     Eliza). Early literature generators include William Chamberlain and Thomas
     Etter's *Racter* (1984), developed in 1988 for the German science competition
     'Jugend forscht', Ferdinand Schmatz and Franz-Josef Czernin's *POE* (1990),
     Rosemary West and Thomas E. Easton's *Thunder Thought* (1988) and Thomas
     Kamphusmann's *Delphi* (1993/1994).
5.   The term 'genre' is indeed problematic if used in the sense of 'literary genre', as
     hypertext literature encompasses all traditional literary genres (see Chapter 1.3)
     and produces adaptations of thematically and formally defined subgenres such as
     the psychological novel, the crime novel, the gothic tale and the epic. Alternative
     terms include 'mode' (of representation; see Jewitt, 2004), 'macromode' (of orga-
     nization; see Ensslin, in preparation), 'medium' and 'media genre'. In this book, I
     will continue to refer to literary hypertext as a genre in the sense of 'literary media
     genre', as its aesthetic principles are largely determined by the materiality and
     techno-structural principles of the computer and the internet.
6.   The referenced page number (0/2) refers to page 2 in section number 0, as desig-
     nated by Nelson (1984).
7.   Notably, no particular emphasis is placed on the visual arts, which would, in a
     direct application of the *Gesamtkunstwerk* concept to hypertext and hypermedia,
     need to play a dominant part.
8.   Intended to emulate the human brain, the *Memex* was designed to operate in terms
     of indexing, associative connection, and creating paths to help retrieve documents,

'snapping from one item instantly to the next that is suggested by association of thoughts' (Bush, 1945/1975: 34).

9. Clothed in varying terminological labels, these concepts are employed by theorists such as Barthes (1970/1987), Foucault (1973), Bakhtin (1984) and Derrida (1981).

10. Admittedly, reading conventional, linear print literature (and I will continue to refer to it as such, not least to mark the intended structural differences to hypertext) also involves retrospective and anticipating thoughts as well as physically realized flashbacks and flashforwards on the part of the reader (by means of turning pages). This adds to the fact that plot organization deliberately disarranges the chronological sequence of an underlying story. In other words, to a certain extent, structural delinearization and perceptive multilinearity are integral components of all literature. Having said that, 'multilinear reading', as used in this study, refers to the unusually high number of options a reader has in navigating through a hypertext as well as the text-inherent encouragement of the implied reader not to proceed in a linear fashion.

11. Wirth's and Simanowski's shared concept of carnivalization is drawn from Bakhtin (1981), who refers to the penetration of the carnivalesque (the disruption and subversion of authority and hierarchy for the sake of entertainment and the release of suppressed energies) into everyday life and the effect it has on literature and language (see Cuddon, 1999).

12. To reference lexias, their titles are italicized and put into square brackets.

13. As opposed to prognoses made by Kuhlen (1991: 14), 'hypermedia' has not replaced 'hypertext'. On the contrary, the two terms have come to be seen as denominators of two different generations of hypertext. Instead of taking over from each other back to back, hypertexts of both generations have been produced until now, depending on the aesthetic effects intended by authors.

14. GUIDE applications were developed in Great Britain to supplement earlier versions of HyperCard (Kuhlen, 1991: 55).

15. Contrary to Conklin's (1987) predictions, tastes and smells have not yet been included in hypermedia's multisensual experience. Tactile sensations, on the other hand, include touch-screen technology and text manipulation by means of mouse and keyboard. One may in fact argue that operating computer technology is no more if not actually less tactile than handling a book.

16. Landow (1992/1997), which is widely held to be perhaps the most significant (albeit not uncontroversial) monographic study of hypertext criticism, ignores hyperdrama entirely.

17. Simanowski describes his notion of hypertextual 'enactment' in terms of the programming of a text-intrinsic, reception-based performance, which essentially causes verbal elements to perform upon activation by the user.

18. For commercial reasons, directors are inclined to make patrons see such dramas sequentially rather than synchronically, making the audience attend two separate performances rather than one and charging separately as well. A similar, mixed approach was taken by Hannah Chissick in the most recent production of Ayckbourn's *House and Garden* at Harrogate (September/October 2005), where the two actions were performed on either side of a soundproof-strengthened safety curtain, which allowed the two audiences to attend only one action at a time. Notably, neither the theatre programme nor any of the reviews familiar to me mention the term 'hyperdrama'.

19. According to Bakhtin (1981: xxxi), the name 'novel' may be given to a work that reveals the limits and artificial constraints of a given literary system. Therefore, the term brings with it a notion of unconventionality, rebellion and experiment, which without further ado vindicates the idea of a hypernovel, the major element of which is defiance of established 'linear' modes of reading and understanding.

20. In his third, revised edition (Landow, 2006), Landow acknowledges the critical countermovement to his convergence theory, without, however, withdrawing it altogether. Instead, he offers a range of new, mostly postcolonialist approaches to hypertext and digital culture.

21. Further criticism of Landow's 'wreader' empowerment has been expressed, for example by Möckel-Rieke (1996), Aarseth (1997) and Rau (2000a). Their major argument is that the actual author-programmer (as an individual or a group) needs to be a master of digital synaesthesia, a technological *Universalgelehrter*, which implies a concept of the author as a writer as well as a numerical programmer or software designer.

22. Heibach (2001) explains that the crucial underlying principle of computer and internet technology is oscillation. She distinguishes between horizontal and vertical oscillation. The former signifies the data transfer and transformations between elements of the same type (e.g. different semiotic processes within the same computer system), whereas the latter describes oscillations between elements of different systems (e.g. human–machine interaction). The problem with Heibach's approach is that both levels mix to an almost indefinite degree in almost every work of digital literature, which complicates categorization and the drawing of clear boundaries between the two basic types of oscillation.

23. I adopt the Brechtian term 'culinary' to describe reading experiences that provide the receiver with 'food' for easy mental 'digestion'. Brecht's idea of an epic theatre broke with the 'culinary', realistic theatre which, in his opinion, set out to create an illusion of reality and thus infiltrated audiences with dominant bourgeois political ideology. In this study, 'culinary' describes any conventional reading experiences that indulge readers in the 'willing suspension of disbelief' by presenting them with traditionally linear text organization. Having said that, as an avid reader of both linear/print and antilinear/electronic literature, it would never occur to me to try to replace the former with the latter, but rather to raise the latter to an equally recognized status.

24. See http://www.berlinerzimmer.de/ (accessed 07/11/05) – also available in English.

25. See http://home.snafu.de/klinger/webgespraech/ (accessed 07/11/05).

26. See http://www.literaturcafe.de/ (accessed 07/11/05).

27. See http://www.bgsu.edu/cconline/ (accessed 20/10/05).

28. See http://www.dichtung-digital.com/ (accessed 20/10/05).

29. See http://www.hyperdis.de/ (accessed 20/10/05).

30. By 'simplex' hypertexts I understand hypertexts that are organized in a straightforward way, in terms of both quantitative scope and qualitative, cognitive demand. They can be read in a relatively short time (less than two hours). Complex hypertexts, on the other hand, comprise large numbers of lexias, which are also interlinked in such intricate ways that it is virtually impossible for any reader to cover all of them, not to mention reading all possible combinations and resulting plotlines. As complexity is relative, the relationship between simplex and complex hypertexts equals that of a continuum (rather than two separate categories).

31. The concept of defamiliarization can be traced as far back as the Romantics, such as Samuel T. Coleridge, who ascribed the effect of poetry to 'awakening the mind's attention to the lethargy of custom, and directing it to the loveliness and wonders of the world before us' (*Biographia Literaria*, Ch. XIV). Similarly, about 100 years later, in his essay 'Art as Technique', Shklovsky developed a similar concept, which he referred to as 'ostranenie': 'The technique of art is to make objects "unfamiliar", to make forms difficult, to increase the difficulty and length of perception because the process of perception is an aesthetic end in itself and must be prolonged' (Shklovsky, 1988: 20).

32. Block *et al.* (2004) position digital poetry in the tradition of concrete poetry.

33. Glazier's concept of transmissibility is roughly synonymous with Block *et al.*'s (2004) notion of networking.

34. Colours, for instance, are culturally contingent. The use of multiple, bright colours, for instance, is considered tasteful in countries such as India, Britain and the USA, whereas in central Europe, monochromous combinations are generally preferred (Taglinger, 2003: 132).

35. The term 'horizon of expectations' denotes the criteria used by readers to evaluate literary texts at any given time. According to Jauss, these criteria are based on a shared set of assumptions and help a certain community of readers to judge a text in a trans-subjective way. As horizons of expectations change over time, Jauss employs the term 'aesthetic distance' to describe the degree to which current readings depart from contemporary interpretations.

2 Hypertext and the Question of Canonicity

1. For a diachronic, etymological approach, see Marino (1996).

2. The problematic nature of this concept is evident, as it reflects the inherent contingency of the canon upon prominent socio-political and aesthetic ideologies, mostly represented by legislative, governing bodies and their executive administrative organs.

3. According to Tenbruck (1962), there are three types of societies: primitive, civilized and modern societies, which he understands in terms of a continuum, along which societies develop structurally. Tenbruck emphasizes that the three types are developmental stages rather than historical periods. Therefore, earlier societies are not necessarily less developed than later societies. As opposed to primitive societies, which largely consist of peasant strata, civilized societies ('Hochkulturen') are characterized by stratification into higher and lower social levels, where the higher strata hold together the lower ones, thus defining a common culture (e.g. religious, legal, oral and linguistic parameters). Modern societies are the most complex of the three, as mainly determined by functional rather than local differentiation, institutional contingency and a plurality of roles assumed by each society member in a variety of functional contexts.

4. The terms 'hypertext', 'hypermedia' and 'cybertext' were excluded from this survey, as the vast majority of occurrences appeared in the context of 'HTML' programming rather than literary discourse.

5. No occurrences of 'hyperpoetry' could be found in *LexisNexis*.

6. 'THES' is short for the weekly *Times Higher Education Supplement*.

7. Clearly, the evidence given in this survey cannot be considered representative for the whole of England or the UK. It would be interesting to see whether the North–South divide traditionally assumed in relation to cultural progressivity might be confirmed or rather, which would be more desirable, refuted.

8. Altogether three sets of SAT exams are done in English schools, at ages 7, 11 and 14 (after the pupils complete a 'key stage'). The SATs are national tests, which do not lead to a qualification but are intended to provide comparison between schools and help with applications to secondary schools and also for preparing streaming procedures for the GCSE (General Certificate of Secondary Education).

9. This observation is based on anecdotal evidence only.

10. The so-called 'Bolter Test' (Bernstein, n.d.) operates by asking the question: 'Can I read [this text] in bed? In the bathtub?' In the case of hypertext, this question has to be denied, which has been one of the main objections raised against hypertext.

11. For consistency's sake, the phenomenon of technological intertextuality can only be mentioned as an aside. Many author-programmers make use of previously written JavaScripts and Java Applets, which are sold or distributed freely on the web. This raises the questions of what true authorship really implies in an electronic environment, and where the boundary lies between radical instrumentalism and technological plagiarism.

3   A Hypertext Canon

1. Bearing in mind that hypertext readings tend to differ greatly from reader to reader, I shall outline the most 'common' features underlying each of the chosen texts rather than supplying fully fledged plot analyses, which may come across as prescriptive readings and, what is more, undermine themselves *per definitionem*.

2. According to Wikipedia, 50 per cent of all webpages are in English, followed by German (over 8 per cent), French (6 per cent), Japanese (5 per cent), Spanish (3 per cent) and Portuguese (2 per cent).

3. The title of the hyperfiction alludes to a pun mingling the name with success at war.

4. This unprecedentedly capricious medley of themes evokes associations with pig-centred novels like George Orwell's *Animal Farm* (1945), Marie Darrieussecq's *Pig Tales: A Tale of Lust and Transformations* (1997) and P. G. Wodehouse's Blandings novels. The spam obsession alludes to the Monty Python sketch 'Spam', first broadcast in 1970.

5. The major themes employed by Günther and Klötgen are clearly reminiscent of Günter Grass's *The Tin Drum*, with its never-growing child narrator and the maternal figure being traumatized by her husband's phallic obsession with eels, which symbolize at once *eros* and *thanatos*, as they feed on cadavers, thus uniting death and sexual instinct.

4   Literary Competence – Conceptual Adaptations

1. Constructivism was preceded by behaviorism and cognitivism, two learning theories that are still applied yet are considered less significant in a subject-centred,

individualist Western society. Siemens (2005) suggests yet another contemporary paradigm, which is supposed to reflect the prerequisites of the networking tendencies, as well as the exponential growth of easily accessible information in the Digital Age. He refers to it as 'connectivism'. However, our contemporary educational parameters, which are directed towards knowledge that should be 'compiled', and 'constructed' in such a way as to make it summatively testable, do not (yet) comply to the implications imposed by connectivism, which works on the basis of epistemological ephemerality and substitutability. Similarly, with regard to curriculum-planning and didactic practice, connectivism has not yet translated into the ideologies of educational institutions. Therefore, Siemens's no doubt plausible anticipations may certainly not go unnoticed, yet cannot be taken as a working basis of this study.

2. Constructivism first emerged in the fields of mathematics and logic. The term will be used in this study primarily in the epistemological sense of radical constructivism, which contravenes traditional philosophy in that it deviates from the fallacy of metaphysical truth and, in lieu, proposes a more pragmatic approach to issues surrounding language, reality, truth and human cognition.

3. Both Piaget and Bruner postulate that learning is an active process. Throughout his studies, Piaget investigated the cognitive development of children and young teenagers. His major observation was that cognitive structures are formed in the *process* of assimilating one's environment to meet existing cognitive structures while simultaneously accommodating pre-existing structures to adjust to newly experienced external structures. Bruner, on the other hand, extended and applied this theory to curriculum design. According to him, all teaching should be based on student learning. His key emphasis lay on how to organize and structure the learning process such as to design curricula along the lines of the learners' needs, interests and readiness. What is absolutely central about Bruner's heritage is the strong belief that new concepts can only be constructed on the basis of current and past knowledge.

4. The term 'human organism' is used by Maturana and Varela, who are based in biology and view human beings in terms of autonomous, self-creating, self-organizing and self-preserving systems.

5. The term *autopoietic* (Greek for 'self-creating') refers to concepts such as self-sufficiency, autonomy, self-referentiality, operational self-containedness and structural determination (Schmidt, 2002: 151). Its major implication is that each subject, who is essentially seen as a self-contained, closed system, continually interacts with its environment and other living systems or organisms and, at the same time, continual changes its own structure. Interaction thus takes place externally and internally.

6. Pike (2003) emphasizes the validity of Rosenblatt's work in contrast to Iser's and other Reader-Response critics, who, rather than focusing on individuals in their social context, 'still seek the aesthetic factor entirely in the text' (Rosenblatt, 1985: 38).

7. According to Schmeck (1983), a learning style is a certain predisposition to display particular kinds of behaviour, which are fed by personality and cognitive style characteristics. Honey and Mumford's four learning styles always apply in combination, but vary in weighting.

8. The term 'flow' refers to a concept introduced by Csikszentmihalyi (1990). In a nutshell, it relates to the capacity for full engagement in the sense of 'losing oneself' in an activity, which entails a maximum degree of concentration, intrinsic motivation and personal gain.

5 Hypertext in the Literature Classroom

1. Schema Theory assumes that human knowledge is stored in so-called information packets (schemas), which contain mental constructs for ideas. Schemas have certain attributes, which they may share with other schemas. They can be perceived as mini-frameworks, into which new conceptual elements can be integrated.

2. An important contribution to hypertext pedagogy has been made by Nielsen (1990, 1994). He concentrates on the general uses of hypertext and hypermedia, both within and beyond education. His perception of the general usability properties of hypertext systems is that they are easy to learn, efficient to use, easy to remember, make few errors, and are pleasant to use. Paradoxically, Nielsen both critiques and adds to the hype surrounding hypertext learning systems without, however, backing up his argument with empirical data.

3. The generally small number of reported cases does, of course, not imply that there has been an overall lack of integrated, exploratory and constructive teaching approaches, with students exploring (i.e. analysing) literary hypertexts against the backdrop of hypertext and poststructuralist criticism and, in applying newly acquired knowledge, creating their own literary hypertexts as part of the assessment.

4. Educational theory has been focusing on motivational questions since the 1960s, when it became clear that behaviorism, which had dominated learning psychology since the beginning of the twentieth century, could not account for any processes that occurred inside the 'black box' of the human mind. In the context of cognitivism, the emphasis was subsequently shifted from extrinsic to intrinsic motivation, typically experienced in children's play (Huizinga, 1939/70; Piaget, 1951; Callois, 1961; Herron and Sutton-Smith, 1971). More recently, particular interest has arisen in so-called autotelic activities (activities which are carried out for their own sake and cause a maximum of concentration, enjoyment and deep learning in the individual) and 'flow' (e.g. Csikszentmihalyi, 1990).

5. The term triangulation refers to a combination of distinct research methods, which are used to arrive at an approximate maximum of empirical objectivity.

6. 'Qualitative' indicates the non-statistical nature of this project. A quantitative, statistical study would only apply given a minimum number of 30 research subjects.

7. For consistency's sake, I use methodical terminology as suggested by Cohen and Manion (1994) and, especially for qualitative research, that of Hammersley *et al.* (1994).

8. Smith and Kollock (1999) use the three terms interaction, communication and coordination to map out the differences between face-to-face and online communication like email, chat and conferencing systems. The terms will be applied in this study to describe actual face-to-face communication in a hypermedia-expanded classroom.

9. For a discussion of language learning through hypertext, see Ensslin (2006).

References

Primary Sources

Amerika, M. (1996) *Grammatron* [online]. Available at: www.grammatron.com [accessed 20 August 2006].

Avenstoup, T. and Lippok, R. (2002) *marbel + matrikel* [online]. Available at: www. marbelundmatrikel.de/ [accessed 20 August 2006].

Ayckbourn, A. (1973) *The Norman Conquests*. London: Chatto & Windus.

Ayckbourn, A. (2000) *House and Garden*. London: Faber & Faber.

Bertram, N. (2002) *Der Kahuna Modus*, CD-ROM, in R. Simanowski (ed), *Literatur. digital. Formen und Wege einer neuen Literatur*. Munich: dtv.

Bly, B. (1997) *We Descend*, CD-ROM. Environment: Storyspace. Cambridge, MA: East-gate Systems.

Böttcher, B. (1997) *looppool – ein Hyperpoetry-Clip* [online]. Weimar University. Available at: www.looppool.de [accessed 20 August 2006].

Brunnauer, R. (2002) *Zwei Tote?*, CD-ROM, in R. Simanowski (ed), *Literatur.digital. Formen und Wege einer neuen Literatur*. Munich: dtv.

Christian, P. (1996) *The Spoonbill Generator* [online]. Available at: www.spoonbill.org [accessed 20 August 2006].

Coverley, M. D. (2000) *Califia*, CD-ROM. Environment: Storyspace. Watertown, MA: Eastgate Systems.

Deemer, C. (1986) *Chateau de mort* [online]. Available at: www.brookes.ac.uk/VL/ theatre/authord.htm [accessed 20 August 2006].

Deemer, C. (1996a) *The Last Song of Violeta Parra* [online]. Available at: www.geocities. com/cdeemer/chile.htm [accessed 30 July 2006].

Deemer, C. (1996b) *The Bride of Edgefield* [online]. Available at: www.ibiblio.org/ cdeemer/intro.htm [accessed 20 August 2006].

Deemer, C. (2002) *The Seagull* [online]. Available at: www.ibiblio.org/cdeemer/ chekindx.htm [accessed 20 August 2006].

Douglas, J. Y. (1994) *I Have Said Nothing* [online]. New York, W. W. Norton & Company. Available at: www.wwnorton.com/pmaf/hypertext/ihsn/i_have_said_ nothing.html [accessed 20 August 2006].

EastEdge (1998) *Tyrell.Hungary* [online]. Available at: www.shiseido.co.jp/s9808tre/ realindex.html [accessed 20 August 2006].

Ehlert, N. and Bauer, W. (2002) *Jetzt? Oder der höchste Augenblick*, CD-ROM, in R. Simanowski (ed), *Literatur.digital. Formen und Wege einer neuen Literatur*. Munich: dtv.

Eisen, A. (1996) *Six Sex Scenes* [online]. Available at: www.geocities.com/penelope4515/ six_sex_scenes/index.htm [accessed 20 August 2006].

Falco, E. (1997) *A Dream with Demons*, CD-ROM. Environment: Storyspace. Watertown, MA: Eastgate Systems.

Freude, A. and Espenschied, D. (1999/2000) *Assoziations-Blaster* [online]. Available at: www.a-blast.org [accessed 20 August 2006].

Ganymed and Nexo of Kystone (2001) *Fraktalroman: Interaktive Literatur für schreibende Leser* [online]. Available at: www.fraktalroman.de [accessed 20 August 2006].

Goldmann, M. (2002) *Schreiben auf Wasser*, CD-ROM, in R. Simanowski (ed), *Literatur. digital. Formen und Wege einer neuen Literatur*. Munich: dtv.

Grigat, G. (1997) *23:40 – das kollektive Gedächtnis* [online]. Available at: www. dreiundzwanzigvierzig.de/cgi-bin/2340index.pl [accessed 20 August 2006].

Günther, D. and Klötgen, F. (1998) *Die Aaleskorte der Ölig* [online]. Available at: www.aaleskorte.de [accessed 20 August 2006].

Guyer, C. (1993) *Quibbling*, CD-ROM. Environment: Storyspace. Watertown, MA: Eastgate Systems.

Hasecke, J. U. (1997) *Generationenprojekt* [online]. Available at: www.generationenprojekt. de [accessed 20 August 2006].

Holeton, R. (2001) *Figurski at Findhorn on Acid*, CD-ROM. Environment: Storyspace. Watertown, MA: Eastgate Systems.

Inglis, G. (1999) *Same Day Test* [online]. Available at: www.bareword.com/sdt/ [accessed 20 August 2006].

Jackson, S. (1995) *Patchwork Girl, Or a Modern Monster*, CD-ROM. Environment: Storyspace. Cambridge, MA: Eastgate Systems.

Joyce, M. (1990) *afternoon, a story*, CD-ROM. Environment: Storyspace. Cambridge, MA: Eastgate Systems (first published 1987).

Joyce, M. (1996) *Twilight, a Symphony*, CD-ROM. Environment: Storyspace. Watertown, MA: Eastgate Systems.

Kendall, R. (1999–2000) *The Seasons* [online]. Watertown, MA: Eastgate Systems. Available at: www.eastgate.com/Seasons/Welcome.html [accessed 20 August 2006].

Klinger, C. (2000) *Beim Bäcker* [online]. Available at: http://home.snafu.de/klinger/ baecker/ [accessed 20 August 2006].

Larsen, D. (1993) *Marble Springs*, CD-ROM. Environment: HyperCard. Watertown, MA: Eastgate Systems. Trial version available at: www.eastgate.com/MS/ Title_184.html [accessed 20 August 2006].

Larsen, D. (2000) *Samplers: Nine Vicious Little Hypertexts*, CD-ROM. Environment: Storyspace. Watertown, MA: Eastgate Systems.

Linke, D. (2002) *Der Apfel*, CD-ROM, in R. Simanowski (ed), *Literatur.digital. Formen und Wege einer neuen Literatur*. Munich: dtv.

Mac, C. (1994) *Unnatural Habitats*, CD-ROM. Environment: Storyspace. Watertown, MA: Eastgate Systems.

McDaid, J. (1992) *Uncle Buddy's Phantom Funhouse*, CD-ROM. Environment: Storyspace. Watertown, MA: Eastgate Systems.

McLaughlin, T. (1995) *Notes towards Absolute Zero*, CD-ROM. Environment: Storyspace. Watertown, MA: Eastgate Systems.

Malloy, J. and Marshall, C. (1996) *Forward Anywhere*, CD-ROM. Environment: Storyspace. Watertown, MA: Eastgate Systems.

Maskiewicz, S. (2001) *Quadrego* [online]. Kiel, Germany. Available at: www.leeon.de/ showroom/Quadrego/start.htm [accessed 20 August 2006].

Meetfactory (1998) *Conversation with Angels* [online]. Available at: http://angels.kiasma. fng.fi/ [accessed 20 August 2006].

Menzer, U. and Orth, S. (2001) *Er/Sie: ein literarisches Internet-Projekt* [online]. Available at: www.soyosigma.de/ersie/ [accessed 20 August 2006].

Morrissey, J. and Talley, L. (2002) *My Name Is Captain, Captain*, CD-ROM. Environment: Flash. Watertown, MA: Eastgate Systems.

Moulthrop, S. (1991) *Victory Garden*, CD-ROM. Environment: Storyspace. Cambridge, MA: Eastgate Systems.

Moulthrop, S. (1997) *Hegirascope* [online]. Baltimore University. Available at: http://iat.ubalt.edu/moulthrop/hypertexts/hgs/ [accessed 20 August 2006] (first published 1995).

Nestvold, R. (1995–2001) *Cutting Edges, Or, A Web of Women* [online]. Available at: www.lit-arts.net/Cutting_Edges/1stpage.htm [accessed 20 August 2006].

Pullinger, K. (2004) *The Breathing Wall*, CD-ROM. London: The Sayle Literary Agency.

Rosenberg, J. (1968–1999) *Diagrams* [online]. Available at: www.well.com/user/jer/diags.html [accessed 20 August 2006].

Ryman, G. (1996) *253, Or: Tube Theatre* [online]. Available at: www.ryman-novel.com [accessed 20 August 2006].

Sanford, C. S. (1996) *Safara in the Beginning* [online]. Available at: http://web.purplefrog.com/~christy/safara/safara2.html [accessed 20 August 2006].

Schreiber, U. (1998) *Das Epos der Maschine* [online]. Available at: http://kunst.im.internett.de/epos-der-maschine/edmdiemaschine.html [accessed 20 August 2006].

Servin, J. (1997) *BEAST* [online]. Available at: www.netzaesthetik.de/Servin/Beast/ [accessed 20 August 2006].

Seyerlein, A. L. (2002) *Die Callas-Box*, CD-ROM, in R. Simanowski (ed), *Literatur. digital. Formen und Wege einer neuen Literatur*. Munich: dtv.

Siffert, C. (1998) *StorySprawl* [online]. Available at: www.storysprawl.com/ [accessed 20 August 2006].

Smith, S. (1991) *King of Space*, CD-ROM. Environment: Storyspace. Watertown, MA: Eastgate Systems.

Strickland, S. (1997) *True North*, CD-ROM. Environment: Storyspace. Watertown, MA: Eastgate Systems.

Swigart, R. (2000) *Down Time*, CD-ROM. Environment: QuickTime. Cambridge, MA: Eastgate Systems.

von Goethe, J. W. (1948–1960), *Goethes Werke*, vols. 1–14. Ed. Erich Trunz. Hamburg: Wegner.

Zeitgenossen (2001) *Yatoo* [online]. Available at: www.zeitgenossen.com/outerspaceip/ [accessed 20 August 2006].

Secondary Sources

Aarseth, E. J. (1997) *Cybertext: Perspectives on Ergodic Literature*. Baltimore: John Hopkins University Press.

Ackermann, E. and Hartman, K. (2000) *Internet and Web Essentials*. Wilsonville, OR: Franklin, Beedle and Associates. Supplementary glossary [online]. Available at: www.webliminal.com/essentials/glossary.htm [accessed 20 August 2006].

Allen, D. (1980) *English Teaching since 1965: How Much Growth?*. London: Heinemann Educational.

Allinson, L. and Hammond, N. (1999) 'A learning support environment: the Hitch-Hiker's Guide', in R. McAleese (ed), *Hypertext: Theory into Practice*. Exeter: Intellect, pp. 53–63.

Amerika, M. (1998) *The book and the beast* [online]. New York: Rhizome.org. Available from: http://rhizome.org/thread.rhiz?thread=226&page=1 [accessed 20 August 2006].

Anthony, A. (2001) 'Square deals and dodgy geezers: after arson and kidnap, Walford hit a lull – so the Tory leadership contest was the most gripping soap in town', *Observer*, 26 August, 20.

Arnold, H. L. (2001) *Text und Kritik (152) Digitale Literatur*. Munich: Richard Boorberg.

Arnold, H. L. and Detering, H. (1997) *Grundzüge der Literaturwissenschaft*. Munich: dtv.

Arnold, M. (1888) 'The study of poetry', in M. Arnold (ed), *Essays in Criticism: Second Series*. London: Macmillan (first published 1880), pp. 1–55.

Ascott, R. (1999) 'Gesamtdatenwerk: connectivity, transformation, and transcendence', in T. Druckrey (ed), *Ars Electronica: Facing the Future: A Survey of Two Decades*. Cambridge, MA: MIT Press, pp. 86–9.

Assmann, A. and Assmann, J. (1987) *Kanon und Zensur. Archäologie der literarischen Kommunikation, II*. Munich: Wilhelm Fink.

Auer, J. (2000) '7 Thesen zur Netzliteratur'. *Dichtung digital* [online]. Available at: www.dichtung-digital.de/IASL-Forum/Auer-20-Jun-00.htm [accessed 20 August 2006].

Auer, J. (2004) 'Screaming screen and binary idealism', in F. W. Block *et al.* (eds), *p0es1s. Ästhetik digitaler Poesie – The Aesthetics of Digital Poetry*. Ostfildern: Hatje Cantz, pp. 277–86.

Auer, J. (2005) ::*Projekte::Netzliteratur//Hyperfiktion* [online]. Available at: http://auer.netzliteratur.net/du/hyperfiction_a.php [accessed 20 August 2006].

Baacke, D. (1999) ' "Medienkompetenz": theoretisch erschließend und praktisch erfolgreich'. *Medien und Erziehung*, 43, (1), 7–12.

Bakhtin, M. (1981) *The Dialogic Imagination: Four Essays* (ed. M. Holquist, trans. C. Emerson and M. Holquist). Austin: University of Texas Press.

Bakhtin, M. (1984) *Problems of Dostoevsky's Poetics* (ed. and trans. C. Emerson). Minneapolis, MN: University of Minnesota Press.

Bandura, A. (1977) *Social Learning Theory*. New York: General Learning Press.

Barron, J. (1995) 'Moving from *Afternoon* to *Twilight*' [online]. Available at: www.poprocks.com/journ/twilight.htm [accessed 19 August 2006].

Barthes, R. (1972) *Mythologies* (trans. A. Lavers). New York: Hill and Wang.

Barthes, R. (1977a) 'The photographic message', in R. Barthes (ed), *Image-Music-Text* (trans. S. Heath). New York: Hill and Wang (first published 1961), pp. 15–31.

Barthes, R. (1977b) 'Rhetoric of the image', in R. Barthes (ed), *Image-Music-Text* (trans. S. Heath). New York: Hill and Wang (first published 1964), pp. 32–51.

Barthes, R. (1977c) 'The death of the author', in R. Barthes (ed), *Image-Music-Text* (trans. S. Heath). New York: Hill and Wang (first published 1968), pp. 142–8.

Barthes, R. (1980) *Leçon/Lektion* (transl. H. Scheffel). Frankfurt/M.: Suhrkamp (first published 1978).

Barthes, R. (1987) *S/Z* (trans. J. Hoch). Frankfurt/M.: Suhrkamp (first published 1970).

Barthes, R. (1990) *Die Lust am Text* (trans. T. König). Frankfurt/M.: Suhrkamp (first published 1973).

Beardsley, M. (1973) 'The concept of literature', in E. John and J. McIver Lopes (eds), *Philosophy of Literature: Contemporary and Classic Readings*. Oxford: Blackwell, pp. 51–8.

Becker, H. B. (1995) 'A new art form: hypertext fiction', in M. L. L. dos Santos (ed), *Cultura & Economia*. Lisbon: Edicões do Instituto de Ciências Sociais, pp. 67–81. Available at: http://home.earthlink.net/-hsbecker/lisbon.html [accessed 20 August 2006].

Beiguelman, G. (2004) 'WYSIWYG or WYGISWYS? (What You See is What You Get or What You Get is What You See: notes on the loss of inscription)', in F. W. Block *et al.* (eds), *pOes1s. Ästhetik digitaler Poesie – The Aesthetics of Digital Poetry*. Ostfildern: Hatje Cantz, pp. 169–80.

Belkin, N. J., Brooks, H. M. and Oddy, R. N. (1982) 'ASK for information retrieval'. *Journal of Documentation*, 38, 61–71.

Bell, A. (forthcoming) ' "Do you want to hear about it?" Exploring possible worlds in Michael Joyce's hyperfiction, afternoon, a story', in M. Lambrou and P. Stockwell (eds), *Contemporary Stylistics*. London: Continuum.

Benjamin, W. (1977) 'Das Kunstwerk im Zeitalter seiner technischen Reproduzierbarkeit', in W. Benjamin (ed), *Illuminationen. Ausgewählte Schriften I*. Frankfurt/M.: Suhrkamp, pp. 136–69.

Benton, M. (2000) 'Canons ancient and modern: the texts we teach'. *Educational Review*, 52, (3), 269–77.

Bernstein, M. (1998) 'Patterns of hypertext' [online]. Watertown, MA: Eastgate Systems. Available at: www.eastgate.com/patterns/Print.html [accessed 20 August 2006].

Bernstein, M. (n.d.) 'Electronic reading' [online]. Watertown, MA: Eastgate Systems. Available at: www.eastgate.com/HypertextNow/archives/Electronic.html [accessed 20 August 2006].

Biggs, J. B. (1979) 'Individual differences in study processes and the quality of learning outcomes'. *Higher Education*, 8, 381–94.

Blackledge, A. (1994) 'Poetry and bias in the primary school'. *Educational Review*, 46, (1), 39–46.

Block, F. W. (2001) 'Website: zum Ort digitaler Literatur im Netz der Literaturen', in H. L. Arnold (ed), *Text und Kritik (152) Digitale Literatur*. Munich: Richard Boorberg, pp. 99–111.

Block, F. W. (2004) 'Eight digits of digital poetics', in F. W. Block *et al.* (eds), *pOes1s. Ästhetik digitaler Poesie – The Aesthetics of Digital Poetry*. Ostfildern: Hatje Cantz, pp. 307–17.

Block, F. W., Heibach, C. and Wenz, K. (2004) *pOes1s. Ästhetik digitaler Poesie – The Aesthetics of Digital Poetry*. Ostfildern: Hatje Cantz.

Bloom, H. (1994) *The Western Canon: The Books and School of the Ages*. New York: Harcourt Brace & Company.

Bly, B. (n.d.) 'I descend into hypertext' [online]. Lubbock, TX: Texas Tech. University. Available at: http://english.ttu.edu/kairos/3.2/response/Kendall/bly.htm [accessed 20 August 2006].

Bolter, J. D. (1991) *Topographic Writing: Hypertext and the Electronic Writing Space*. Cambridge, MA: MIT Press.

Bolter, J. D. (1992) 'Literature in the electronic writing space', in M. Tuman (ed), *Literacy Online: The Promise (and Peril) of Reading (and Writing) with Computers*. Pittsburgh, PA: University of Pittsburgh Press, pp. 19–42.

Bolter, J. D. (2001) *Writing Space: Computers, Hypertext, and the Remediation of Print*. Mahwah, NJ: Lawrence Erlbaum Associates.

Bootz, P. (2004) 'Reader/readers', in F. W. Block *et al.* (eds), *p0es1s. Ästhetik digitaler Poesie – The Aesthetics of Digital Poetry*. Ostfildern: Hatje Cantz, pp. 93–122.

Bridgham, F. (2000) 'Gesamtkunstwerk', in M. Konzett (ed), *Encyclopedia of German Literature*. Chicago: Fitzroy Dearborn, pp. 337–8.

Bruner, J. S. (1977) 'Wie das Kind lernt, sich sprachlich zu verständigen'. *Zeitschrift für Pädagogik*, 23, 829–44.

Bühler, K. (1934) *Sprachtheorie: Die Darstellungsfunktion der Sprache*. Jena: Fischer.

Bukatman, S. (1994) 'Virtual textuality'. *Artforum*, January 1994, 13–14.

Bush, V. (1975) 'As we may think', in V. Bush (ed), *Endless Horizons*. Washington, DC: Public Affairs Press (first published 1945), pp. 16–38.

Calliope Inc. (2005) *The Thoreau Project* [online]. Available at: www.calliope.org/thoreau/thoreau.html [accessed 20 August 2006].

Callois, R. (1961) *Man, Play and Games*. New York: Free Press of Glencoe.

Calvi, L. (2001) 'Hypertext and comics: towards an aesthetics of hypertext', in K. Grønbæk (ed), *Proceedings of the Twelfth ACM Conference on Hypertext and Hypermedia*. Aarhus: ACM Press, pp. 135–7.

Carr, F. L. (1999) 'Interview with Mark Bernstein' [online]. Fairfax, VA: George Mason University. Available at: http://chnm.gmu.edu/ematters/issue3/bernstein/bernstein1.html [accessed 20 August 2006].

Chance, P. (1992) 'The rewards of learning'. *Phi Delta Kappan*, 73, 200–7.

Chaouli, M. (2001) 'Was bedeutet: online lesen? Über die Möglichkeit des Archivs im Cyberspace', in H. L. Arnold (ed), *Text und Kritik (152) Digitale Literatur*. Munich: Richard Boorberg, pp. 65–74.

Chomsky, N. (1964) *Current Issues in Linguistic Theory*. The Hague: Mouton.

Chomsky, N. (1965) *Aspects of the Theory of Syntax*. Cambridge, MA: MIT Press.

Clarke, S., Dickinson, P. and Westbrook, J. (2004) *The Complete Guide to Becoming an English Teacher*. London: Paul Chapman Publishing.

Cohen, L. and Manion, L. (1994) *Research Methods in Education*. London: Routledge.

Collins, A., Brown, J. S. and Newman, S. E. (1989) 'Cognitive apprenticeship: teaching the craft of reading, writing and mathematics', in L. B. Resnick (ed), *Knowing, Learning, and Instruction: Essays in Honor of Robert Glaser*. Hillsdale, NJ: Lawrence Erlbaum Associates, pp. 1–35.

Conklin, J. (1987) 'Hypertext – an introduction and survey'. *IEEE Computer*, 20, (9), 17–41.

Constantinou, O. (2005) 'Multimodal discourse analysis'. *Journal of Sociolinguistics*, 9, (4), 602–18.

Coover, R. (1992) 'The end of books'. *New York Times Book Review*, 21 June, 23–5.

Coover, R. (1993) 'Hyperfiction: novels for the computer'. *New York Times Book Review*, 29 August, 1–12.

Coover, R. (1999) 'Literary hypertext: the passing of the Golden Age' [online]. Available at: http://nickm.com/vox/golden_age.html [accessed 20 August 2006].

Corey, S. (1949) 'Action research, fundamental research and educational practices'. *Teachers' College Record*, 50, 509–14.

Cramer, F. (2001) 'sub merge {my $enses;: ASCII Art, Rekursion, Lyrik in Programmiersprachen', in H. L. Arnold (ed), *Text und Kritik (152) Digitale Literatur*. Munich: Richard Boorberg, pp. 112–23.

Cramer, F. (2004) 'Digital code and literary text', in F. W. Block *et al.* (eds), *p0es1s. Ästhetik digitaler Poesie – The Aesthetics of Digital Poetry*. Ostfildern: Hatje Cantz, pp. 263–76.

Crane, G. (2005) *The Perseus Digital Library* [online]. Available at: http://www.perseus. tufts.edu/ [accessed 20 August 2006].

Csikszentmihalyi, M. (1990) *Flow: The Psychology of Optimal Experience*. New York, NY: Harper & Row.

Cuddon, J. A. (1999) *The Penguin Dictionary of Literary Terms and Literary Theory*. London: Penguin.

Culler, J. (1975) *Structuralist Poetics: Structuralism, Linguistics and the Study of Literature*. London: Routledge & Kegan Paul.

Cumming, A. and Sinclair, G. (1991) 'Conceptualizing hypermedia curricula for literary studies in schools', in P. Delany and G. P. Landow (eds), *Hypermedia and Literary Studies*. Cambridge, MA: MIT Press, pp. 315–28.

Cunningham, D. J., Duffy, T. M. and Knuth, R. A. (1993) 'The textbook of the future', in C. McKnight *et al.* (eds), *Hypertext: A Psychological Perspective*. Chichester: Ellis Horwood, pp. 19–50.

Daiber, J. (1999) 'Literatur und Nicht-Linearität: ein Widerspruch in sich?', in K. Eibl and F. Jannidis (eds), *Jahrbuch für Computerphilologie*. Paderborn: mentis, pp. 21–39. Available at: www.computerphilologie.uni-muenchen.de/jahrbuch/jb1/daiber.html [accessed 20 August 2006].

Davenport, E. (1978) 'Why theorize about literature?', in P. Hernadi (ed), *What Is Literature?*. Bloomington, IN: Indiana University Press, pp. 35–46.

de Beaugrande, R. and Dressler, W. U. (1981) *Einführung in die Textlinguistik*. Tübingen: Niemeyer.

Deci, E. and Ryan, R. (1985) *Intrinsic Motivation and Self-Determination in Human Behavior*. New York: Plenum.

Deemer, C. (1994) 'What is hypertext?' [online]. Chapel Hill, NC: ibiblio. Available at: www.ibiblio.org/cdeemer/hypertxt.htm [accessed 20 August 2006].

Deemer, C. (1996) 'Hyperdrama and virtual development: notes on creating new hyperdrama in cyberspace'. *Theatre Central Presents*, 1, (3) [online]. Chapel Hill, NC: ibiblio. Available at: www.ibiblio.org/cdeemer/virtdev.htm [accessed 20 August 2006].

Deemer, C. (n.d.) 'The new hyperdrama: how hypertext scripts are changing the parameters of dramatic storytelling' [online]. Chapel Hill, NC: ibiblio. Available at: www.ibiblio.org/cdeemer/newhype.htm [accessed 20 August 2006].

Delany, P. and Landow, G. P. (1991) *Hypermedia and Literary Studies*. Cambridge, MA: MIT Press.

Deleuze, G. and Guattari, F. (1987) *A Thousand Plateaus: Capitalism and Schizophrenia* (trans. and foreword B. Massumi). Minneapolis, MN: University of Minneapolis Press.

Dell, G. S. (1986) 'A spreading activation theory of retrieval in sentence production'. *Psychological Review*, 93, 283–321.

Dell, G. S., Schwartz, M. F., Martin, N., Saffran, E. M. and Gagnon, D. A. (1997) 'Lexical access in aphasic and nonaphasic speakers'. *Psychological Review*, 104, 801–38.

DeMan, P. (1983) *Blindness and Insight. Essays in the Rhetoric of Contemporary Criticism*. Minneapolis, MN: University of Minnesota Press.

Derrida, J. (1976) *Of Grammatology* (trans. G. C. Spivak). Baltimore: Johns Hopkins University Press.

Derrida, J. (1981) *Dissemination* (trans. B. Johnson). Chicago: University of Chicago Press.

Dery, M. (1996) *Escape Velocity: Cyberculture at the End of the Century*. London: Hodder and Stoughton.

Dewe, B. and Sander, U. (1996) 'Medienkompetenz und Erwachsenenbildung', in A. V. Rein (ed), *Medienkompetenz als Schlüsselbegriff*. Bad Heilbrunn: Klinkhardt, pp. 115–42.

DeWitt, S. L. (1999) 'Defining links', in S. L. DeWitt and K. Strasma (eds), *Contexts, Intertexts, and Hypertexts*. Cresskill, NJ: Hampton Press, pp. 65–116.

DeWitt, S. L. and Strasma, K. (1999) *Contexts, Intertexts, and Hypertexts*. Cresskill, NJ: Hampton Press.

Dobson, T. (1999) 'Mind the gap: reading literary hypertext' [online]. Charlottesville, VA: University of Virginia. Available at: http://www.iath.virginia.edu/ach-allc.99/proceedings/dobson.html [accessed 20 August 2006].

Douglas, J. Y. (1992) 'Maps, gaps, and perceptions. What hypertext readers (don't) do'. *Perforations*, 3, (1) [online]. Available at: http://web.nwe.ufl.edu/~jdouglas/perforations.pdf [accessed 20 August 2006].

Douglas, J. Y. (1993) 'Where the senses become a stage and reading is direction: performing the texts of virtual reality and interactive fiction'. *The Drama Review*, 37, (4), 18–37.

Douglas, J. Y. (1994) ' "How do I stop this thing": closure and indeterminacy in interactive narratives', in G. P. Landow (ed), *Hyper/Text/Theory*. Baltimore: Johns Hopkins University Press, pp. 159–88.

Duffy, T. M. and Knuth, R. A. (1990) 'Hypermedia and instruction: where is the match?', in D. H. Jonassen and H. Mandl (eds), *Designing Hypermedia for Learning*. Heidelberg: Springer, pp. 199–225.

Duguay, K. (1999) 'Sites of conflict: the challenges of hypertextualizing composition in the college writing class', in S. L. DeWitt and K. Strasma (eds), *Contexts, Intertexts, and Hypertexts*. Cresskill, NJ: Hampton Press, pp. 15–38.

Eagleton, T. (1983) *Literary Theory: An Introduction*. Minneapolis, MN: University of Minnesota Press.

Eco, U. (1989) *The Open Work* (trans. A. Cancogni). Cambridge, MA: Harvard University Press.

Edwards, D. M. and Hardman, L. (1989) ' "Lost in hyperspace": cognitive mapping and navigation in a hypertext environment', in R. McAleese (ed), *Hypertext: Theory into Practice*. London: Intellect Limited, pp. 105–12.

Eichenbaum, B. (1965) 'Theory of the formal method', in L. T. Lemon and M. J. Reis (eds), *Russian Formalist Criticism*. Lincoln, NE: University of Nebraska Press (first published 1926), pp. 99–140.

Eliot, T. S. (1932) *Selected Essays, 1917–1932*. London: Faber & Faber.

Eliot, T. S. (1972) 'Tradition and the individual talent', in T. S. Eliot (ed), *The Sacred Wood: Essays on Poetry and Criticism*. London: Methuen (first published 1919), pp. 47–59.

Empson, W. (1930) *Seven Types of Ambiguity*. London: Chatto and Windus.

Ensslin, A. (2004) 'Reconstructing the deconstructed: hypertext and literary education'. *Language and Literature*, 13, (4), 307–33.

Ensslin, A. (2005a) *Leeds Hypertext Project* [online]. Leeds: University of Leeds. Available at: www.german.leeds.ac.uk/HTproject/04/index.htm [accessed 20 August 2006].

Ensslin, A. (2005b) 'Women in wasteland – gendered deserts in T. S. Eliot and Shelley Jackson'. *Journal of Gender Studies*, 14, (3), 205–16.

Ensslin, A. (2006) 'Literary hypertext in the foreign language classroom: a case study report'. *Language Learning Journal*, 33, 13–21.

Ensslin, A. (in preparation) 'Towards hyperstylistics: expanding the toolkit'.

Fendt, K. (2001) 'Leser auf Abwegen: Hypertext und seine literarisch-ästhetischen Vorbilder', in H. L. Arnold (ed), *Text und Kritik (152) Digitale Literatur*. Munich: Richard Boorberg, pp. 87–98.

Fiderio, J. (1988) 'A grand vision'. *Byte*, 13, (10), 237–43.

Fish, S. (1980) *Is There a Text in this Class? The Authority of Interpretive Communities*. Cambridge, MA: Harvard University Press.

Flender, J. and Christmann, U. (2002) 'Zur optimalen Passung von medienspezifischen Randbedingungen und Verarbeitungskompetenzen / Lernstrategien bei linearen Texten und Hypertexten', in N. Groeben and B. Hurrelmann (eds), *Medienkompetenz: Voraussetzungen, Dimensionen, Funktionen*. Weinheim: Juventa, pp. 201–30.

Flower, L. S. and Hayes, J. R. (1971) 'A cognitive process theory of writing'. *College Composition and Communication*, 32, (4), 365–87.

Foucault, M. (1973) *The Order of Things: An Archeology of the Human Sciences*. New York: Vintage.

Fricke, H. (1981) *Norm und Abweichung: Eine Philosophie der Literatur*. Munich: CH Beck.

Gadamer, H.-G. (1979) *Truth and Method*. London: Sheed and Ward.

Gates, J. E. (1997) 'Literature in electronic format: the traditional English and American canon'. *Choice: Current Reviews for Academic Libraries*, 34, (8), 1279–96.

Gendolla, P. and Schäfer, J. (2001) 'Auf Spurensuche: Literatur im Netz, Netzliteratur und ihre Vorgeschichte(n)', in H. L. Arnold (ed), *Text und Kritik (152) Digitale Literatur*. Munich: Richard Boorberg, pp. 75–86.

Genette, G. (1980) *Narrative Discourse* (trans. J. E. Lewin). Oxford: Cornell University Press.

Genette, G. (1997) *Palimpsests: Literature to the Second Degree* (trans. C. Newman and C. Doubinsky). New York: University of Nebraska Press (first published 1982).

Glazier, L. P. (2002) *Digital Poetics: The Making of E-Poetries*. Tuscaloosa, AL: The University of Alabama Press.

Glazier, L. P. (2004) 'The conditional text: siting the "poetry" in e-poetry', in F. W. Block *et al.* (eds), *p0es1s. Ästhetik digitaler Poesie – The Aesthetics of Digital Poetry*. Ostfildern: Hatje Cantz, pp. 57–78.

Goldberg, D. (1998) 'Comments on *Patchwork Girl*' [online], in G. P. Landow (ed), *Cyberspace, Hypertext, & Critical Theory*. Providence, RI: Brown University. Available at: www.cyberartsweb.org/cpace/ht/pg/dgpatch.html [accessed 20 August 2006].

Gramsci, A. (1957) *The Modern Prince and Other Writings*. New York: International Publishers.

Greco, D. (1996) 'Hypertext with consequences: recovering a politics of hypertext' [online]. Chapel Hill, NC: University of North Carolina. Available at: www. aristarkhova.org/landow/cpace//ht/greco1.html [accessed 20 August 2006].

Greimas, A. J. (1985) 'The love life of the hippopotamus: a seminar with A. J. Greimas', in M. Blonsky (ed), *On Signs*. Baltimore: Johns Hopkins University Press, pp. 341–62.

Griffith, V. (1996) 'Media futures: hyperfiction reader delights in a plot that never thickens'. *Financial Times*, 4 March, 25.

Groebel, J. (1997) 'Medienentwicklung und Medienkompetenz – welche Themen für wen?', in Enquete-Kommission: Zukunft der Medien (eds), *Medienkompetenz im Informationszeitalter*. Bonn: ZV, pp. 111–19.

Groeben, N. (1982) *Leserpsychologie: Textverständnis – Textverständlichkeit*. Münster: Aschendorff.

Groeben, N. (2002) 'Dimensionen der *Medienkompetenz*: deskriptive und normative Aspekte', in N. Groeben and B. Hurrelmann (eds), *Medienkompetenz: Voraussetzungen, Dimensionen, Funktionen*. Weinheim: Juventa, pp. 160–97.

Groeben, N. and Hurrelmann, B. (2002) *Medienkompetenz: Voraussetzungen, Dimensionen, Funktionen*. Weinheim: Juventa.

Grossman, W. (1997) 'Underground fiction' [online]. *Salon Magazine*. Available at: www.salonmagazine.com/march97/21st/london970320.html [accessed 20 August 2006].

Grübel, R. (1997) 'Wert, Kanon und Zensur', in H. L. Arnold and H. Detering (eds), *Grundzüge der Literaturwissenschaft*. Munich: dtv, pp. 601–22.

Guertin, C. (1998) 'Carolyn Guyer, Quibbling' [online]. *Queen Bees and the Hum of the Hive*. Available at: http://beehive.temporalimage.com/archive/12arc.html [accessed 20 August 2006].

Guertin, C. (2000) 'Three-dimensional dementia: M. D. Coverley's *Califia* and the aesthetics of forgetting' [online]. *Riding the Meridian*. Available at: www.heelstone.com/meridian/guertin/3DD1.htm [accessed 20 August 2006].

Guillory, J. (1993) *Cultural Capital: The Problem of Literary Canon Formation*. Chicago: University of Chicago Press.

Günther, H. (1987) 'Die Lebensphasen eines Kanons – am Beispiel des sozialistischen Realismus', in A. Assmann and J. Assmann (eds), *Kanon und Zensur. Archäologie der literarischen Kommunikation, II*. Munich: Wilhelm Fink, pp. 138–48.

Guyer, C. (1992) 'Something about *Quibbling*, a hyperfiction'. *Leonardo Electronic News*, 3, (1), 258.

Haas, G. (2001) *Handlungs- und produktionsorientierter Literaturunterricht: Theorie und Praxis eines anderen Literaturunterrichts für die Primar – und Sekundarstufe*. Seelze-Velber: Kallmeyersche.

Habermas, J. (1983) *Moralbewußtsein und kommunikatives Handeln*. Frankfurt/M.: Suhrkamp.

Habermas, J. (1995) 'Notizen zur Entwicklung der Interaktionskompetenz', in J. Habermas (ed), *Vorstudien und Ergänzungen zur Theorie des kommunikativen Handelns*. Frankfurt/M.: Suhrkamp, pp. 187–225.

Hahn, A. (1987) 'Kanonisierungsstile', in A. Assmann and J. Assmann (eds), *Kanon und Zensur. Archäologie der literarischen Kommunikation, II*. Munich: Wilhelm Fink, pp. 28–37.

Halliday, M. A. K. and Hasan, R. (1976) *Cohesion in English*. London: Longman.

Hammersley, M. (1993) 'On the teacher as researcher', in M. Hammersley (ed), *Educational Research: Current Issues*. London: Paul Chapman, pp. 21–31.

Hammersley, M., Gomm, R. and Woods, P. (1994) *Educational Research Methods: Study Guide*. Milton Keynes: The Open University.

Hammond, N. (1993) 'Learning with hypertext: problems, principles and prospects', in C. McKnight *et al.* (eds), *Hypertext: A Psychological Perspective*. New York: Horwood, pp. 50–69.

Haraway, D. (1991) *Simians, Cyborgs and Women: The Reinvention of Nature*. New York: Routledge.

Harpold, T. (1991) 'The contingencies of the hypertext link'. *Writing on the Edge*, 2, 126–39. Available at: www.newmediareader.com/cd_samples/WOE/Harpold.html [accessed 20 August 2006].

Hayles, N. K. (2002) *Writing Machines*. Cambridge, MA: MIT Press.

Hazlitt, W. (1822/2002) 'On going on a journey'. *New Monthly Magazine*. Available at: www.gutenberg.org/dirs/etext02/table10.txt [accessed 20 August 2006].

Heibach, C. (2001) 'Ins Universum der digitalen Literatur: Versuch einer Typologie', in H. L. Arnold (ed), *Text und Kritik (152) Digitale Literatur*. Munich: Richard Boorberg, pp. 31–42.

Heibach, C. (2003) *Literatur im elektronischen Raum*. Frankfurt/M.: Suhrkamp.

Heibach, C. (2004) 'Conversations on digital aesthetics: synopsis of the Erfurt discussions', in F. W. Block *et al.* (eds), *p0es1s. Ästhetik digitaler Poesie – The Aesthetics of Digital Poetry*. Ostfildern: Hatje Cantz, pp. 38–56.

Heim, M. (1987) *Electronic Language: A Philosophical Study of Word Processing*. New Haven: Yale University Press.

Hernadi, P. (1978) *What Is Literature?*. Bloomington: Indiana University Press.

Herron, R. and Sutton-Smith, B. (1971) *Child's Play*. New York: Wiley.

Hinderaker, A. (2002) 'It has no beginning, it has no end: a novel approach plays havoc with literary convention' [online]. *Stanford Magazine*, 6. Available at: www.stanfordalumni.org/news/magazine/2002/novdec/showcase/review.html [accessed 20 August 2006].

Hirsch, Jr., E. D. (1978) 'What isn't literature?', in P. Hernadi (ed), *What Is Literature?*. Bloomington: Indiana University Press, pp. 24–34.

Honey, P. and Mumford, A. (1982) *Manual of Learning Styles*. London: P. Honey.

Howell, G. (1990) 'Hypertext meets interactive fiction: new vistas in creative writing', in R. McAleese and C. Green (eds), *Hypertext: State of the Art*. Oxford: intellect, pp. 136–41.

Huizinga, J. (1970) *Homo Ludens: A Study of the Play Element in Culture*. New York: Harper & Row (first published 1939).

Hurrelmann, B. (2002) 'Medienkompetenz: Geschichtliche Entwicklung, dimensionale Struktur, gesellschaftliche Einbettung', in N. Groeben and B. Hurrelmann (eds), *Medienkompetenz: Voraussetzungen, Dimensionen, Funktionen*. Weinheim: Juventa, pp. 301–14.

Hymes, D. (1971) *On Communicative Competence*. Philadelphia, PA: University of Pennsylvania Press.

Iser, W. (1971) 'Indeterminacy and the reader's response in prose fiction', in J. H. Miller (ed), *Aspects of Narrative: Selected Papers from the English Institute*. New York: Columbia University Press, pp. 1–45.

Iser, W. (1974) 'The reading process: a phenomenological approach', in R. Cohen (ed), *New Directions in Literary History*. Baltimore, MD: Johns Hopkins University Press, pp. 274–94.

Iser, W. (1978) *The Act of Reading: A Theory of Aesthetic Response* (trans. W. Iser). Baltimore, MD: Johns Hopkins University Press.

Ivo, H. (1971) 'Allgemeine Lernziele des Literaturunterrichts', in G. Wilkending (ed), *Literaturunterricht: Texte zur Didaktik*. Munich: Piper, pp. 170–205.

Jackson, S. (n.d.) 'Stitch bitch: the Patchwork Girl' [online]. Cambridge, MA: MIT. Available at: http://web.mit.edu/comm-forum/papers/jackson.html [accessed 20 August 2006].

Jakobson, R. (1960) 'Closing statement: linguistics and poetics', in T. A. Sebeok (ed), *Style in Language*. Cambridge, MA: MIT Press, pp. 350–77.

Jakobson, R. and Tynyanov, Y. (1928/1971), 'Problems in the study of literature and language', in L. Matejka and K. Pomorska (eds), *Readings in Russian Poetics: Formalist and Structuralist Views*. Cambridge, MA: MIT Press, pp. 79–81.

Jauss, H. R. (1982) *Theory and History of Literature, Vol. 2: Toward an Aesthetic of Reception* (trans. T. Bahti). Minneapolis, MN: University of Minnesota Press.

Jensen, E. (1996) *Brain-based Learning*. Del Mar, CA: Turning Point.

Jensen, E. (1998) *Teaching with the Brain in Mind*. Alexandria, VA: Association for Supervision and Curriculum Development.

Jerz, D. (2000) 'What is interactive fiction?' [online]. Greensburg, PA: Seton Hill University. Available at: http://jerz.setonhill.edu/if/intro.htm [accessed 20 August 2006].

Jewitt, C. (2004) 'Multimodality and new communication technologies', in P. Levine and R. Scollon (eds), *Discourse and Technology: Multimodal Discourse Analysis*. Washington, DC.: Georgetown University Press, pp. 184–95.

John, E. and McIver Lopes, D. (2004) *Philosophy of Literature: Contemporary and Classic Readings. An Anthology*. Oxford: Blackwell.

Johnson-Eilola, J. (1994) 'Reading and writing in hypertext: vertigo and euphoria', in C. L. Selfe and S. Hilligoss (eds), *Literacy and Computers: The Complications of Teaching and Learning with Technology*. New York: MLA, pp. 195–219.

Jonassen, D. H. (1986) 'Hypertext principles for text and courseware design'. *Educational Psychologist*, 21, (4), 269–92.

Jonassen, D. H. (1987) 'Assessing cognitive structure: verifying a method using pattern notes'. *Journal of Research and Development in Education*, 20, (3), 1–14.

Jonassen, D. H. (1989) 'Designing hypertext for learning', in E. Scanlon and T. O'Shea (eds), *New Directions in Educational Technology*. New York: Springer, pp. 123–31.

Jonassen, D. H. (1990) 'Semantic network elicitation: tools for structuring hypertext', in R. McAleese and C. Green (eds), *Hypertext: State of the Art*. Oxford: intellect, pp. 136–41.

Jonassen, D. H. (1991) 'Effects of semantically structured hypertext knowledge bases on users' knowledge structures', in C. McKnight *et al.* (eds), *Hypertext in Context*. Cambridge: CUP, pp. 153–68.

Jonassen, D. H. and Mandl, H. (1990) *Designing Hypermedia for Learning*. Heidelberg: Springer.

Jones, L. (2004) 'Secrets of the labyrinth: Lewis Jones hails a Spanish masterpiece as gripping as it is profound'. *Daily Telegraph*, 19 June, 8.

Jones, T. (1989) 'Incidental learning during information retrieval: a hypertext experiment', in H. Maurer (ed), *Computer Assisted Learning*. Berlin: Springer, pp. 235–53.

Joyce, M. (2002a) *Of Two Minds: Hypertext Pedagogy and Poetics*. Ann Arbor, MI: University of Michigan Press.

Joyce, M. (2002b) 'Siren shapes: exploratory and constructive hypertext', in M. Joyce (ed), *Of Two Minds: Hypertext Pedagogy and Poetics*. Ann Arbor, MI: University of Michigan Press (first published 1988), pp. 39–60.

Kac, E. (1996) *New Media Poetry: Poetic Innovation and New Technologies*. Special issue of *Visible Language*, 30, (2). Providence, RI: Rhode Island School of Design.

Kaplan, N. and Moulthrop, S. (1993) 'Seeing through the interface: computers and the future of composition', in G. P. Landow and P. Delany (eds), *The Digital World: Text-based Computing in the Humanities*. Cambridge, MA: MIT Press, pp. 253–70.

Keep, C., McLaughlin, T. and Parmar, R. (1993–2000) 'Barthes: death of the author' [online]. Charlottesville, VA: University of Virginia. Available at: www3.iath.virginia.edu/elab/hfl0226.html [accessed 20 August 2006].

Kemmis, S. (1993) 'Action research', in M. Hammersley (ed), *Educational Research: Current Issues*. London: Paul Chapman, pp. 177–90.

Kermode, F. (1985) *Forms of Attention*. Chicago: University of Chicago Press.

Kermode, F. (1990) *The Oxford Anthology of English Literature, Vol. I*. Oxford: O.U.P.

Koskimaa, R. (2000) *Digital Literature: From Text to Hypertext and beyond* [online]. Jyväskylä: Jyväskylä University. Available at: www.cc.jyu.fi/~koskimaa/thesis/thesis.shtml [accessed 20 August 2006].

Kress, G. and van Leeuwen, T. (2006) *Reading Images: The Grammar of Visual Design*. 2nd edn. Oxford: Routledge.

Kuhlen, R. (1991) *Hypertext: Ein nicht-lineares Medium zwischen Buch und Wissensbank*. Berlin: Springer.

Lamarque, P. and Olsen, S. H. (1994) *Truth, Fiction, and Literature*. Oxford: OUP.

Landow, G. P. (1992) *The Dickens Web*, CD-ROM. Environment: Storyspace. Cambridge, MA: Eastgate Systems.

Landow, G. P. (1994) 'What's a critic got to do? Critical theory in the age of hypertext', in G. P. Landow (ed), *Hyper/Text/Theory*. Baltimore: Johns Hopkins University Press, pp. 1–50.

Landow, G. P. (1997) *Hypertext 2.0: The Convergence of Contemporary Critical Theory and Technology*. Baltimore: Johns Hopkins University Press (first published 1992).

Landow, G. P. (2005) *The Postcolonial Web* [online]. Available at: www.postcolonialweb.org/ [accessed 20 August 2006].

Landow, G. P. (2006) *Hypertext 3.0: New Media and Critical Theory in an Era of Globalization*. Baltimore: The Johns Hopkins University Press.

Landow, G. P. and Lanestedt, J. (1992) *In Memoriam Web*, CD-ROM. Environment: Storyspace, Cambridge, MA: Eastgate Systems.

Lang, N. (1998) 'Multimedia', in W. Faulstich (ed), *Grundwissen Medien*. Munich: Fink, pp. 296–313.

Lanham, R. (1989) 'The electronic word: literary study and the digital revolution'. *New Literary History*, 20, 265–90.

Lanham, R. (1993) *The Electronic Word: Democracy, Technology, and the Arts*. Chicago: Chicago University Press.

Larsen, D. (1992) *Hyperpoems and Hyperpossibilities*. Unpublished MA Dissertation. University of Colorado.

Leavis, F. R. (1936) *Revaluation: Tradition and Development in English Poetry*. London: Chatto & Windus.

Leavis, F. R. (1948) *Education & the University: A Sketch for an 'English School'*. London: Chatto & Windus.

Lee, S. (2005) 'How do I cool down the overheated medium? Reading Stuart Moulthrop's *Hegirascope 2*' [online]. *Dichtung-digital*. Available at: www.dichtung-digital.com/2005/2-Lee.htm [accessed 20 August 2006].

Leggett, J. L., Schnase, J. L. and Kacmar, C. J. (1990) 'Hypertext for learning', in D. H. Jonassen and H. Mandl (eds), *Designing Hypermedia for Learning*. Heidelberg: Springer, pp. 27–37.

Liu, A. (2005) *Voice of the Shuttle* [online]. Santa Barbara, CA: University of California. Available at: http://vos.ucsb.edu/index.asp [accessed 20 August 2006].

Löser, P. (1999) 'Hypertext im Diskurs: Kritische Ergänzungen zur Diskussion um das Genre literarischer Hypertexte und zur Art und Weise, in der sie ihren Gegenstand formt' [online]. *Dichtung-digital*. Available at: www.dichtung-digital.com/Autoren/Loeser/30-Nov-99/ [accessed 20 August 2006].

Ludwig, H.-W. (1994) *Arbeitsbuch Lyrikanalyse*. Tübingen: Narr.

Lyas, C. (1969) 'The semantic definition of literature'. *Journal of Philosophy*, 66, (3), 81–95.

McAleese, R. (1990) 'Concepts as hypertext nodes: the ability to learn while navigating through hypertext nets', in D. H. Jonassen and H. Mandl (eds), *Designing Hypermedia for Learning*. Heidelberg: Springer, pp. 97–116.

McAleese, R. (1999a) *Hypertext: Theory into Practice*. Exeter: intellect.

McAleese, R. (1999b) 'Navigation and browsing in hypertext', in R. McAleese (ed), *Hypertext: Theory into Practice*. Exeter: intellect, pp. 5–38.

McKillop, A. M. and Myers, J. (1999) 'The pedagogical and electronic contexts of composing in hypermedia', in S. L. DeWitt and K. Strasma (eds), *Contexts, Intertexts, and Hypertexts*. Cresskill, NJ: Hampton Press, pp. 65–116.

Mackintosh, H. (2003) 'Noah Wardrip Fruin: Noah Wardrip Fruin is co-editor of the *New Media Reader*'. *Guardian*, 5 June, 25.

McKnight, C., Dillon, A. and Richardson, J. (1990) 'A comparison of linear and hypertext formats in information retrieval', in R. McAleese and C. Green (eds), *Hypertext: State of the Art*. Oxford: intellect, pp. 10–19.

McKnight, C., Dillon, A. and Richardson, J. (1991) *Hypertext in Context*. Cambridge: CUP.

McLuhan, E. and Zingrone, F. (1995) *Essential McLuhan*. New York: Basic Books.

McLuhan, M. (1962) *The Gutenberg Galaxy: The Making of Typographic Man*. Toronto: University of Toronto Press.

McLuhan, M. (1964) *Understanding Media: The Extensions of Man*. New York: McGraw Hill.

Manuel, J. (2005) 'Teenagers, imaginative literature, and learning: exploring the place and significance of "books" in adolescent experience' [online]. Vancouver: Simon Fraser University. Available at: www3.educ.sfu.ca/conferences/ierg2005/viewabstract.php?id=171 [accessed 20 August 2006].

Marchionini, G. and Shneiderman, B. (1988) 'Finding facts versus browsing knowledge in hypertext systems'. *Computer*, 21, (1), 70–80.

Marino, A. (1996) *The Biography of 'The Idea of Literature' from Antiquity to the Baroque*. Albany: State University of New York Press.

Marx, S. (2002) *Triangulating Shakespeare* [online]. San Luis Obispo, CA: College of Liberal Arts. Available at: http://cla.calpoly.edu/-smarx/Shakespeare/triang/index.html [accessed 20 August 2006].

Maskiewicz, S. (2004) *ColoRama* [online]. Available at: www.leeon.de/showroom/toolbox/colorama/colorama.htm [accessed 20 August 2006].

Matthews, R. J. (1978) 'Literary works express propositions', in P. Hernadi (ed), *What Is Literature?*. Bloomington: Indiana University Press, pp. 102–12.

Maturana, H. R. (1980) 'Autopoiesis: reproduction, heredity and evolution', in M. Zeleny (ed), *Autopoiesis, Dissipative Structures, and Spontaneous Social Disorders*. Boulder, CO: Westview, pp. 48–80.

Maturana, H. R. (1982) *Erkennen: Die Organisation und Verkörperung von Wirklichkeit*. Braunschweig: Vieweg.

Maturana, H. R. and Varela, R. J. (1980) *Autopoiesis and Cognition*. Boston, MA: Reidel.

Maturana, H. R. and Varela, R. J. (1998) *The Tree of Knowledge: The Biological Roots of Human Understanding*. Boston, MA: Shambhala.

Miall, D. S. and Dobson, T. (2001) 'Reading hypertext and the experience of literature' [online]. *Journal of Digital Information*, 2, (1). Available at: http://jodi.ecs.soton.ac.uk/Articles/v02/i01/Miall/ [accessed 20 August 2006].

Möckel-Ricke, H. (1996) 'Der virtuelle Text', in M. Klepper, R. Mayer and E.-P. Schneck (eds), *Hyperkultur. Zur Fiktion des Computerzeitalters*. Berlin: de Gruyter, pp. 68–80.

Mon, F., Höllerer, W. and de la Motte, M. (1960) *movens. Dokumente und Analysen zur Dichtung, bildenden Kunst, Musik, Architektur*. Wiesbaden: Limes.

Montfort, N. (2003) *Twisty Little Passages*. Cambridge, MA: MIT Press.

Moody, G. (1992) 'The hyperpoem; what do you get if you cross a poem with an Apple Mac?'. *Guardian*, 17 September, 33.

Morgan, W. and Andrews, R. (1999) 'City of text? Metaphors for hypertext in literary education'. *Changing English*, 6, (1), 81–92.

Morris, P. (1994) *The Bakhtin Reader*. London: Edward Arnold.

Moulthrop, S. (1993) 'You say you want a revolution? Hypertext and the laws of media', in E. Amiron and J. Unsworth (eds), *Essays in Postmodern Culture*. New York: OUP, pp. 69–97.

Moulthrop, S. (1995) 'Traveling in the breakdown lane: a principle of resistance for hypertext'. *Mosaic*, 28, (4): 55–77. Available at: http://iat.ubalt.edu/moulthrop/essays/breakdown.html [accessed 20 August 2006].

Moulthrop, S. (1997) 'What if the word still won't be still?' [online]. Baltimore, MD: Baltimore University. Available at: http://iat.ubalt.edu/moulthrop/hypertexts/hgs/HGSAbout.html [accessed 20 August 2006].

Moulthrop, S. and Kaplan, N. (1994) 'They became what they beheld: the futility of resistance in the space of electronic writing', in C. L. Selfe and S. Hilligoss (eds), *Literacy and Computers: The Complications of Teaching and Learning with Technology*. New York: MLA, pp. 220–7.

Müller-Oberhäuser, G. (2002) 'Lesesozialisation und Enkulturation im Viktorianischen England am Beispiel der Artusliteratur für junge Leser', in N. Groeben and B. Hurrelmann (eds), *Medienkompetenz: Voraussetzungen, Dimensionen, Funktionen*. Weinheim: Juventa, pp. 25–43.

Murray, J. H. (1997) *Hamlet on the Holodeck: The Future of Narrative in Cyberspace*. New York: Free Press.

Nelson, T. H. (1984) *Literary Machines 93.1*. Sausalito: Mindful Press.

Nelson, T. H. (1992) 'Opening hypertext: a memoir', in M. C. Tuman (ed), *Literacy Online: The Promise (and Peril) of Reading and Writing with Computers*. Pittsburgh, PA: University of Pittsburgh Press, pp. 43–57.

Nielsen, J. (1990) *Hypertext and Hypermedia*. Boston: Academic Press.

Nielsen, J. (1996) *Multimedia, Hypertext und Internet. Grundlagen und Praxis des elektronischen Publizierens* (trans. K. Lagrange and M. Linster). Braunschweig: Vieweg.

Norman, D. A. (1976) *Studies in Learning and Self-Contained Educational Systems, 1973–1976*. Washington, DC: Office of Naval Research, Advanced Research Projects Agency.

Norton, D., Zimmermann, B. B. and Lindemann, N. (1999) 'Developing hyperphoric grammar to teach collaborative hypertexs', in S. L. DeWitt and K. Strasma (eds), *Contexts, Intertexts, and Hypertexts*. Cresskill, NJ: Hampton Press, pp. 177–202.

Nunan, D. (1991) *Language Teaching Methodology: A Textbook for Teachers*. Hemel Hempstead: Prentice Hall.

Odin, J. K. (n.d.) 'Unraveling the tapestry of *Califia*: a journey to remember history' [online]. Available at: www.altx.com/ebr/reviews/rev12/r12odi.htm [accessed 20 August 2006].

O'Donnell, H. (1984) 'Where does adolescent literature belong?'. *English Journal*, 73, (7), 84–6.

Ohmann, R. (1971) 'Speech acts and the definition of literature'. *Philosophy and Rhetoric*, 4, 1–19.

Ong, W. J. (1982) *Orality and Literacy. The Technologizing of the Word*. London: Methuen.

Paefgen, E. K. (1999) *Einführung in die Literaturdidaktik*. Stuttgart: Metzler.

Palgrave, F. T. (1861) *The Golden Treasury of the Best Songs and Lyrical Poems in the English Language*. London: Macmillan.

Palgrave, F. T. (1897) *Landscape in Poetry from Homer to Tennyson, with Many Illustrative Examples*. London: Macmillan.

Paul, C. (1995) *Unreal City: A Hypertext Guide to T. S. Eliot's The Waste Land*, CD-ROM. Environment: Storyspace. Cambridge, MA: Eastgate Systems.

Pavlov, I. P. (1927) *Conditioned Reflexes*. London: Routledge and Kegan Paul.

Piaget, J. (1951) *Play, Dreams and Imitation in Childhood*. New York: Norton.

Picot, E. (2004) 'Hyperventiliterature: the Breathing Wall' [online]. *The Hyperliterature Exchange*. Available at: http://hyperex.co.uk/reviewbreathingwall.php [accessed 20 August 2006].

Pike, M. A. (2003) 'From personal to social transaction: a model of aesthetic reading in the classroom'. *Journal of Aesthetic Education*, 37, (2), 61–72.

Pike, M. A. (2004) *Teaching Secondary English*. London: Paul Chapman.

Pope, A. (1737) *Imitations of Horace*. London: T. Cooper.

Popper, K. (1963) *Conjectures and Refutations: The Growth of Scientific Knowledge*. London: Routledge.

Powell, T. (1999) *HTML. The Complete Reference*. Berkeley: McGraw-Hill Osborne Media.

Preece, P. (1976) Mapping cognitive structure: a comparison of methods'. *Journal of Educational Psychology*, 68, 1–8.

Raible, W. (1992) *Junktion: Eine Dimension der Sprache und ihre Realisierungsformen zwischen Aggregation und Integration*. Heidelberg: Winter.

Rau, A. (2000a) *What You Click Is What You Get: Die Stellung von Autoren und Lesern in interaktiver digitaler Literatur*. Berlin: dissertation.de.

Rau, A. (2000b) 'Wreader's digest – how to appreciate hyperfiction' [online]. *Journal of Digital Information*, 1, (7). Available at: http://jodi.tamu.edu/Articles/v01/i07/Rau/#death [accessed 20 August 2006].

Reich, K. (1998) 'Thesen zur konstruktivistischen Didaktik'. *Pädagogik*, 7, (8), 43–6.

Reinfried, M. (2000) 'Can radical constructivism achieve a viable basis for foreign language teaching? – A refutation of the Wolff-Wendt-Theorem' [online]. Göttingen: Göttingen University. Available at: http://webdoc.gwdg.de/edoc/ia/eese/artic20/marcus/8_2000.html [accessed 20 August 2006].

Renshaw, C. (2000) 'One on one with Michael Joyce' [online]. *Pif Magazine*, 32. Available at: www.pifmagazine.com/vol32/i_m_joyce.shtml [accessed 20 August 2006].

Richards, I. A. (1929) *Practical Criticism: A Study of Literary Judgement*. London: Routledge & Kegan.

Richardson, P. (1998) 'Literacy, learning and teaching'. *Educational Review*, 50, (2), 115–34.

Rimmon-Kenan, S. (1989) 'How the model neglects the medium: linguistics, language, and the crisis of narratology'. *Journal of Narrative Technique*, 19, (1), 157–66.

Rosenblatt, L. M. (1976) *Literature as Exploration*. New York: Noble and Noble.

Rosenblatt, L. M. (1985) 'The transactional theory of the literary work: implications for research', in C. R. Cooper (ed), *Researching Response to Literature and the Teaching of Literature*. Norwood, NY: Ablex, pp. 33–53.

Rötzer, F. (1998) *Digitale Weltentwürfe: Streifzüge durch die Netzkultur*. Munich: Carl Hanser.

Rumelhart, D. E. and Ortony, A. (1977) 'The representation of knowledge in memory', in R. C. Anderson, R. J. Spiro and W. E. Montague (eds), *Schooling and the Acquisition of Knowledge*. New York: John Wiley & Sons, pp. 99–135.

Ryan, G. (1999) 'Epistemic conversations: creating Socratic dialogue in hypertext', in S. L. DeWitt and K. Strasma (eds), *Contexts, Intertexts, and Hypertexts*. Cresskill, NJ: Hampton Press, pp. 233–64.

Ryan, M.-L. (1999) *Cyberspace Textuality: Computer Technology and Literary Theory*. Bloomington, Indiana University Press.

Ryan, M.-L. (2000) 'Narrative as puzzle!? – an interview with Marie-Laure Ryan' [online]. *Dichtung-digital*. Available at: www.dichtung-digital.de/Interviews/Ryan-29-Maerz-00/index.htm [accessed 20 August 2006].

Ryan, M.-L. (2001) *Narrative As Virtual Reality: Immersion and Interactivity in Literature and Digital Media*. Baltimore: Johns Hopkins University Press.

Ryan, M.-L. (2004) *Narrative across Media: The Languages of Storytelling*. Lincoln, NE: University of Nebraska Press.

Ryan, R. and Deci, E. (1996) 'When paradigms clash: comments on Cameron and Pierce's claim that rewards do not undermine intrinsic motivation'. *Review of Educational Research*, 66, (1), 33–8.

Sandbothe, M. (1997) 'Interaktivität – Hypertextualität – Transversalität', in S. Münker and A. Roesler (eds), *Mythos Internet*. Frankfurt/M.: Suhrkamp, pp. 56–82.

Saul, M. L. (1999) 'The limitations of hypertext in the composition classroom', in S. L. DeWitt and K. Strasma (eds), *Contexts, Intertexts, and Hypertexts*. Cresskill, NJ: Hampton Press, pp. 39–64.

Schmeck, R. R. (1983) 'Learning styles of college students', in R. Dillon and R. R. Schmeck (eds), *Individual Differences in Cognition: Vol. I*. New York: Academic Press, pp. 233–79.

Schmidt, S. J. (1987) 'Abschied vom Kanon? Thesen zur Situation der gegenwärtigen Kunst', in Assmann and J. Assmann (eds), *Kanon und Zensur. Archäologie der literarischen Kommunikation, II*. Munich: Wilhelm Fink, pp. 336–47.

Schmidt, S. J. (2002) 'Vom Text zum Literatursystem: Skizze einer konstruktivistischen (empirischen) Literaturwissenschaft', in H. v. Foerster, E. v. Glasersfeld, P. M. Hejl, S. J. Schmidt and P. Watzlawick (eds), *Einführung in den Konstruktivismus*. Munich: Piper, pp. 147–66.

Schnierer, P. P. (2000) ' "graphic novels", cyber "fiction", multiform "stories" – virtual theatre and the limits of genre', in B. Reitz and S. Rieuwerts (eds), *Proceedings, Anglistentag 1999 Mainz*. Trier: Wissenschaftlicher Verlag, pp. 535–47.

Schnierer, P. P. (2001) 'Hyperdrama – prototypes, current practice, problems', in B. Reitz and H. Stahl (eds), *What Revels Are in Hand? Assessments of Contemporary Drama in English in Honour of Wolfgang Lippke*. Trier: Wissenschaftlicher Verlag, pp. 139–52.

Schnierer, P. P. (2003) 'Modernist at best: poeticity and tradition in hyperpoetry', in K. Stierstorfer (ed), *Beyond Postmodernism: Reassessments in Literature, Theory, and Culture*. Berlin: de Gruyter, pp. 91–9.

Schweikle, G. and Schweikle, I. (1990) *Metzler Literatur Lexikon*. Stuttgart: Metzler.

Seidel, E. J. (1996) 'Patchwork Girl: the hypertextuality of scars' [online]. *Cyberspace, Hypertext, & Critical Theory*. Available at: www.cyberartsweb.org/cpace/ht/pg/espatch.html [accessed 20 August 2006].

Selden, R. (1985) *A Reader's Guide to Contemporary Literary Theory*. Brighton: Harvester.

Shavelson, R. (1974) 'Methods for examining representations of subject matter structure in students' memory'. *Journal of Research in Science Teaching*, 11, (3), 231–49.

Shklovsky, V. (1988) 'Art as technique', in D. Lodge (ed), *Modern Criticism and Theory*. London: Longman, pp. 16–30.

Shklovsky, V. (1991) 'The novel as parody', in V. Shklovsky (ed), *Theory of Prose*. Normal, IL: Dalkey Archive Press (first published 1925), pp. 147–70. Available from: www.centerforbookculture.org/context/no1/shklovsky.html [accessed 20 August 2006].

Short, E. (2001) 'What is interactive fiction?' [online]. Available at: http://emshort.home.mindspring.com/whatsif.html [accessed 20 August 2006].

Siegel, D. (1997) 'Foreword', in N. Heinle (ed), *Designing with JavaScript: Creating Dynamic Web Pages*. Sebastopol, CA: Songline Studios and O'Reilly & Associates.

Siemens, G. (2005) 'Connectivism: a learning theory for the digital age' [online]. *International Journal of Instructional Theory and Distance Learning*, 2, (1). Available at: www.itdl.org/Journal/Jan_05/article01.htm [accessed 20 August 2006].

Simanowski, R. (1999a) 'Dirk Günthers und Frank Klötgens "Die Aaleskorte der Ölig" ' [online]. *Dichtung-digital*. Available at: www.dichtung-digital.com / Simanowski / 18-Aug-99/abstract.htm [accessed 20 August 2006].

Simanowski, R. (1999b) 'Perspektiven einer Ästhetik der digitalen Literatur' [online]. *Dichtung-digital*. Available at: www.dichtung-digital.de/Simanowski/5-Okt-99/index.htm [accessed 20 August 2006].

Simanowski, R. (1999c) 'Die Ordnung des Erinnerns. Kollektives Gedächtnis und digitale Präsentation am Beispiel der Internetprojekte *Das Generationenprojekt* und *23:40*' [online]. *Dichtung-digital*. Available at: www.dichtung-digital.com/Simanowski/30-Dez-99/index.htm [accessed 20 August 2006].

Simanowski, R. (2000a) 'Urs Schreibers "Das Epos der Maschine": Wenn konkrete Poesie digital wird' [online]. *Dichtung-digital*. Available at: www.dichtung-digital.de/2000/Simanowski/23-Aug [accessed 20 August 2006].

Simanowski, R. (2000b) 'Operations of writing: interview with Stuart Moulthrop' [online]. *Dichtung-digital*. Available at: www.dichtung-digital.com / Interviews / Moulthrop-22-Nov-00/ [accessed 20 August 2006].

Simanowski, R. (2000c) ' "Beim Bäcker". Collaborative Sex und soziale Ästhetik' [online]. *Dichtung-digital*. Available at: www.dichtung-digital.com/2000/Simanowski/15-Feb/ [accessed 20 August 2006].

Simanowski, R. (2001a) 'Laudatio zum Wettbewerb Literatur.digital 2001 von DTV und T-Online' [online]. *Dichtung-digital*. Available at: www.dichtung-digital.com/Verschiedenes/Events/dtv-laudatio.htm [accessed 20 August 2006].

Simanowski, R. (2001b) 'Multiple Personality Disorder als Bildschirmkombination' [online]. *Dichtung-digital*. Available at: www.dichtung-digital.com/2001/11/30-Reviews/quadrego.htm [accessed 20 August 2006].

Simanowski, R. (2001c) 'Digitale Literatur? Links für Eilige' [online]. *Dichtung-digital*. Available at: www.dichtung-digital.com/Einsteigeressay/ [accessed 20 August 2006].

Simanowski, R. (2001d) 'Interview with Stefan Maskiewicz' [online]. *Dichtung-digital*. Available at: www.dichtung-digital.com/2001/11/30-Wettbewerb/maskiewicz.htm [accessed 20 August 2006].

Simanowski, R. (2002a) *Literatur.digital. Formen und Wege einer neuen Literatur*. Munich: dtv.

Simanowski, R. (2002b) *Interfictions. Vom Schreiben im Netz*. Frankfurt/M.: Suhrkamp.

Simanowski, R. (2002c) 'Hypertext: Merkmale, Forschung, Poetik' [online]. *Dichtung-digital*. Available at: www.01media.de/2002/07/31-Simanowski/Simanowski-Hypertext.htm [accessed 20 August 2006].

Simanowski, R. (2002d) 'Zeitgenossen: "Yatoo". Audiovisueller Hypertext als Roll-over-Lovepoem' [online]. *Dichtung-digital*. Available at: www.dichtung-digital. com/2002/01–21-Simanowski.htm [accessed 20 August 2006].

Simanowski, R. (2004) 'Death of the author? Death of the reader!', in F. W. Block *et al.* (eds), *pOes1s. Ästhetik digitaler Poesie – The Aesthetics of Digital Poetry*. Ostfildern: Hatje Cantz, pp. 17–92.

Skinner, B. F. (1953) *Science and Human Behavior*. New York: Macmillan.

Smith, C. F. (1991) 'Reconceiving hypertext', in G. E. Hawisher and C. L. Selfe (eds), *Evolving Perspectives on Computer and Composition Studies*. Urbana, IL: NCTE, pp. 224–52.

Smith, M. A. and Kollock, P. (1999) *Communities in Cyberspace*. London: Routledge.

Snyder, I. (1997) *Page to Screen: Taking Literacy into the Electronic Era*. Sydney: Allen and Unwin.

Sommers, E. A. (1985) 'Integrating composing and computing', in J. L. Collins and E. A. Sommers (eds), *Writing On-Line: Using Computers in the Teaching of Writing*. Upper Montclair, NJ: Boynton/Cook, pp. 3–10.

Spiller, N. (2002) *Cyber_Reader: Critical Writings for the Digital Era*. London: Phaidon.

Stanford Poynter Project (1995–2005) [online]. Available at: http://www.poynterextra. org/et/i.htm [accessed 20 August 2006].

Stanton, N. A. and Stammers, R. B. (1990) 'Learning styles in a non-linear training environment', in R. McAleese and C. Green (eds), *Hypertext: State of the Art*. Oxford: intellect, pp. 114–20.

Stanzel, F. K. (1984) *A Theory of Narrative*. Cambridge: CUP.

Stenhouse, L. (1975) *An Introduction to Curriculum Research and Development*. London: Heinemann.

Stibbs, A. (1998) 'Language in art and art in language'. *Journal of Art and Design Education*, 17, (2), 201–9.

Stock, B. (1983) *The Implications of Literacy. Written Language and Modes of Interpretation in the Eleventh and Twelfth Centuries*. Princeton, NJ: Princeton University Press.

Storrer, A. (2002) 'Coherence in text and hypertext'. *Document Design*, 3, (2), 156–68.

Strasma, K. (1999) 'Hypertext unplugged: using hypertext in any writing context', in S. L. DeWitt and K. Strasma (eds), *Contexts, Intertexts, and Hypertexts*. Cresskill, NJ: Hampton Press, pp. 203–32.

Suter, B. (1999) *Hyperfiktion und interaktive Narration im frühen Entwicklungsstadium zu einem Genre*. Zurich: update.

Suter, B. (2000) Untitled contribution to the IASL Kommunikationsforum *Netzkommu-nikation in ihren Folgen* [online]. *Dichtung-digital*. Available at: www.dichtung-digital. com/IASL-Forum/Suter-20-Jun-00.htm#1 [accessed 20 August 2006].

Suter, B. (2001) *Cyberfiction* [online]. Available at: www.cyberfiction.ch [accessed 20 August 2006].

Suter, B. and Böhler, M. (1999) *Hyperfiction. Hyperliterarisches Lesebuch*. Basel: Stroemfeld.

Sutter, T. (1999) *Systeme und Subjektstrukturen. Zur Konstitutionstheorie des interaktionistischen Konstruktivismus*. Opladen: Westdeutscher Verlag.

Sutter, T. and Charlton, M. (2002) 'Medienkompetenz – einige Anmerkungen zum Kompetenzbegriff', in N. Groeben and B. Hurrelmann (eds), *Medienkompetenz: Vor-aussetzungen, Dimensionen, Funktionen*. Weinheim: Juventa, pp. 129–47.

Taglinger, H. (2003) *Jetzt lerne ich HTML: Der einfache Einstieg in die eigene Webseite*. Munich: Markt + Technik.

Tenbruck, F. H. (1986) *Geschichte und Gesellschaft*. Berlin: Duncker & Humblot.

Theunert, H. (1999) 'Medienkompetenz. Eine pädagogisch und altersspezifisch zu fassende Handlungsdimension', in F. Schell, E. Stolzenburg and H. Theunert (eds), *Medienkompetenz: Grundlagen und pädagogisches Handeln*. Munich: KoPäd, pp. 50–9.

Toolan, M. (1998) *Language in Literature*. London: Arnold.

Tosca, S. P. (1999) 'Michael Joyce: *Twilight, a Symphony*' [online]. *Dichtung-digital*. Available at: www.dichtung-digital.com/Tosca/15-Juli-99/twilight.htm [accessed 20 August 2006].

Tulodziecki, G. (1997) *Medien in Erziehung und Unterricht*. Bad Heilbrunn: Klinkhardt.

Tulodziecki, G. (1998) 'Entwicklung von Medienkompetenz als Erziehungs- und Bildungsaufgabe'. *Pädagogische Rundschau*, 52, (6), 693–711.

Tuman, M. C. (1992) *Word Perfect: Literacy in the Computer Age*. Pittsburgh, PA: University of Pittsburgh Press.

Turkle, S. (1996) 'Constructions and reconstructions of the self in virtual reality', in T. Druckrey (ed), *Electronic Culture: Technology and Visual Representation*. New York: Aperture, pp. 354–65.

Turner, V. W. (1974) *Dramas, Fields and Metaphors: Symbolic Action in Human Society*. Ithaca, NY: Cornell University Press.

van Dijk, T. A. (1980) *Textwissenschaft*. Munich: dtv.

Varela, F. J. (1979) *Principles of Biological Autonomy*. New York: North Holland.

Vaughan, W. (1999) *William Blake*. Princeton, NJ: Princeton University Press.

Vitanza, V. J. (1996) *CyberReader*. Boston, MA: Allyn and Bacon.

von Glasersfeld, E. (2002) 'Konstruktion der Wirklichkeit und des Begriffs der Objektivität', in H. von Foerster, E. von Glasersfeld, P. M. Hejl, S. J. Schmidt and P. Watzlawick (eds), *Einführung in den Konstruktivismus*. Munich: Piper, pp. 9–40.

Vygotsky, L. S. (1978) *Mind in Society*. Cambridge, MA: Harvard University Press.

Vygotsky, L. S. (1986) *Denken und Sprechen*. Frankfurt/M.: Fischer (first published 1934).

Wardrip-Fruin, N. and Montfort, N. (2003) *The New Media Reader*. Cambridge, MA: MIT Press.

Waters, J. (1992) 'Dallas on the Liffey'. *Guardian*, 31 January, 23.

Watson, J. B. (1912) 'Psychology as the behaviorist views it'. *Psychological Review*, 20, 158–77.

Weber, B. (2004) 'Fewer noses stuck in books in America, a survey finds'. *New York Times*, 8 July [online]. Available at: www.nytimes.com/2004/07/08/books/08READ.html?ex=1247025600&en=0478807a580f2a85&ei=5090&partner=rssuserland [accessed 20 August 2006].

Webopedia [online]. Available at: www.webopedia.com [accessed 20 August 2006].

Wellek, R. and Warren, A. (1956) *Theory of Literature*. New York: Harcourt, Brace & World.

Wenz, K. (1998) 'Verschiebungen und Transformationen: Mark Amerikas "Grammatron"' [online]. *Netzliteratur.net*. Available at: www.netzliteratur.net/wenz/wenz_amerika.htm [accessed 20 August 2006].

Wenz, K. (2000) 'Vom Leser zum User? Hypertextmuster und ihr Einfluss auf das Leseverhalten'. *Sprache und Datenverarbeitung*, 24, (1), 2000, 23–34.

Wenz, K. (2001) 'Eine Lese(r)reise: moving text into e-space', in H. L. Arnold (ed), *Text und Kritik (152) Digitale Literatur*. Munich: Richard Boorberg, pp. 43–53.

Werning, R. (1998) 'Konstruktivismus: eine Anregung für die Pädagogik?'. *Pädagogik*, 7, (8), 39–41.

Whalley, P. (1990) 'Models of hypertext structure and learning', in D. H. Jonassen and H. Mandl (eds), *Designing Hypermedia for Learning*. Heidelberg: Springer, pp. 61–7.

Wikipedia: The Free Encyclopedia [online]. Available at: www.wikipedia.org [accessed 20 August 2006].

Wilkending, G. (2002) 'Das Mädchen als Subjekt der Lektüre und als Objekt pädagogischer Einwirkung', in N. Groeben and B. Hurrelmann (eds), *Medienkompetenz: Voraussetzungen, Dimensionen, Funktionen.* Weinheim: Juventa, pp. 44–70.

Willems, G. (2000) *Der Weg ins Offene als Sackgasse. Zur jüngsten Kanondebatte und zur Lage der Literaturwissenschaft.* Bonn: Bouvier.

Williams, J. (1999) 'Texture, topology, collage, and biology in Patchwork Girl' [online]. *Cyberspace, Hypertext, & Critical Theory.* Available at: www.cyberartsweb.org/cpace/ht/pg/jwpatch.html [accessed 20 August 2006].

Wimsatt, J. I. (1978) 'The mirror as metaphor for literature', in P. Hernadi (ed), *What Is Literature?.* Bloomington: Indiana University Press, pp. 127–40.

Wingert, B. (1996) 'Kann man Hypertexte lesen?', in D. Matejovski and F. Kittler (eds), *Literatur im Informationszeitalter.* Frankfurt/M.: Campus Verlag, pp. 185–218.

Winko, S. (1997) 'Literarische Wertung und Kanonbildung', in H. L. Arnold and H. Detering (eds), *Grundzüge der Literaturwissenschaft.* Munich: dtv, pp. 585–600.

Winko, S. (1999) 'Lost in Hypertext? Autorkonzepte und neue Medien', in F. Jannidis, G. Lauer, M. Martinez and S. Winko (eds), *Rückkehr des Autors. Zur Erneuerung eines umstrittenen Begriffs.* Tübingen: Niemeyer, pp. 511–33.

Winko, S. (2002) 'Literarische Wertung – literarischer Kanon' [online]. Kiel: Kiel University. Available at: www.literaturwissenschaft-online.uni-kiel.de/veranstaltungen/einfuehrungsvorlesungen/2002/Literarische_Wertung.pdf [accessed 20 August 2006].

Wirth, U. (1997) 'Literatur im Internet. Oder: Wen kümmert's, wer liest?', in S. Münker and A. Roesler (eds), *Mythos Internet.* Frankfurt/M.: Suhrkamp, pp. 319–37.

Wirth, U. (2000) 'Super-scroll-back: b' [online]. *Dichtung digital.* Available at: www.dichtung-digital.com/Interscene/Wirth/ [accessed 20 August 2006].

Wirth, U. (2001) 'Der Tod des Autors als Geburt des Editors', in H. L. Arnold (ed), *Text und Kritik (152) Digitale Literatur.* Munich: Richard Boorberg, pp. 54–64.

Zancanella, D., Hall, L. and Pence, P (2000) 'Computer games as literature', in A. Goodwyn (ed), *English in the Digital Age: Information and Communications Technology and the Teaching of English.* London: Cassell, pp. 87–102.

Ziefle, M. (1998) 'Effects of display resolution on visual performance'. *Human Factors,* 40, (4), 554–68.

Index